I0800947

RECODING THE CITY

jovis

RECODING THE CITY

Thinking, Planning, and Building the City of the Nineteenth Century

Britta Hentschel, Harald R. Stühlinger [eds.]

jovis

RECODING THE CITY
An Introduction

Britta Hentschel, Harald R. Stühlinger

The city of the nineteenth century is a phenomenon that intrigues scholars from various disciplines as it has lately come to be seen to represent the basic configuration of the European city *per se*. This book seeks to tie in with this, analyzing a phenomenon in the genesis of the city in the nineteenth century—in Europe and overseas—that has not been discussed so far, but is, especially in terms of urbanism and city planning, a pressing and fundamental one: the rewriting of the historic city center—or rather, the recoding of the city.

According to the Italian semiotician, essayist, philosopher, literary critic, and novelist Umberto Eco (1932–2016), architecture is a factor of communication. He assumes that an architectural code is an abstract model that aims to be recognized. All objects convey something, even if they are not in use.[1] So according to Eco—and according to us—architecture operates as a system of signs that can be read, deciphered and understood. However, this also implies that an architectural system of signs can be changed, and that its meaning can be converted. Therefore, a built object is coded and can be recoded.

Architectural codes offer the option of different readings of a building over time. The work of an architect is confronted with the changeability of readings and changes in communication. Every architectural object offers various versions of coding that can be intended or even unforeseen.

Umberto Eco differentiates between two types of code: firstly, syntactic codes that derive from the structural conditions at the denotation of spaces, and secondly, semantic codes that describe functions, such as *roof*, *terrace*, *stairs*, or *window*, or architectural elements such as *column*, *pediment*, or *tympanum*, as well as the articulation of room typologies like *bedroom*, *kitchen*, or *hall*, and architectural typologies such as *castle*, *villa*, *hospital*, *school* or *train station*.[2]

Codes, then, are nothing more than iconological, stylistic, or rhetorical lexica or thesauruses. But Eco offers a third type of coding, one which he calls *styling*, that changes the reading of an entire building. Its function stays the same, but the way the building is seen within a system of buildings changes. Its significance among the other buildings is converted.

Umberto Eco concludes that architecture might emanate from architectural codes, but in reality leans on another system of coding that is not part of the architecture itself, but part of the reading and perception of architecture.[3] This third type of coding or styling that Eco depicts demands a wider embedding. It works not only for individual buildings but also, and above all, for architecture in a context: hence the city.

The editors of this book are convinced that a coding of architecture as described by Umberto Eco—or also as by his French colleague Roland Barthes (1915–1980), who assumes that a code produces structures and thus meaning[4]—can and must be transferred to the larger context of the city. When the German art historian Günther Bandmann (1917–1975) says that architecture bears meaning and reference,[5] it is doubly true for the city. It is the aim of this book to analyze and discuss the various aspects of the coding and recoding of the urban space. We have chosen the nineteenth century as the object of investigation because we are certain that it presents multiple aspects and mechanisms of coding due to the radical social, political, technical, and urban changes that occurred between 1798 and 1914. It also introduces new elements in respect of representational needs, housing different social classes, and public hygiene. The "long nineteenth century"[6] produced not only a wealth of ideas about the city, but was also the period of the largest wave of urbanization yet seen in Europe. Urban planning debates and activities are therefore focusing more intensively than ever on the nineteenth-century city. The founding of the nation-states in Europe, industrialization, and the increased mobility that went along with them were accompanied by radical social changes. The hegemony of the aristocracy was replaced by a self-assured bourgeoisie, and the working class was formed into a revolutionary and potentially threatening third force. Participation in the shaping of society—and thus also of urban space—became the central maxim for the multitude of protagonists involved. New functions—such as governmental and administrative centers, production plants, and focal points for modern cultural and social life—not only promoted the physical expansion of the developing capitals and metropolises, but also required a new coding of existing structures to enable them to serve as modernized platforms for city life and urban society.

This publication aims to inquire into the divergent intentions and claims of the new protagonists of shaping the city who emerged in the nineteenth century, and into the associated mechanisms which enabled them to inscribe themselves into existing urban structures, overwrite them, or even rewrite them if needed. Against the background of escalating competition between cities and vigorous image-building, public space grew in importance to become a medium that conveyed significance—and it also became a battleground for ideas and demands. Spurred on by new legislation, novel building regulations, emerging manuals on urban design, and the building speculation that was particularly rife in the liberal economic system, the appearance of cities changed drastically. The associated new coding and recoding of the city ranged from local interventions such as the erection of monuments to wide-ranging surgical urban-planning operations that created new contexts of significance within historically developed cities. On the basis of criteria such as public hygiene, security, modern traffic volumes, and assertions of prestige status, the historic city was physically modified and charged with layers of meaning, and was used both as a screen for the projection of an ideal image and as a demarcation line between a wide range of different interests. In parallel with these radical urban upheavals, which were also accompanied by the development of new media such as photography and film, the disciplines of historic monument preservation, urban planning, and sociology also emerged.

The procedure of coding and recoding of urban space can doubtless be found in every epoch—from the Roman Pantheon,[7] to King Louis XIV of France, who exploited coding to his own ends to the maximum,[8] to the present day—but, as the various chapters of the book emphasize, the nineteenth century especially is very rich in this complex process.

The starting point regarding the subject of the book was an international conference on the urban recoding process in the nineteenth century at the Federal Institute of Technology (ETH Zürich) in Zurich, Switzerland, organized by the editors of this book in 2015. Subsequently, a smaller group of scholars was asked to intensify their research on the phenomenon of recoding and to contribute essays under a blind peer-review procedure.

What left us thunderstruck was the fact that all the researchers, including ourselves, focused on the second half of the nineteenth century. At first sight, the period of 1800 until 1850 seems to be less fruitful for investigations into the phenomenon of recoding the city. However, we are convinced that especially the Napoleonic occupations throughout Europe, the recoding of the formerly sovereign capitals, and the following years of the Restoration provide interesting and demanding ground for future investigations.[9]

In the first chapter of the book, focused on Urban Development, Dragan Damjanović explores the shaping of Zagreb into the Croatian national capital through the recoding of the historic monuments in the center of the city, while Sarah Whiting analyzes the neighborhoods of Chicago and Florian Hutterer examines the coding potential of the *Hobrechtplan* of 1862 for Berlin. Britta Hentschel focuses on the shifting of the urban layout of Rome as a result of the construction of the *Vittoriano*, a monument in honor of Italy's first king.

The second chapter, on Urban Agents, offers insight into a wide range of stakeholders operating in and recoding the city centers of Vienna (Richard Kurdiovsky), London (Irina Davidovici), Budapest (Ágnes Anna Sebestyén) and Paris (Bradley Fratello) with fairly different intentions and claims to authority.

Designing the City, the third chapter of the book, assembles essays on urban theory, planning instruments, and urban hygiene. Katrin Albrecht and Lukas Zurfluh compare and discuss the manuals of Rudolph Eberstadt und Raymond

Unwin, while Anna Minta analyzes the social concepts behind American town planning debates. Laila Seewang and Harald R. Stühlinger investigate the power of the recoding of sanitation infrastructure.

It is the aim of this publication to offer a representatively wide range of different approaches toward an understanding of the phenomenon of recoding the city in the nineteenth century. We thank the Swiss National Science Foundation, the Department of Architecture of ETH Zurich, and its Institute of History and Theory of Architecture (gta) for their financial support. Special thanks go to Laurent Stalder, Ita Heinze-Greenberg, and Vittorio Magnago Lampugnani, as well as to Ralph-Miklas Dobler, Gregory Grämiger, Nadia Göntem-Wachtel, Gregor Harbusch, Cornelia Jöchner, Karl Kegler, Niklas Naehrig, Lothar Schmitt, Rainer Schützeichel, Daniela Spiegel, Anselm Wagner, and Mechthild Widrich.

Furthermore, we are grateful for the support of our publisher jovis, thanking in particular Verena Pfeiffer-Kloss, Doris Kleilein, Jessica Glanz, and Susanne Rösler.

Endnotes

1 Umberto Eco, "Funktion und Zeichen. Semiologie der Architektur" in *Architektur als Zeichensystem*, ed. Alessandro Carlini and Bernhard Schneider (Tübingen: Wasmuth Verlag, 1971), pp. 19–68, here pp. 21–22. The identical text by Eco on semiotics in architecture can be found in Umberto Eco, *Einführung in die Semiotik*, trans. Jürgen Trabant (Munich: Fink Verlag, 1972), pp. 295–356.

2 Eco, *Funktion und Zeichen*, pp. 46–50.

3 Ibid., p. 51.

4 Roland Barthes, S/Z (Frankfurt a M.: Suhrkamp Verlag 1976); see pp. 23–26 and pp. 256–258 on Barthes's theory of the five codes. Barthes distinguishes between the hermeneutic code, the proairetic code, the semantic code, the symbolic code, and the cultural code. Beyond that, we would like to point to literature regarding architecture as a medium of communication, but not necessarily involving the term "code," recommending Matthias Ross, *Weltbilder aus Stein. Architektur als politisches Kommunikationsmittel in Brüssel—eine kulturgeographische Analyse* (Passau: Passauer Schriften zur Geographie, 2015) as a brief (and the most recent) introduction to this wider topic.

5 Günter Bandmann, "Ikonologie der Architektur," in *Jahrbuch für Ästhetik und allgemeine Kunstwissenschaft*, ed. Heinrich Lützeler (Cologne: Universitäts-Verlag, 1951), pp. 67–109, here p. 86.

6 The "long nineteenth century" is a term coined to describe the period between the years 1789 and 1914 by the British historian and author Eric Hobsbawm (1917–2012), adapting the concept of Fernand Braudel's 1949 notion of "Le long seizième siècle" and elaborated in three books: Eric Hobsbawm, *The Age of Revolution: Europe: 1789–1848* (London: Weidenfeld & Nicolson, 1962); Hobsbawm, *The Age of Capital: 1848–1875* (London: Weidenfeld & Nicolson, 1975); and Hobsbawm *The Age of Empire: 1875–1914* (London: Weidenfeld & Nicolson, 1987).

7 For example, see Richard Sennett, *Fleisch und Stein. Der Körper und die Stadt in der westlichen Zivilisation* (Berlin: Suhrkamp Verlag, 1997), pp. 111–155.

8 See Peter Burke, *Ludwig XIV. Die Inszenierung des Sonnenkönigs* (Berlin: Wagenbach Verlag, 2005).

9 In general, the history of urbanism in the nineteenth century focuses strongly on the second half of the century. One of the few exceptions among the latest publications in this field is Cornelia Jöchner, *Gebaute Entfestigung. Architekturen der Öffnung im Turin des frühen 18. und 19. Jahrhunderts* (Berlin: De Gruyter, 2015).

URBAN DEVELOPMENT

1

THE SHAPING OF ZAGREB INTO THE CROATIAN NATIONAL CAPITAL

Rebuilding, Aestheticization, and Croatization of the Historical City Core in the Long Nineteenth Century

Dragan Damjanović

Introduction

During the nineteenth century Zagreb, a small provincial town located near the southern border of the Habsburg Empire, developed into the main Croatian national center. The number of people in the town grew tenfold from around 8,000 in 1810 to 80,000 in 1910. Although it could not measure up in size to other large nineteenth-century Central European cities such as Vienna, Budapest, or Prague, Zagreb went through a rapid development which was considerably influenced by its status as a national center and the political capital of Croatia.

The city was formed as a single administrative unit in 1850 through the amalgamation of several settlements, of which the most important were Kaptol and Gradec (the Upper Town). They were located on two adjacent hills and separated by the Medveščak stream. The eastern part of the old city core, Kaptol, was mostly owned by institutions associated with the Catholic Church. It housed a Franciscan monastery, a seminary, the homes of the canons of the cathedral chapter, and the huge fortified archbishop's palace alongside the cathedral, all located on Kaptol Street, the main street running north—south. On the other hand, Gradec—the western part of Zagreb's old city core—was inhabited by aristocrats and bourgeois families, and served as the administrative center of the city and of the Habsburg province of the Kingdom of Croatia and Slavonia in general. The city council and all of the Croatian autonomous institutions (the Croatian Parliament, ministerial departments, and Viceroy or *Ban*) had their seats in this part of Zagreb, mostly located around the central Saint Mark's Square (named after the gothic parish church located at its northern side) or in its immediate vicinity.

The Lower Town, which had begun to develop south of Kaptol and Gradec in the eighteenth century, took on the role of the city's new economic and cultural

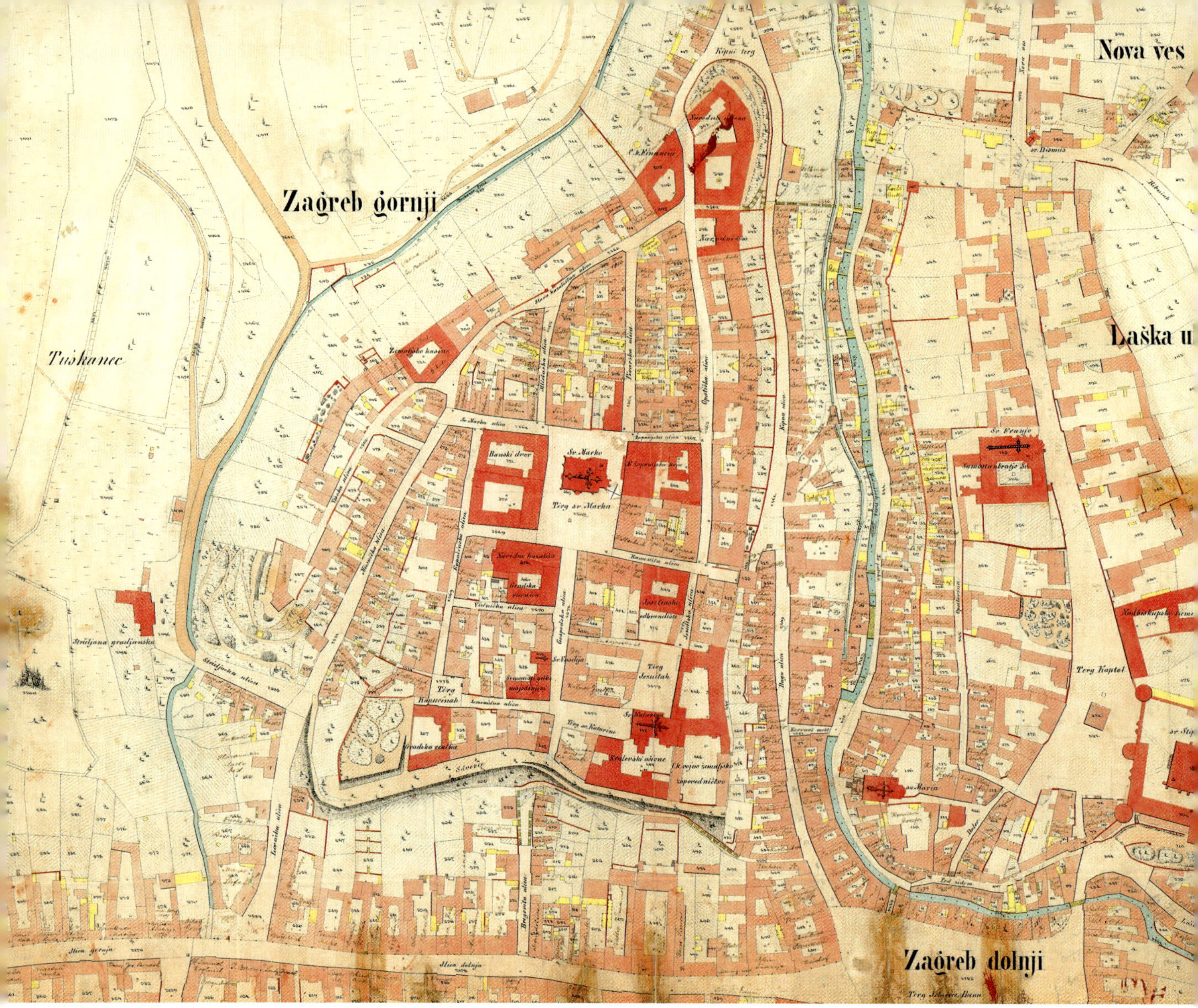

[1] Anton Kieszwetter, Cadastral Map of the center of Zagreb (Gradec/Upper Town and Kaptol), 1862. Public buildings were marked with dark red.

Source: Museum of the City of Zagreb, collection of plans.

center during the nineteenth century. It was erected in a flat, unbuilt area, and its core was structured as a U-shaped belt of gardens and parks that was filled with the buildings of various public institutions (education, museum, transport, health, and sports institutions). On the northern edge of the Lower Town, just beneath Kaptol and Gradec, the main commercial street Ilica and the new main city square, the Ban Jelačić Square, developed. The size of the new part of the city by far exceeded that of the old nucleus, the development of which was running more and more behind. Nevertheless, the old city core underwent considerable transformation over the course of the nineteenth century **[1]**.[1]

In this text attention will focus on the processes that caused this transformation: the reform of central administrative bodies of the Habsburg Monarchy and the rebuilding of the fortifications as key factors in the transformation of the center in the first half of the nineteenth century, and the concentration of

[2] Former Jesuit Monastery, circa 1900.

Source: Ivan Bogavčić's collection of postcards, Zagreb.

public institutions in the Upper Town and the desire for aestheticization and national recoding of the area as the main factors for change in the second half of the same century.

The Urban Transformation of Zagreb in the First Half of the Nineteenth Century

Of all the reform measures initiated in Vienna that influenced the transformation of central parts of Zagreb at the end of the eighteenth and in the first half of the nineteenth centuries, the reforms of the emperor Joseph II (1780–90) undoubtedly had the most profound impact on the development of the city. Of particular importance, primarily for the urban transformation of Gradec, was the secularization of parts of church property, and the closure of monasteries and certain churches and chapels. It enabled new construction in this densely built part of town, as well as the housing of both old and new public institutions.

All the monasteries that existed in Gradec were dissolved during the 1770s and 1780s. The Jesuit monastery was abolished first and all the real estate which had belonged to this order became state property. In 1784 the main monastery building became the location of the *Generalcommando*, the supreme Military Frontier authority in Croatia and Slavonia [2]. Of the Jesuit school institutions, the grammar school building maintained its role while the preparatory seminary building was converted into the Aristocratic Boarding School in 1796.[2]

The buildings and land of other dissolved monasteries became either temporary or permanent state property—that is, the property of the *Ärar* (Treasury). Some buildings were converted, some removed, and their plots used to construct residential and public buildings. The St. Claire monastery building in Opatička Street, dissolved in 1782, was first turned into a post office, and then into the financial administration building for Croatia.[3] The Capuchin monastery, which was dissolved last, in 1788, remained in the hands of the state for only a short period, and was later purchased by the County of Zagreb and sold into private ownership.[4]

While monastery buildings could at least be partially adapted to accommodate public institutions or for residential purposes, the churches standing next to them were not as fortunate, and most of them were dismantled. Out of all the churches that once stood in Gradec only two were preserved—the Parish Church of St. Mark, and the building that was first the Jesuit church, then the Grammar School church, and which finally became the University Church of St. Catherine. The Capuchin Church, St. Clare's Church, and St. Ursula's Chapel were demolished and the private residential palaces of Croatian noble families were constructed on their plots.[5]

In the same period, a series of aristocratic palaces was built in Gradec on the former city fortifications. This positioning enabled the creation of gardens on a sort of a miniature glacis, a green area beneath the town walls. Streets on the western and eastern margins of the Upper Town—Demetrova, Opatička, and partially also Visoka and Vranyczanyjeva—thus began to fill up with the monumental Neoclassical palaces belonging to the most influential Croatian families of the period: Drašković, Hellenbach, Sermage, Jelačić, and others.

Parts of the fortifications that could not be used for new residential construction—the city gates—were removed for traffic and aesthetic reasons. Only the eastern gate, known as the Stone Gate, survived thanks to the fact that it contained (and continues to contain) a chapel with a worshiped icon of the Madonna.

Under the town walls on the north and south sides of Gradec, a part of the former glacis was used in 1813 and 1839–45 to create the first public promenades (as in Vienna, where the intervention was on a much larger scale).[6] Similar interventions were made at the base of the town walls of Kaptol, where Bishop Aleksandar Alagović designed a spacious bishop's park, today called Ribnjak.[7] These were the first attempts at the aestheticization of the city's urban space, an indicator of the growth of communal awareness which would have a far stronger influence on the transformation of public spaces in the second half of the nineteenth century.

Stylistic Purification, Aestheticization and National Recoding of Churches

After the Austro-Hungarian Compromise of 1867 and the Croato-Hungarian Compromise of 1868, Croatia managed to obtain an inner autonomy in the Hungarian part of the Monarchy, which accelerated the demographic and urban development of its capital, Zagreb. Due to immigration from various parts of the Monarchy, its population became more diverse. It was still predominantly Catholic (around 90% throughout the nineteenth century) and the majority were Croat (68.22% of the population in 1880 and 75.58% in 1910).[8] However, the German language remained, until the turn of the century, the main language spoken by the economic and intellectual elite.

The focal point of urban development became the Lower Town, but both the state and the municipal government made a great effort to encourage the development of older parts of the city and their physical and visual integration with the new ones. A part of that effort was the monumentalization and aestheticization of buildings in old parts of Zagreb.

Out of all the buildings in the old city core, the ones that underwent the most profound transformation during the second half of the nineteenth century were the churches, which reflects the position held by the Catholic Church in Croatia (and Austria-Hungary in general) at the time, and the crucial role it played in the formation of Croatian national identity. As part of the campaign to make historic buildings more impressive so that they could honorably act as the "crown" of the Croatian capital, all medieval and Baroque churches were redesigned through Neo-Gothic, Neo-Renaissance and Neo-Byzantine restorations (which was a very widespread practice in Central Europe during this period).[9]

The period of restoration of monuments in Zagreb began with the intervention in the parish church of St. Mark in the Upper Town (1876–1882), prompted by the Bishop of Đakovo, Josip Juraj Strossmayer, then the most important patron of Croatian art and science. He succeeded in convincing Zagreb City Council not to demolish this building, as had been planned in order to make a spacious square in the center of the Upper Town, but rather to engage the famous Viennese Neo-Gothic expert Friedrich von Schmidt to carry out its restoration.

The church was rebuilt in the Neo-Gothic style. The completed restoration work reflects the aesthetic, stylistic and preservationist views of Historicism. It was motivated primarily by the aim of reconstructing the presumed original appearance of the building. Returning to the "original"—but actually idealized and never-existing—state led to the removal of most works of art from post-medieval periods not only in this church but also in most other restored buildings, all in the drive to achieve unity and purity of style. The principles of unity and purity of style dominated the restoration of monuments in every part of continental Europe. In Austria-Hungary, Schmidt played the key role in spreading this type of restoration,[10] so it is no wonder Strossmayer chose him to restore Zagreb's medieval monuments.

The key element of the church's new look was the roof made of glazed polychrome tiles with the coat-of-arms of the Triune Kingdom of Croatia, Slavonia and Dalmatia (the official name of Croatia at the time) and of the city of Zagreb, framed by motifs from Slavonian vernacular textile work. Although severely criticized for excessive coloristic effects after completion, it was immediately accepted by the citizens of Zagreb and became a new national symbol, due especially to the

[3] St. Mark's Parish Church, 2009
The roof is covered with polycrome glazed tiles in the motif of the Croatian and Zagreb coats of arms.

Photograph by the author.

fact that the coat of arms of Croatia did not contain the Hungarian crown of Saint Stephen (which was then the official version of the coat of arms used by the state).[11]

Without a doubt a clear political message lay behind the idea of placing such a roof on St. Mark's Church. The capital of Croatia strove to display unequivocally visible national heraldic symbols which referred to Croatian national consciousness. The message (from Bishop Strossmayer and the Zagreb city government to the Croatian and Hungarian authorities) was all the more explicit because the church was the highest-situated building in the city, and because it was surrounded by the seats of the main autonomous Croatian institutions: that of the *Ban*, of the Government, and of the Parliament.[12] [3]

With this intervention, St. Mark's Church was nationally recoded: it was *Croatized*. Just as Croatian became the official language of administration and as the population of the city became more and more linguistically Croatized, there was in the same way a tendency to put a national stamp on the most important architectural monuments as well. In Austria-Hungary, an empire marked by constant ethno-confessional conflicts, national recoding of monuments had great political importance, even more so because Zagreb was not just the political capital of Croatia but also the cultural capital of all Croats.

Although it sounds strange that the *Croatization* of St. Mark's Church was realized by a Viennese, German-born architect, it reflects the status Schmidt enjoyed at the time. The quality of his work was more important than his national identity. Furthermore, Croatian national identity was primarily built after Croato-Hungarian settlement in opposition to Hungarians and not to Austrian Germans, and it was also a matter of prestige to employ an architect from Vienna, the main capital of the Monarchy, on the Zagreb project.

Thanks to the restoration of St. Mark's Church, Strossmayer managed to achieve the dominance of Schmidt and his school in the restoration of monuments in Croatia, which lasted until the World War I. It led, first of all, the way to the restoration of Zagreb's Cathedral, the most significant Gothic medieval monument in Croatia. Again, the key role in the entire process was played by Bishop Strossmayer, who wanted to give the main church of the Croatian capital a look *worthy* of its role, and to restore the building to its *original* state, which again meant that all additions made in post-medieval epochs had to be removed.

The job was again assigned to Schmidt, who finished his designs for the restoration in 1878. His disciple Herman Bollé initiated the restoration work in November 1879. It was then that Bollé, originally from Cologne, moved to Zagreb and soon became the city's leading architect.[13]

The restoration changed the appearance of Zagreb Cathedral considerably—it received a new Neo-Gothic façade with tall towers. Simultaneously, its roof was covered, just like the roof of St. Mark's Church, with glazed tiles again based on motifs taken from Croatian vernacular textile—but politically much more neutral, without a coat of arms. While the restoration of St. Mark's Church was financed by municipal authorities that favored the opposition, the restoration of the cathedral was financed for the most part by the Archdiocese of Zagreb (which was close to the government) and by government funds. Therefore, the *Croatization* of architectural elements on the cathedral was not as emphasized. National recoding had to be mitigated for political reasons, as the Croatian government led by Narodna stranka (People's Party), and *Ban* Dragutin Khuen-Hédervàry (in office 1883–1903) was pro-Hungarian and avoided connections with Croatian nationalism.

While the national recoding, aestheticization, and monumentalization of important church buildings in Zagreb were parallel processes in the 1870s and early 1880s, from the mid-1880s restoration efforts concentrated only on aestheticization due to the new political circumstances and the diminishing influence of Bishop Strossmayer.

National symbols became far less accentuated, as attested by projects realized after the earthquake that hit Zagreb on November 9, 1880, causing considerable damage to numerous buildings and thus encouraging the aestheticization and monumentalization of all the other churches in Gradec and Kaptol. The medieval Franciscan Church was restored in the Neo-Gothic style, the parish church of St. Mary of Dolac in the German Neo-Renaissance style, and the Baroque St. Catherine's Church in the Neo-Baroque style, while the Greek-Catholic Church, a simple, modest Neoclassical building, was completely transformed in the Neo-Byzantine style.

The choice of style depended primarily on the function of the building and the date it was built. Catholic churches were rebuilt in styles that dominated the architecture of western Christianity—Neo-Gothic, Neo-Renaissance and Neo-Baroque—while the Eastern Rite church was rebuilt in the Neo-Byzantine style. The Neo-Gothic was particularly widespread as the first Croatian art historian, Iso Kršnjavi, tried to promote it as the Croatian national style in the early 1880s. Since Croatia's Gothic heritage was in part destroyed during the Ottoman wars of the sixteenth and seventeenth centuries, and the buildings that survived were considered too modest to be worthy models, Kršnjavi tried

[4] Zagreb Gradec/Upper Town with the Inner Department and Parliament building in the middle, 2013.

Photograph by the author.

to create the national style through the combination of elements from Gothic and vernacular Croatian architecture. He promoted the complete rebuilding of the Kaptol area in this style; however, his ideas could not be implemented due to lack of funds.[14]

Gradec as Croatia's Political Acropolis

As can be seen, the first half of the nineteenth century was a time when public, administrative, cultural, and social institutions began to concentrate in the Upper Town area. This process intensified in the second half of the same century. Beyond the previously mentioned institutions that started to occupy former monastery buildings, local government bodies bought an entire series of properties—mostly private mansions located in prominent positions from an urbanistic point of view. Already in 1808, a newly built mansion on the main St. Mark's Square was bought from the Kulmer family for the seat of the regional government in Croatia and of the *Ban*.[15] Soon numerous other purchases followed.

The Croato-Hungarian Settlement of 1868 accelerated the process of the concentration of public services in Gradec, thanks to the creation of a whole range of new public institutions that strove to be located as near as possible to the main centers of power: the *Ban* and the Parliament. All departments of the Croatian Provincial Government, along with many other public institutions, were housed there.

The state property portfolio not only continued to grow, but soon started to be rebuilt as well. The largest part of the work was undertaken for purely utilitarian reasons: lack of space. A large number of buildings were given more floors or new wings; however, some of them saw their facades and/or interior modified, which is a clear indication of how the need for aestheticization, noticeable at the time in church architecture, was reflected in public architecture as well.

The most important example of this process is the modification of the palace of the Department for Religious and Educational Affairs, situated in the former Vojkffy-Paravić mansion at 10 Opatička Street on Gradec. The palace was rebuilt in 1892–96 on the initiative of the then-head of Department Iso Kršnjavi, in accordance with the project of his favorite architect Herman Bollé. Its interior was richly furnished, and the central, so-called Golden Hall was decorated with scenes from Croatian history, which emphasized the political position of Croatia in the Austro-Hungarian Monarchy.[16] In this case the *Croatization* of architecture was implemented in the decoration of the interior.

The expansion of the building of the Internal Department and the Parliament (1908–11) represents a sort of culmination of the process of concentrating Croatian public institutions in Gradec. The new palace comprised the former Zagreb County Palace and five private houses that were torn down in order to make room for the new part of the building, which in the end took up the entire block in the very center of the Upper Town.

In a period when Modernism had already started to penetrate Croatian architecture, the style that was chosen for this building was Neoclassicism with some Art Nouveau elements, to fit in, as explained by government officials of the time, with the architectural milieu of the Upper Town. However, the new palace, due to its height, was totally oversized for the area and as a result considerably damaged its urban cohesion.[17] [4]

The expansion of state administration in the end completely "ate up" the central block of Zagreb's historic nucleus. It reflects the process of the bureaucratization of society, but at the same time the existence of the idea, though not entirely developed, of preserving the specific appearance of the Upper Town.

Aestheticization of Private Palaces and Public Spaces in the Upper Town and Kaptol

The concentration of administrative services in the Upper Town which occupied, as could be seen, numerous previously residential buildings, considerably stalled economic and demographic growth in this part of the city. Therefore, it is not surprising that in the nineteenth century not even one single bank decided to open its office in the Upper Town, and only a very small number of shops managed to stay open.

The remaining residential parts of the Upper Town, however, still maintained a certain prestige, especially the streets near the former walls where houses could have private parks and gardens.

Demographic and social changes were very fast—almost all the old aristocratic palaces changed hands. Some were purchased by public institutions, and others became the property of the new bourgeoisie. Some mansions, mostly those with modest Baroque facades, were also transformed in the late nineteenth and early twentieth centuries for the same reason that churches and public buildings were restored—the need to make them more spacious and lavishly decorated. An especially interesting example was the rebuilding of the Pongratz Palace at 22 Visoka Street. The building, the central part of which is a medieval tower rebuilt at the end of the eighteenth century, was extended in 1902–1903 by Fellner & Helmer, a respectable Viennese atelier specializing in the construction of theatres and department stores, which undoubtedly demonstrated the status of the family in Zagreb society.[18]

[5] Friedrich von Schmidt and Herman Bollé, *Pillar of Immaculata*, 1879–81.

Source: National and University Library, Zagreb, collection of postcards.

In tandem with the aestheticization of public and residential buildings there was a tendency to aestheticize open, public spaces as well. However, very few public monuments were erected, mostly for political reasons. Croatian authorities, in order to show their loyalty to Vienna and, especially, to Budapest, did not raise monuments to controversial national heroes next to their administrative palaces. Instead, they were placed in the new part of the city, the Lower Town, on the initiative of either oppositional municipal authorities or private financiers. Over the course of the entire nineteenth century only two totally non-political public sculptures were displayed in the old parts of the city, in Grič Park and on Jesuit Square, where a sculpture of a fisherman was incorporated in Viktor Kovačić's architectural composition (1908–1909). This was a pure and simple aestheticization of (public) space, as is clearly evident from the total political neutrality of the sculpture and the entire composition—which is understandable since the decoration was financed by the army (the Imperial and Royal Corps Command, or *K. u. K. Korps-kommando*).[19] A similar, somewhat earlier example is the construction of the pillar of Immaculata with a fountain in front of the cathedral in Kaptol (1879–1881), designed by Friedrich von Schmidt and built by Herman Bollé. [5]

Prior to the First World War (1910–1912), partly from a similar urge for aestheticization, and partly to achieve a better integration of the Upper and the Lower Town, the new architectural infrastructure of the South Promenade was built and the new Zakmardi's Steps were realized in a certain kind of modernized Neo-Romanesque style, in accordance with Hugo Ehrlich's project, who concurrently built new steps along the North Promenade as well.[20]
However, due to the difference in altitude, neither the new steps nor the funicular that had already been built in 1889 at the bottom of Bregovita/Tomićeva Street brought the successful integration of the Upper Town with the new urban centre lying on flat land, thanks to which there were no major alterations to the urban matrix of Gradec in the second half of the nineteenth century.

The Urban Transformation of Kaptol

Secularization, which sped up the processes of the urban transformation of Gradec in the first half of the nineteenth century, had almost no effect on Kaptol. Not a single monastery, church or chapel in this part of town was dissolved. Furthermore, the existing walls and gates around Kaptol were not removed in that period and the area next to them was not as suitable for the construction of residential buildings as it had been in Gradec, as the walls faced the polluted Medveščak stream on the west side, and most parts of the walls on the east side had already been incorporated into the houses of the canons of the Zagreb Cathedral Chapter.
For this reason, the urban transformation of this part of the city and its physical unification with the rest of Zagreb only began in the 1860s, when the city gates were removed. In the end, however, it was far more comprehensive than the interventions in Gradec.
Even though Kaptol also lies at a somewhat higher altitude than the Lower Town, it is nevertheless positioned much lower than the Upper Town, which eventually enabled its stronger integration with the new part of Zagreb. The monumentality and luxuriousness of new bourgeois residential, business, and public buildings in the Lower Town strongly influenced the urge to make the old part of Zagreb equally monumental. This tendency was most pronounced in Kaptol, since the clash between the old and the new was most evident in this most neglected part of town: the south-west corner of Kaptol (Dolac and Tkalčićeva Street) was situated directly behind the north row of the new monumental palaces on the central Ban Jelačić Square.
Plans for the thorough urban renovation of this area began to appear in the final years of the nineteenth century. The first design (along with scale models that have not been preserved) was the work of the city engineer Milan Lenuci for the Millennium Exhibition in Budapest 1896, which was then published by Josef Stübben in 1897 in the respected Berlin journal *Deutsche Bauzeitung*. Traffic and health concerns were listed as main reasons for the demolition of the old neighborhood, as well as aesthetic ones—the desire to replace narrow alleys with wide and modern city streets, just like in other

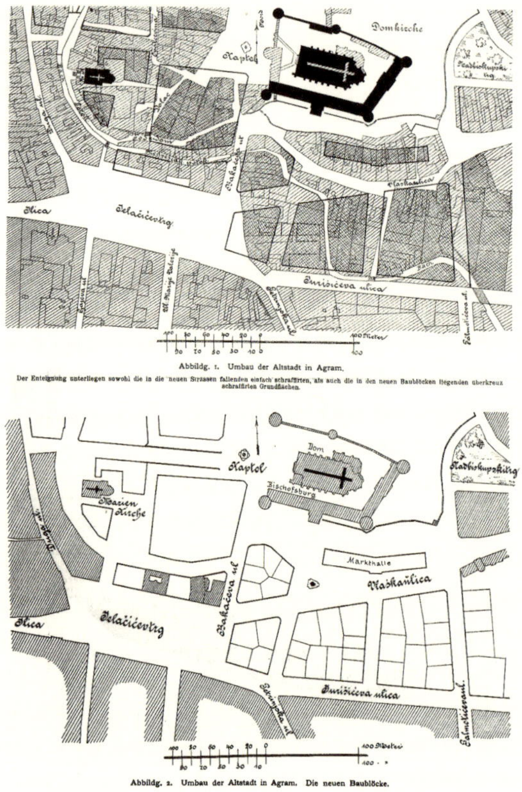

[6] Milan Lenuci, Design for the urban renewal of Kaptol and surrounding areas, 1895–96.

Source: *Deutsche Bauzeitung* XXXI/53 (1897), p. 333.

European metropolises.[21] Lenuci's plan envisaged the demolition of all buildings in Kaptol located north of Ban Jelačić Square and west of the cathedral, as well as of houses in Vlaška Street and also to some extent in Jurišićeva Street in the Lower Town, south of the archbishop's palace. This would open up views of this building and of the cathedral, in a similar way as had been done in many other cities—especially in Germany, where cathedrals were being "liberated" from nearby structures (a process known as *Freilegung*). Such an intervention would also "liberate" the parish church of St. Mary from adjacent structures, and to its north there would be a street, in the text referred to as "Prospektstraße", which would lead directly to the cathedral and thus enable its visual opening towards the west [6].[22] However, due to a lack of funding, a complete transformation of this neglected part of Zagreb was not effected until the 1920s, when only the south-western part of Kaptol (Dolac) was demolished and in place of the picturesque neighborhood a new town market was built.[23]

Prior to the World War I, the only demolition of larger extent realized in Kaptol was the removal of the western part of the archbishop's fort with the so-called Bakač Tower. Built in the early sixteenth century to provide protection from Ottoman assaults, its role as a fortification was obviously no longer relevant. [7] The initiative to remove this part of the fort had been mooted since the 1860s, but in the period when the restoration of the cathedral was coming to an end in 1901 intense discussions about its future were revived. Although many Croatian historians were opposed to the idea, it was realized in 1906–07 [8].

As soon as it was torn down it became evident that the wrong decision had been made, irreversibly destroying the picturesqueness of Kaptol. For this reason a public competition for designs to rebuild this part of town was organized in 1908. Viktor Kovačić, the champion of Croatian modern architecture, won the competition with a design that anticipated not only construction of a new wall and a tower in front of the cathedral, but also, just as in Lenuci's design, a complete rebuilding of south-western part of Kaptol and of Vlaška Street. The planned intervention was justified on functional, utilitarian, traffic, and health grounds, but the material factor of lack of money stopped the works, and so the area in front of the cathedral has retained to this day the vague contours it gained after demolitions in the early twentieth century.[24]

[7] left: Hermann Fickert, Photograph of Zagreb cathedral before its restoration and the removal of western part of the archbishop's fort, 1880.

Source: Museum of the City of Zagreb, collection of photographs.

[8] right: Zagreb Cathedral after its restoration and the removal of the western part of archbishop's fort, circa 1910.

Source: Jura Gašparac's collection of postcards, Zagreb.

Concluding Remarks

Although Kovačić's project remained unrealized, discussions stirred by the demolition of Bakač Tower gave impetus to the founding of the Provincial Committee for the Preservation of Artistic and Historic Monuments in Croatia and Slavonia in 1910. Due to this newly formed institutional framework and to a new approach to the conservation of monuments, attitudes toward the buildings located in the historical nucleus of Zagreb changed significantly. Even though interventions, in some cases very destructive ones, continued, the awareness of the need to preserve Gradec and Kaptol intensified and led to the creation of a legal framework which protected these parts of the city.[25]

Endnotes

1 On Zagreb nineteenth century urbanism, see: Aleksander Laslo, "Zagreb, 1880–1918. Modern Architectural Town Planning in Zagreb," in *Shaping the Great City. Modern Architecture in Central Europe, 1890–1937,* ed. Eve Blau and Monika Platzer (Munich, London, New York: Prestel, 1999), pp. 136–139; Snješka Knežević, "Milan Lenuci and the Urbanism of Zagreb," in *Project Zagreb. Transition as Condition, Strategy, Practice*, ed. Eve Blau and Ivan Rupnik (Barcelona: Actar, 1997), pp. 84–89.

2 Lelja Dobronić, *Zagrebački Kaptol i Gornji grad nekad i danas* (Zagreb: Školska knjiga, 1986), pp. 206–14, pp. 226–235.

3 Dobronić, *Zagrebački*, p. 272.

4 Emilij Laszowski, Stari i novi Zagreb (Zagreb: Hrvatski štamparski zavod, 1925), p. 171; Dobronić, *Zagrebački*, pp. 195–96.

5 Dobronić, *Zagrebački*, pp. 173, 190–94, p. 264.

6 Harald Stühlinger, *Der Wettbewerb zur Wiener Ringstraße. Entstehung, Projekte, Auswirkungen* (Basel: Birkhäuser, 2015), p. 36.

7 Bojana Bojanić Obad Šćitaroci and Mladen Obad Šćitaroci, *Gradski perivoji Hrvatske u 19. stoljeću. javna perivojna arhitektura hrvatskih gradova u europskom kontekstu* (Zagreb: Šćitaroci, Arhitektonski fakultet, 2004), pp. 134–36; Ivan Kampuš and Igor Karaman, *Zagreb through a Thousand Years, from Ancient Settlements to Modern City* (Zagreb: Školska knjiga, 1995), pp. 162–63; Krešimir Regan, "Preporodno doba" in *Povijest grada Zagreba*, ed. Slavko Goldstein and Ivo Goldstein (Zagreb: Novi liber, 2012), pp. 252–297 (pp. 279–283).

8 Tomislav Timet, *Stambena izgradnja Zagreba do 1954. godine*, (Zagreb: JAZU, 1961), pp. 50-54.

9 József Sisa, "Neo-Gothic Architecture and Restoration of Historic Buildings in Central Europe: Friedrich Schmidt and his School," *Journal of the Society of Architectural Historians* 61/2 (2002): pp. 170–187.

10 Walter Frodl, *Idee und Verwirklichung. Das Werden d. staatl. Denkmalpflege in Österreich* (Vienna, Cologne, Graz: Böhlau, 1988), p. 144.

11 Janko Barlè, *Povijest župa i crkava zagrebačkih 1* (Zagreb, 1896), 9; Dragan Damjanović, "Schmidt-Bolléova obnova crkve u drugoj polovici 19. stoljeća" in *Crkva sv. Marka u Zagrebu: arhitektura, povijest, obnova*, ed. Petar Puhmajer (Zagreb: Hrvatski restauratorski zavod, 2013), pp. 63–96.

12 Dragan Damjanović, "Polychrome Roof Tiles and National Style in Nineteenth-century Croatia," *Journal of the Society of Architectural Historians*, 70/4 (2011): pp. 466–491.

13 Ana Deanović and Željka Čorak, *Zagrebačka katedrala* (Zagreb: Kršćanska sadašnjost, 1988); Dragan Damjanović, *Arhitekt Herman Bollé* (Zagreb: Leykam International, Muzej za umjetnost i obrt, 2013), pp. 132–187.

14 Damjanović, *Arhitekt*, pp. 121-123.

15 Dobronić, *Zagrebački*, pp. 173, 175–76; Kampuš and Karaman, *Zagreb*, p. 155.

16 Olga Maruševski, *Iso Kršnjavi kao graditelj* (Zagreb: Društvo povjesničara umjetnosti Hrvatske, 1986), pp. 185–202; Olga Maruševski, *Iso Kršnjavi. Kultura i politika na zidovima palače u Opatičkoj 10* (Zagreb: Hrvatski institut za povijest, 2002).

17 Dobronić, *Zagrebački*, p. 294; Lelja Dobronić, "Povijest palače Hrvatskoga sabora," *Radovi Instituta za povijest umjetnosti* 17/2 (1993): pp. 89–105; Darja Radović Mahečić, "Sekvenca secesije – arhitekt Lav Kalda," *Radovi Instituta za povijest umjetnosti* 30 (2006): pp. 241–64.

18 Dragan Damjanović, Iskra Iveljić, "Arhitektonski atelijer Fellner & Helmer i obitelj Pongratz" (Architecture Studio Fellner & Helmer and the Pongratz Family), *Radovi Instituta za povijest umjetnosti* 39 (2015): pp. 121-134.

19 Snješka Knežević, *Zagrebu u središtu* (Zagreb: Barbat, 2003), pp. 275-277.

20 Žarko Domljan, *Hugo Ehrlich* (Zagreb: Društvo povjesničara umjetnosti Hrvatske, 1979), pp. 58-63.

21 Tanja Damljanović Conley and Emily Gunzburger Makaš, "Shaping Central and Southeastern European Capital Cities in the Age of Nationalism," in *Capital Cities in the Aftermath of Empires: Planning in Central and Southeastern Europe*, ed. Emily Gunzburger Makaš and Tanja Damljanović Conley, (London: Routledge, 2010), pp. 1–28 (at p.10).

22 Josef Stübben, "Der Umbau der inneren Stadt Agram," *Deutsche Bauzeitung* XXXI/53 (1897): pp. 330–31, 333; Knežević, *Zagrebu*, pp. 264–65; Snješka Knežević, "Nadbiskupski/Langov trg: mijene i poništenje," *Radovi Instituta za povijest umjetnosti* 28 (2004): pp. 250–69 (261–62); Snješka Knežević, "Milan Lenuci", pp. 85–86.

23 Zlatko Jurić, Martina Strugar, "Karlo Vajda i Vjekoslav Bastl – Detaljna regulacijska osnova i arhitektonski projekti tržnice na Dolcu u Zagrebu, 1925–1927. godine," *Radovi Instituta za povijest umjetnosti* 33 (2009): pp. 307–318; Zlatko Jurić and Martina Strugar, "Karlo Vajda i Vjekoslav Bastl: Izgradnja tržnice na Dolcu u Zagrebu, 1928–1936," *Prostor* 19, 1[41] (2011): pp. 200–213.

24 Knežević, *Zagrebu u središtu*, pp. 265–272. Olga Maruševski, "Kovačić u kontekstu svog vremena," in *Arhitekt Viktor Kovačić. Život i djelo*, ed. Miroslav Begović (Zagreb: Hrvatska akademija znanosti i umjetnosti, Hrvatski muzej arhitekture, 2003), pp. 29–50 (34–38); Zlatko Jurić, "Viktor Kovačić – prolog u regulaciju Kaptola, 1908," *Prostor* 13, 1[29] (2005): pp. 23–39.

25 This work has been fully supported by the Croatian Science Foundation under project 4153 Croatia and Central Europe: Art and Politics in the Late Modern Period (1780–1945).

URBAN LARGESSE
Chicago's Scalar Simultaneity

Sarah M. Whiting

Globalism's Scales

NASA's "blue marble" photograph, which was first beamed back to earth from Apollo 17 in 1972, permitted the world's inhabitants to apprehend the earth as a singular entity: it was the first time one could "see" our world as a whole. The world has only been getting smaller ever since. Air travel from the US to Europe used to require a refueling stopover in Nova Scotia. Today, one can fly direct from Dubai to Auckland, provided one is willing to sit for seventeen hours and fifteen minutes. Meanwhile, satellite technology permits us to communicate instantaneously across the globe, provided one is willing to disregard time zones. In short, even if the pace of globalization has been breathtaking, it has nevertheless permitted us to grasp the scale of this new world—or at least to grasp the concept of a single world.

Grasping the scale of a city and what "city" means for us as metropolitan citizens, however, isn't as obvious. The geography of cities can never be reduced to the neatness of a globe or a blue marble. Our inability to grasp the totality of the metropolitan whole is due to the tension between physical, urban delineations and non-physical economic, social, and political ones. Our direct understanding of the urban retains the scale of our human experience, even though the urban constantly immerses us in utterly non-scalar information—data, climate details, economic indicators and other kinds of facts and figures. The vastness of mass production and the commensurate scale of commodity exchange that emerged with industrialization only exacerbated the challenges of urban agglomeration: the social, political and economic tensions that arose when the urban began exceeding the scale of the village or town.

NASA's photo allowed us to comprehend the globe as an object: calling it the "blue marble" made the world something we could all understand, bringing its scale down to a little glass ball that we could conceivably just slip into a pocket.

Cities, however, cannot be rendered as viewable objects as easily as all that. It's true that Manhattan can be photographed as a whole—from Google Earth the island borough does *sort* of look like a boat or a whale, caught between two rivers—but there is no visual that captures all of New York City.

Instead, cities tend to be condensed in other ways: not as objects but through *urban narratives*—myths, monikers and metaphors that permit us to tame a given unruly metropolis as "the Big Apple," the "City of Lights," the "City of Big Shoulders," and the like. These narratives are shortcuts—Post-It notes that try to capture complexity within a single phrase.

Infrastructure similarly parses cities into organizations that we're able to get our heads around: grids, avenues, streets, and squares—*urban figures* that lasso the urban realm, taming it. And that taming is the urban designer's dual role: first, the job of making the city work as a complex organism, and second, the job of translating that organism to the public at large, the city's metropolitan inhabitants.

Translating is, in fact, a far better term for this task than *taming*. Urban design translates the worlds of economics, politics, social relations, culture and physical history into physical forms that will, ideally, not break our urban histories but rather will extend them into new chapters. Idealized, abstract, totalizing narratives are critical for advancing our urban futures, but they can also be the urban designer's version of the Post-It note: singular visions of a "green city," or a "horizontal city," or a "generic city" that capture the imagination—but in such a way that they gloss over the complexity that underlies any city, particularly economic complications. Cities are made up of individual parcels of land. This economic parcelization of the land can often be at odds with the social intricacies of urban life. Particularly within the American context, platting, or land division, is where the individual butts right up against the collective, and vice versa.

As architectural historian Alan Colquhoun already pointed out more than forty years ago, however, global capital has further complicated this tension between the individual and the collective, as demonstrated by private capital's subsuming of ever-greater areas of any given city: "If one looks at any modern city, one cannot help being struck by the fact that much of it consists of large pieces of real estate, each of which is financed and organized as a single entity."[1] And the legibility of these large pieces is becoming ever harder to discern. Where once one could point to the Waterside Generating Plant between Thirty-eighth Street and Fortieth Street in Manhattan and identify that entire superblock as being Consolidated Edison's property, today entire city zones are owned by conglomerates that develop these zones as small cities complete unto themselves within a larger metropolitan environment (to wit: Hudson Yards, "the largest private real estate development in the history of the United States and the largest development in New York City since Rockefeller Center."[2])

Paralleling this scalar expansion has been a second form of capitalized urbanism: the homogenization of urban development across the world, particularly evident with retail development but increasingly with residential and office

[1] A Starbucks on every corner of the world, 2017.

Source: wikicommons.

development as well. What was first a phenomenon of finding a Starbucks [1] on a corner of every city has become a repetition of identical commercial areas: the very same global retail chains proliferate in the very same way in and around Houston, Beijing, Madrid, and Budapest. Such standardization compensates for the fiscal risks that conglomerates take with their rapid, rampant development. It creates an international urban familiarity: whole cities have become like the hotel atria that Andreas Gursky has photographed all over the world. Only the caption identifiers distinguish his shots of the Grand Hyatt in Shanghai from the Hyatt Regency in Atlanta.

But here we hit a curious paradox: development is more and more homogenized and this sameness breeds a comfortable familiarity among the world's inhabitants—or at least the inhabitants of the globalized "first world." At the same time, given the way that markets work, high-priced items still require a certain individualization in order for the price to be justified. The paradox, then, is that urban development walks a fine line between repetition and difference. One way it does so is through narrative, so we return again to the significance of the urban narrative. Just as the city adopts narratives of big apples and big shoulders, neighborhoods acquire character through particularized nomenclature.

It is striking how many urban designers, from the most radical to the most conservative and across the last century, advocate an "ideal unit." Whether or not they call it a neighborhood, that's essentially what they mean. Neighborhoods are typically defined by their *walkability* (a ten-minute radius), *amenities* (grocery stores, parks and schools), *character* (hip, bohemian, boomer, live-work), or *population* (an "ideal" range of 3,000 to 5,000 inhabitants). The homogeneity of this "ideal" population is a socio-economic-political by-product that we cannot ignore—in other words, it's almost inevitable that neighborhoods are homogeneous communities.

The neighborhood is certainly an urban inevitability: it is the physical organization of the scale of social interaction that exceeds the family but that is part of a daily or weekly routine, whether tied to schools, groceries, or other amenities. At the same time, the neighborhood concept should not prevent understanding or promoting the city in broader, more synthetic terms. Neighborhoods are, in essence, little villages, and now, well into the twenty-first century, it is essential to ensure that as urbanists, we are working collectively to advance urban thinking beyond a pre-industrial model. Cities should be more than agglomerations of hamlets.

To counter this overwhelming tendency to render cities into collections of small-scale entities, the remainder of this text will examine three moments in Chicago's history when there were attempts to conceive of and design that city at multiple scales simultaneously: the Chicago Plan of 1909, the Quarter Section competition of 1913, and the Near South Side Plan of 1946. None of these examples took root; even so, they offer up possible models for advancing a multi-scalar form of urban design. And they do so in a context that is decidedly neighborhood-oriented. In Chicago, novelists, politicians and chefs can agree on one thing, perhaps only one thing: Chicago is a city of neighborhoods.

Chicago aggregates neighborhoods that are characterized by geography (*Uptown*), ethnicity (*Greektown*), economy (*Printers' Row*), and history (*Bronzeville*). But Chicago, with its mile-square gridding (a powerful remnant of the Northwest Ordinance of 1787) and its flat, expansive geography (Lake Michigan severs one edge of the city's otherwise flat endlessness) lends itself particularly well to being parsed into neighborhoods.

Chicago 1909: The Burnham Plan

Chicago has long capitalized upon its identity as a city of neighborhoods. In 1942, the Chicago Plan Commission published "Forty-Four Cities in the City of Chicago." Another Chicago Plan Commission report, "Building New Neighborhoods," published the following year, proposed new subdivision design standards and redevelopment strategies with the stated purpose of making "suburban-style residences in the city that would keep Chicagoans in Chicago."[3] This is the same Chicago Plan Commission that was formed in tandem with Burnham's Chicago Plan of 1909. Then-Mayor Fred Busse appointed 328 men, representing the city's business and social interests, to promote

[2] Jules Guérin, *Chicago Civic Center*, 1909 (from: the Burnham Plan of Chicago).

Source: https://upload.wikimedia.org/wikipedia/commons/1/1f/BurnhamPlanOfChicago-CivicCenterPlaza-JulesGuerin.jpg

Burnham's plan. From one to forty-four in thirty-three years: *make no little plans became make a whole lot of little cities.*

The backlash to Burnham's Plan didn't take thirty-three years, however; it began almost immediately after the Plan's completion. Already in 1911, landscape architect Jens Jensen described Burnham's Plan as "inhuman, imperialistic, and undemocratic."[4] Progressive planners, sociologists, settlement house activists, community leaders, and designers all coalesced around a critique of what they perceived to be the business-first single-mindedness of the Chicago Plan Commission leaders. Reacting to what they saw to be the Plan's problem—its singularity—they advocated multiplication.

"Organize the whole" versus "break down the parts" remains a dichotomy that's all too familiar today: *singular versus plural; imperial versus democratic.* Cities can't be reduced to binaries. Sure, it's easy to focus solely on one of Jules Guerin's bird's eye views of the 1909 Plan [2]. These watercolors dramatize Burnham's baroque boulevards, centering on the colossal Civic Center. But the Plan's brilliance is that it already introduced multiple scales: regionally scaled forest preserves, a city-scaled park along the waterfront, and playgrounds dispersed throughout the city. Critics mistook coherence for singularity and, rather than embracing the multi-scalar aspects of the plan, they advocated for what really amounts to a balkanized alternative.

Burnham's Plan wasn't singular versus plural: it was both at once. That's what neighborhood boosters forgot when they grew anxious about the Plan's scale. And it's what they continue to forget when they focus only on neighborhood planning. Burnham's famous mandate "make no little plans; they have no magic to stir men's blood" did not mean that the Chicago Plan overlooked the small: it merely absorbed many plans into its multi-scalar logic.

[3] Walter D. Moody, *Wacker's Manual of the Plan of Chicago book cover*, reprint of 1911 original.

Source: https://buildingchicago.files.wordpress.com/2014/09/wackers-manual-cover-sept-20142.jpg

Chicago 1913: The Quarter Section Competition

The Chicago Plan Commission also recognized that while planning is a work of formal and spatial design, policy and education are equally crucial in a plan's adoption and long-term maintenance. Strategic offshoots of the Plan were developed in order to inform the general public, creating an audience for urban design for years to come. Walter Moody, managing director of the Chicago Plan Commission, especially recognized this public responsibility: in addition to organizing "Nehemiah Day Services," which coordinated 80 ministers in delivering sermons that tied the Plan to the Old Testament's prophecy "therefore we, His servants, will arise and build," Moody produced and distributed *Wacker's Manual of the Plan of Chicago* [3], a condensed version of the Plan, which was dispersed to every public school eighth grader (every thirteen-year-old child) in the city of Chicago between 1911 and the mid-1920s. Consequently, through World War II, at least, most Chicago adults had had a civic education that had included detailed study of the Burnham Plan.

Despite this public relations effort to help educate Chicagoans about the Plan and about planning more generally, backlash against its perceived singularity unmoored a flotilla of smallness in Chicago, culminating in the hundreds of neighborhoods used by today's real estate maps of the city. While the American planner and sociologist Clarence Perry is widely credited with coining both the concept and the term "neighborhood unit" in a study he did for New York's Regional Plan Association in 1929,[5] already as early as 1913, the Chicago City Club sponsored an urban design competition promoting a neighborhood urbanism of the "quarter section"—a quarter mile square, or 160 acres. The terms of the competition defined a community or neighborhood as being primarily residential, with a bit of civic and commercial use added in. The imaginary site, which was eight miles from Chicago's center, was only for a residential community, as it was connected to places of work by rail.[6] In short, the competition promoted but a fraction of a city—the competition press release even specified that it aimed to "encourage landowners and capitalists to promote social welfare by developing ideal suburbs."[7]

While some of the proposals isolated these fractions from their surroundings, creating isolated mini-cities that foreshadowed the cul-de-sac suburban planned developments all too familiar to us today (the most extraordinary version being an intricate, snowflake-like plan submitted by Louis Boynton), several schemes capitalized on Chicago's generous grid, creating new urban subdivisions that were not isolated like suburbs but were instead integral to the city. Architect William Drummond, who was placed second, coined the term "neighborhood unit" in his submittal.[8] Drummond used the neologism in his project description, explaining that the neighborhood unit should approximate the size of the quarter section, operating as a social and political unit with the aim of re-establishing a coherent civil society:

"The citizen is to-day [sic] removed from an effective voice in the political expression of the city, because he now uses no consistent and orderly method of local expression. The very mass of the city makes it a prey to spoilsmen. The real intelligence of the community is inoperative and frequent "reform" movements to improve conditions are baffled. The organization of the entire city into working units would bring about systematic activity and a broad civic unity of purpose."[9]

For Drummond, the twentieth-century city should be a collection of these neighborhood units. For him, the unit was a means of taming the industrialized metropolis so that it could continue to grow, while also fostering the civic ties that were being tested by modernism. Each neighborhood unit had its own amenities, but each was seamlessly woven into Chicago's fabric, rather than called out physically as an independent entity. As he noted, the American context discourages community ownership and planning, unlike parallel situations in both Germany and England. For Drummond, the neighborhood unit offered a means of negotiating the context of twentieth-century urban capitalism.

Also included among the competition schemes that redesigned the city, rather than suburbanizing it, was Frank Lloyd Wright's "non-competitive" entry [4], submitted after the deadline (not desiring to "compete," Wright still wanted to demonstrate his intelligence regarding the solution), which integrated multiple densities, ranging from apartment buildings to "seven- and eight-room houses, better class." Wright's scheme pin-wheeled buildings around intersections, allying with the larger Chicago grid but introducing spatial variety throughout the quarter section, particularly in its interior.

Wright's design maintained the overriding orthogonality of the Chicago grid system, but eschewed monotony by introducing what he called "picturesque variety." He introduced the "quadruple block plan," which adopted a square rather than rectangular block subdivision for the plan's single-family homes. By placing only four houses on a single small block, Wright was able to offer each house its own orientation. He rotates the four around an inner core of shared utilities, thereby guaranteeing a degree of privacy while also ensuring visual variety: quoting Wright's text explaining the layout, he says "His building is in unconscious but necessary grouping with three of his neighbors," looking out upon harmonious groups of other neighbors, no two of which would present to him the same elevation even were they all cast in one mold. "A succession of buildings of any given length by this arrangement presents the aspect of well-grouped buildings in a park, of greater picturesque variety than is possible where façade follows façade."[10] Wright created a picturesque relationship between buildings and park without sacrificing the grid or green space. An internal park system, financed by the sale of the residential property, weaves its way through the subdivision, ordering recreational features such as playgrounds, athletic

[4] Frank Lloyd Wright, *Plan of Quarter Section*, as published in A.B. Yeomans, ed., *City Residential Land Development* (Chicago: University of Chicago Press, 1916).

Source: http://www.averyreview.com/content/3-issues/10-10/8-chicagos-multi-scalar-alternatives/whiting-03.jpg

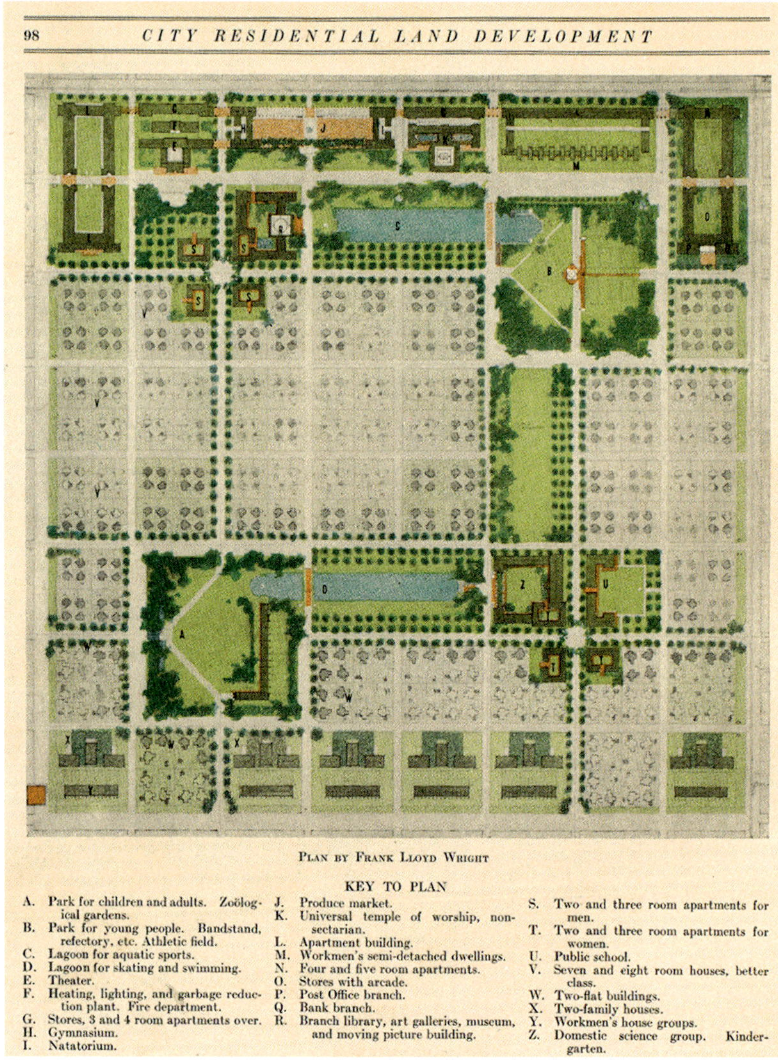

fields, and a music pavilion. Balanced, although not entirely symmetrically, around a diagonal axis across the site, the park subtly segregates the residential from the civic and commercial sections of the subdivision. It also differentiates residential zones of seven- or eight-room houses, two-flat buildings, workmen's houses, and women's and men's apartment buildings. With this park, Wright's proposal surpasses both the tower in the park and suburban residential development strategies. The park reaches to the edges of the superblock but, unlike the green carpets that Le Corbusier would design a decade later, this one is strategically programmed: it combines low-rise and medium-rise densities with non-residential programming to perpetually animate the entire subdivision. While the park system blocks some streets, it never creates cul-de-sacs and refuses to turn its back on Chicago.[11] While Wright's Quarter-Section Plan for the 1913 Competition was never executed, it demonstrates how development can work within the logic of the Chicago grid without being entirely subsumed by that grid: Wright's scheme offers an urbanism of its own that emerges from the larger gridded urbanism within Chicago's DNA.

Burnham, Drummond and Wright animated and even deliberately agitated the neighborhood-city relationship. The residential areas that they envisioned were not isolated from the broader context of the city; these architects were not proposing self-sufficient islands, but smaller-scaled pieces of the city that were dependent upon yet other pieces of the city, which in turn, depended upon them.

Chicago 1946: The Near South Side Plan

Writing at the end of the 1940s, planner Reginald Isaacs, who was then Director of the Planning Staff of Michael Reese Hospital in Chicago and would go on to chair the planning department at Harvard, was appalled by the prevailing obsession with neighborhoods. He was particularly struck by the failure of the neighborhood proponents to recognize the impossibility of reproducing a rural community within an urban environment.[12] Rural communities typically center on a single school and a single church, and their attendant, relatively homogeneous population. For urban organizations, on the other hand, such homogeneity is not only less likely but also anathema to what a city is: a mash-up of vibrant (if unpredictable) cultural exchanges.

While Isaacs was the most ardent critic of neighborhood planning, he wasn't alone in spotting an incompatibility between the neighborhood ideal and the urban real: as Perry's neighborhood unit reached its twentieth anniversary, it was reviewed by sociologists, architects, planners, and historians. In a nuanced article laying out the complexities of urban neighborhood planning, Lewis Mumford acknowledged that it was relatively easy to plan communities as suburban bubbles, but far more challenging to integrate them into a larger urban fabric.[13] Isaacs furthered this argument, honing in on a more volatile kind of integration: "The neighborhood," he wrote, "is an excellent device and framework for the organization and enforcement of covenants and deed restrictions against FHA's inharmonious groups. Today, the fear of minority group infiltration is substituted for a common denominator of neighborhood consciousness."[14] Isaacs recognized that neighborhood boosterism could be deployed as a seemingly innocent cover for discrimination; the May 1948 Supreme Court case Shelley v. Kraemer was a unanimous ruling declaring that a court may not constitutionally enforce a "restrictive covenant" that prevents people of certain race from owning or occupying property. Isaacs posited that without that tool, fearful residents would turn to claims of neighborhood and community "definition" to prevent integration. And his assumptions were not unfounded: developer J.C. Nichols, who had largely depended on restrictive covenants in drawing up the deed restrictions for his suburban developments around Kansas City, wrote with all sincerity in a *Time Magazine* article that "when you rear children in a good neighborhood, they will go out and fight Communism."[15] As Isaacs

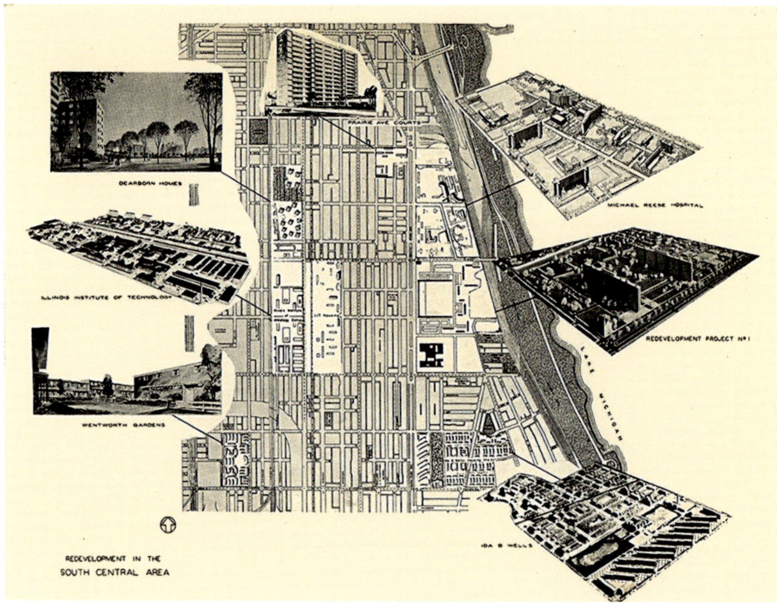

[5] South Side Planning Board, "Redevelopment in the South Central Area," in John McKinlay, *Redevelopment Project No. 1*, 1949.

Source: http://www.averyreview.com/content/3-issues/10-10/8-chicagos-multi-scalar-alternatives/whiting-04.jpg

noted in response, "[Nichols] is representative of many who, disregarding the mobility of urban life, say that the Negro, Pole, Jew, Mexican, Italian, and other "inharmonious" persons shall continue to live in his confined ghetto and that the neat division of a "neighborhood" unit around him is just what is wanted."[16] But if not neighborhood planning, then what? As Planning Director of Michael Reese, Isaacs was deeply involved with Chicago's Near South Side Plan, one of the few truly modern plans to be implemented in the United States. The South Side Planning Board, which was founded in 1946, was a nonprofit organization initiated by IIT and Michael Reese Hospital that architecture critic Ada Louise Huxtable described—with clear astonishment—as being composed of "Catholic, Protestant, Jewish, Negro, Labor, Railroad, Industrial-Commercial, Real Estate, and Public Housing" interests, all focused on the replanning of a seven-square-mile area of Chicago just south of the Loop.[17] The South Side Planning Board wasn't a government entity; it wasn't an elected body; it had no given powers. In short, the SSPB was the very model of the civic associations that had so fascinated Alexis de Tocqueville in his trip across America a century earlier: as he had noted, these uniquely American societal organizations enabled, channeled, and also masked various interlocking regimes of economic and political power. The South Side Planning Board was an alliance of academics from IIT and the University of Chicago, business leaders from Chicago's Loop, and neighborhood clergy and community organizers, even including the editor in chief of the *Chicago Defender*, the country's most prominent black newspaper. The Board's resulting Near South Side Plan [5], developed and partially implemented over the span of about a decade, transformed the area that Huxtable pointedly called the largest slum in North America into a district of

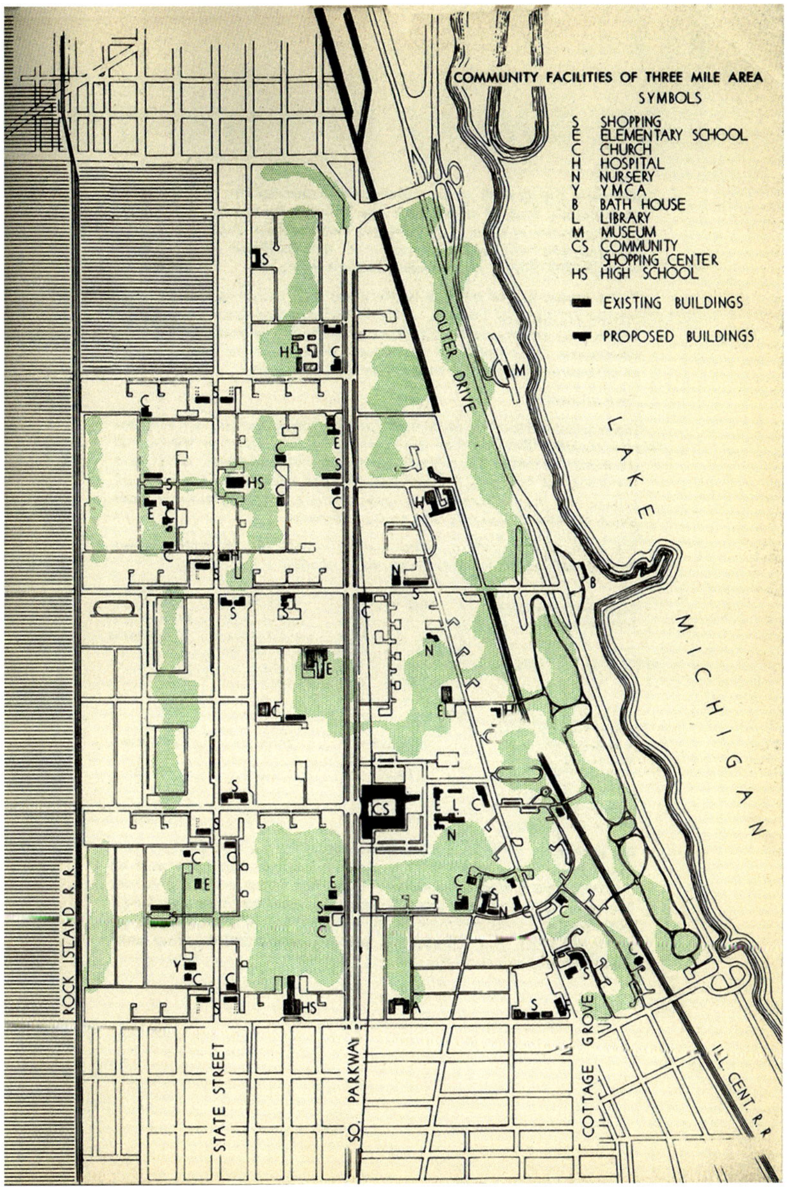

[6] South Side Planning Board, "Community Facilities of Three Mile Area," in *An Opportunity for Private and Public Investment in Rebuilding Chicago*, 1947.

Source: http://www.averyreview.com/content/3-issues/10-10/8-chicagos-multi-scalar-alternatives/whiting-05.jpg

modern campuses that included, in addition to IIT and Michael Reese Hospital, a Catholic school, public housing, private housing, and a shopping center. Each institution's boards (the hospital, the university, and the Chicago Housing Authority) were, like the South Side Planning Board itself, composed of different but overlapping constituencies. Each campus varied the building types on its land, lending each the feel of a small city. Because none of the campuses was fenced, the entire seven-square-mile area had this same varied quality. Housing campuses combined townhouses, rowhouses, and slabs, ranging from seven to fourteen stories high, and included small community buildings. Institutions, whether the hospitals or the university, were collections of buildings. Landscape architects who collaborated on the plan included Hideo Sasaki and Alfred Caldwell, among others. As with Frank Lloyd Wright's Quarter Section scheme and the Burnham Plan, the plan's components—and each separate campus's components—were connected by a fluid, landscaped system [6], including defined gardens, playgrounds, and green circulation arteries, and collecting the entire South Side Plan into a dynamic whole.

As the Near South Side's various campuses stretched and reached into one another, they also stretched and reached into the city's existing grid. Platted in 1830, Chicago was squarely set within the gridiron tradition systematized by Thomas Jefferson's 1785 Northwest Ordinance, which subdivided the Western Territories into townships of thirty-six square miles. This gridded system divided the landscape into commodifiable parcels, thereby facilitating rapid (and rampant) land speculation.

Despite the implied rigor of the grid's mathematical substrate, Chicago's blocks are not entirely homogeneous:

"The blocks may be made 300 feet square, and usually not over 320 feet by 400 feet, with a 20-foot alley running the long dimension of the block. The principal streets are usually made 80 feet in width, though frequently as much as 100 feet where the greater width appears to be needed or desirable, and the less important intersecting streets are seldom given a width of less than 60 feet. An alley is usually placed in each block, 20 feet in width and paralleling the principal street system.... Unless planned differently, the whole system is laid out on cardinal directions...."[18]

The phrase "usually," oft-repeated within the pages of *The Manual of Surveying Instructions*, suggests regularity but admits aberration. If New York's unyielding grid "forces Manhattan's builders to develop a new system of formal values, to invent strategies for the distinction of one block from another,"[19] Chicago's is essentially the opposite: the grid itself is manipulated in order to distinguish one project from another. Because Chicago emerged from a territorial organization (unlike Manhattan's, which is limited to its island configuration), its logic lies at a scale much greater than its urbanism—and this telescoping between the Jeffersonian grid and local practices of subdivision resulted in non-standard parcelization: the *usual* Chicago block is 266 by 600.[20]

The campus projects that defined the Near South Side Plan were all bigger than the usual block, but the consolidation of plats through different means of land aggregation (ranging from backroom transactions to passing inaugural urban renewal legislation at the state level) was done with the conviction that the urban environment could (and should) foster a different kind of urban citizen: a citizen living in and defining an emancipated city-state.[21]

Chicago 2017: Scaling Urbanism

And that's precisely the challenge of urban design: it is easier to see cities as agglomerations of villages, perfected atolls, securing our identities and ideals. But overconfidence in where "we" live and work as being different from where "they" live and work is more than risky. It balkanizes the social contract. It places the city as a whole at risk.

Chicagoans may coalesce around their various sports teams, but do they ever really coalesce around a broad understanding of how the city defines them as members of an urban public? The continued and extreme violence in the Englewood/South Side areas of Chicago over recent years has intensified anxiety regarding the city and a greater desire to differentiate "safe" neighborhoods from those zones of violence, echoing some of the discriminatory sentiments that Reginald Isaacs noted more than sixty years ago.

The campuses built in the 1940s and '50s as part of the Near South Side Plan—IIT, Michael Reese Hospital, Mercy Hospital, Lake Meadows, Prairie Shores, Prairie Avenue Courts, Dearborn Homes – did not "take" as a model. With a few exceptions, including Carl Sandburg Village, developed north of the Loop in the '60s, most of the housing, public and private, of the sixties was singular in its typology, particularly the vast arrays of homogeneous towers (Stateway Gardens, Robert Taylor Homes) that came to symbolize public housing in Chicago. Why didn't the model continue? How much of the reason depends upon the fact that the advocates moved on? Henry Heald, the President of IIT, left to become chancellor of NYU and later the head of the Ford Foundation; Mies stepped down as Head of Architecture at IIT; Reginald Isaacs left Michael Reese for Harvard; Martin Meyerson left the University of Chicago for Penn; and Elizabeth Woods, the outspoken head of the CHA, was ousted for her pro-integrationist stance. The devastating effect of this cast-change at the South Side Planning Board reveals the vulnerable flipside to American urbanism's dependence on civic associations. The rich variety and connectivity that had marked the Near South Side's projects, what I have referred to elsewhere as a *bas-relief urbanism*, disappeared.[22] This lively bas-relief had constantly reminded the collective public of this seven-square-mile area that they didn't belong to one building, but to many; not to one campus, but to an area; not to one neighborhood, but to a city.

Have architects and urban designers become numbed by the seductive salve of the neighborhood unit? Have we become fearful of the social contract itself? Is the "making of no small plans" taboo today? Is there, in fact, an urbanism of the neighborhood today? Or, for that matter, of the city?

It's a particularly urgent moment now to confront these questions by looking back on these multi-scalar experiments: the Burnham Plan, Drummond and Wright's Quarter Section plan, and the Near South Side Plan. The evidence of the experiment on the Near South Side is fast disappearing: Keck and Keck's Prairie Avenue Courts have been demolished; Michael Reese is being demolished; and historicist townhomes have sprouted up on the Lake Meadows campus, with rumors that the SOM-designed slabs will be torn down. Similar historicist townhomes have replaced the Robert Taylor Homes and Stateway Gardens already, as the city has shifted its public housing strategy to HOPE VI mixed-income, New Urbanist-inspired developments. While the mixing of incomes is laudable, the program's admitted inability to replace low income housing stock availability one-to-one repeats one of the social support crimes of urban renewal: when the density of the slums was not replaced with modern public housing. The concomitant shift from modernism to historicism makes modernism the straw man in this complicated story.

And therein lies the challenge. It's the same challenge that has faced the city ever since industrialization increased urban scale: how best to design *modern, metropolitan living*. As we move decidedly into the twenty-first century, the anachronism between our conception of the contemporary subject and our concept of the contemporary city becomes ever more pronounced. Countering the assumption that the best solution for urban living is the neighborhood does not mean eliminating the significant role of the immediate or intimate scale. But it is also critical not to create a false identity of immediate scale (a false sense of neighborliness) in a world defined by larger-scaled relations, whether those of global capital or simply global access. Each urban citizen constitutes his or her city out of overlapping environments and experiences, particularly now that the virtual world has become such an integral part of our everyday lives. It's much like political philosopher Nancy Fraser's understanding of the public sphere: the public sphere is not a singular realm that operates in a binary relation with the private sphere. Instead, the public is constituted of multiple publics—different constituencies that constantly overlap, morph, and combine into additional constituencies, all of which both form public discourse and also constantly challenge it.[23] In other words, despite desires to bracket people into singular and often binary categories (Democrat/Republican, male/female, white collar/blue collar…) it is impossible to keep people so tightly parsed in the same way and for the same reasons that it is impossible to keep neighborhoods so tightly parsed.

In recent writing, Fraser has taken up the challenge of understanding the effect of transnationalism on this understanding of the public sphere. The loosening of the singular relationship between the sovereign state and its citizens makes it difficult to see how any publics can engage in an effective political discourse: "If the modern territorial state no longer possesses the administrative ability to steer 'its' economy, ensure the integrity of 'its' national environment, and provide for the security of 'its' citizens, then how should we understand the capacity component of efficacy today?"[24] In this recent work, Fraser sees the contemporary challenges of fluid national borders, fluid ideologies, and fluid media, but also the challenge of the engines behind access to information and the opinions that follow.

Scaling Fraser's argument down—from nations to neighborhoods—the parallels are striking. Pan-city activism (think: race, crime, income disparity, environment) is ever more urgent. By centering urban identity on neighborhood definition, we overlook the extent to which the socio-political topographies of any neighborhood are a product of the city that neighborhood sits in. It doesn't take a village. It takes a city… a new kind of city that isn't afraid of its largesse, its rough edges, and the idiosyncrasies of its ever-more vociferous cultural micro-climates.

Thank you to Harald R. Stühlinger and Britta Hentschel for their invitation to deliver this talk at their inspiring Recoding the City conference at the ETH, and thank you to Ron Witte, James Graham, and Vittorio Magnago Lampugnani for their insightful feedback on earlier manifestations of this research.

Endnotes

1 Alan Colquhoun, "The Superblock," in *Essays in Architectural Criticism* (Cambridge, MA: MIT Press 1981), p. 83; first written in 1971, and first published in *Arquitectura moderna y cambio historio: Ensayos 1962–76* (n.p.: Barcelona, Gustavo Gili, 1978).

2 Hudson Yards developers, "The Story," (website), http://www.hudsonyardsnewyork.com/about/the-story/

3 Carl Smith "The Plan of Chicago: Heritage," Encyclopedia of Chicago online edition, http://www.encyclopedia.chicagohistory.org/pages/300009.html. Also see Chicago Plan Commission, "Building New Neighborhoods: Subdivision Design and Standards," (Chicago: Chicago Plan Commission, July 1943).

4 From "Regulating City Building," *The Survey*, 18 November, 1911, pp. 13–14, quoted in Gwendolyn Wright, *Moralism and the Model House* (Chicago: University of Chicago Press, 1980), p. 263.

5 Clarence Perry, *The Neighbourhood Unit*, ([New York: Regional Plan Association], 1929; repr. London: Routledge/Thoemmes, 1998), pp. 25–44.

6 A.B. Yeomans, ed., *City Residential Land Development: Studies in Planning. Competitive Plans for Subdividing A Typical Quarter Section of Land in the Outskirts of Chicago*, (Chicago: University of Chicago Press, 1916).

7 As cited in Donald Leslie Johnson "Origin of the Neighbourhood Unit," in *Planning Perspectives* 17 (2002): p. 231.

8 Ibid., pp. 227–245.

9 William Drummond in "Plan by William Drummond," in Yeomans, *City Residential Land Development*, p. 43

10 Frank Lloyd Wright, "Plan by Frank Lloyd Wright," in Yeomans, *City Residential Land Development*, p. 99 (emphasis Wright's).

11 Albert Pope, *Ladders* (New York: Princeton Architectural Press and Rice School of Architecture, 1996).

12 Reginald Isaacs, "Are Urban Neighborhoods Possible?" *The Journal of Housing*, vol. 5, issue 7, (July 1948): p. 178.

13 Lewis Mumford, "The Neighborhood and the Neighborhood Unit," *Town Planning Review*, vol. 24, (January 1954): p. 261.

14 Reginald Isaacs, "The Neighborhood Theory: An Analysis of its Adequacy," *The Journal of the American Institute of Planners*, (Spring 1948): p. 19.

15 *Time Magazine* "The Country Clubber," December 1, 1947, as quoted in Isaacs, "Are Urban Neighborhoods Possible?" p. 178. See Sara Stevens's *Developing Expertise: Real Estate and Architecture in Metropolitan America* (New Haven: Yale University Press, 2016) for more about Nichols and other American developers.

16 Ibid.

17 Ada Louise Huxtable, *Two Cities: Planning in North and South America*, Museum of Modern Art. Exhibition #352, June 24–September 21, 1947.

18 Bureau of Land Management, *The Manual of Surveying Instructions of 1947* (Washington, D.C.: Bureau of Land Management, 1947), p. 352. (Emphasis added.)

19 Rem Koolhaas, *Delirious New York* (New York: Monacelli Press, 1984), pp. 20–21.

20 Homer Hoyt, *One Hundred Years of Land Values in Chicago: The Relationship of the Growth of Chicago to the Rise in Its Land Values 1830-1933* (Chicago: University of Chicago Press, 1933), pp. 428–429.

21 Please see my "Bas-Relief Urbanism: Chicago's Figured Field," in Phyllis Lambert, ed., *Mies in America* (New York, Harry N. Abrams, 2001), pp. 642-691 for a more detailed explication of the means by which plats were assembled into large parcels for these projects.

22 Ibid.

23 See Nancy Fraser, "Rethinking the Public Sphere. A Contribution to the Critique of Actually Existing Democracy," Social Text, No. 25/26, (1990): pp. 56–80.

24 Nancy Fraser, "Transnationalizing the Public Sphere," in Kate Nash, ed. *Transnationalizing the Public Sphere* (Cambridge, Polity Press, 2014), 32.

WHAT KIND OF CODE?
Berlin's Hobrechtplan from 1862 and the Term "Code"

Florian Hutterer

The *Bebauungsplan für Berlin und seine Umgebungen*[1] of 1862 [1] was a milestone in the urban development of Berlin. Never again would a single plan reconfigure such a large area. The plan itself is not an independently developed work but the result of negotiation, and to a certain extent followed a planning practice which in part approximates to today's planning procedures. Nevertheless, the *Hobrechtplan* has barely been explored. In a two-year project at TU Berlin[2], a team of urban planners and art historians has tried to at least partially close this gap in the research. For the project, it was important to examine not only the 1862 plan, but also the underlying ideas, as well as the built city and its later transformations up until the present. Therefore, the theoretical concept of the *Hobrechtian Berlin* was introduced in order to meet the multidimensionality of the subject under investigation. *Hobrechtian Berlin* means, on one hand, the limited area of the city developed on the basis of the plan. On the other hand, it includes various urban developments that have been realized since the *Bebauungsplan* was drawn up. The term combines planning, spatial development, and value propositions.

This article focuses on particularly to the key term *recoding*, and therefore the term "code." In communication science, a code in the broadest sense means a language. Communication is based on the exchange of information generated by the sender according to a particular code, which the recipient interprets using the same code. Two widely used associations are considered here—programing language as a code in computer science, and DNA as a genetic code—to examine which interpretation of code and thus recoding applies to the prominent *Bebauungsplan* of 1862. The plan is thus assessed according to its character as a work of urban planning and according to its impact on the urban grid and structure. Is it a program by a good engineer, who coded or recoded the city of Berlin? Or is it part of a Berlin city-genetics, which has created a

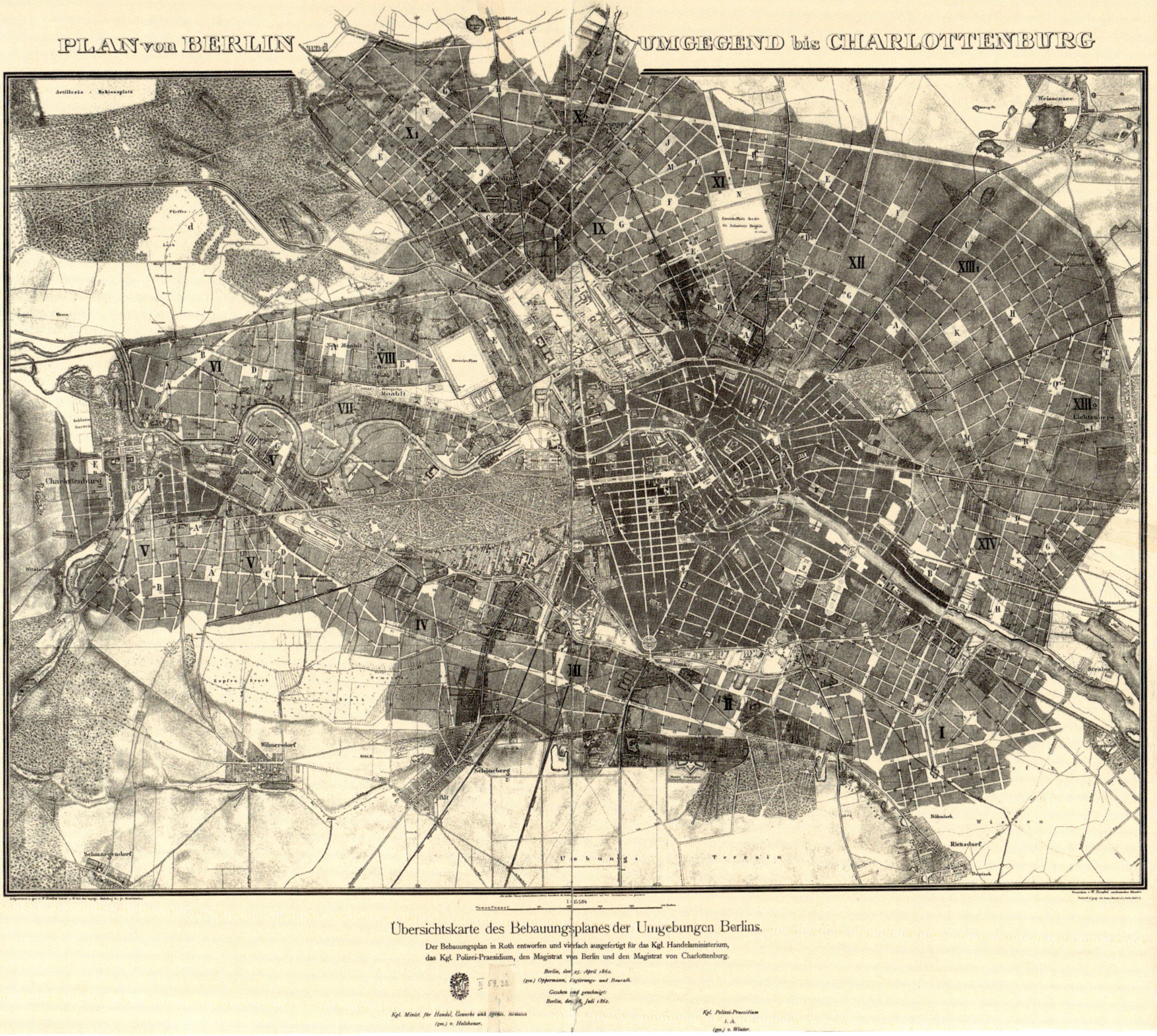

[1] James Hobrecht (designer), Ferdinand Böhm (drafter), general plan of Berlin, 1862. It comprises the fourteen sections of the city extension plan.

Source: Zentral- und Landesbibliothek Berlin.

viable and mutable structure over generations? To answer these questions, the essential content of the development plan will be identified and described using built examples as well as predecessor and successor planning. We approach the code in three sections—genesis of the document, spatial impact of the plan, and transformation of the city—to understand the multidimensional character of the *Hobrechtian Berlin*. Along the way, we will consider the role of James Hobrecht in the planning process: Was he the genius engineer and founder of modern Berlin, or a part of the city's planning elite, involved in a long progression of urban development?[3]

The genesis of the document

If we look at the plan as a document, we can see some basic facts. A city extension surrounds the existing city, transforming the Tiergarten park and Friedrichshain from peripheral leisure areas to inner-city parks and unifying two separate cities, Berlin and Charlottenburg, into one city-region. The plan relates to the old arterial roads which are commonly the borders of the fourteen divisions of the plan, but provides it with a polycentric structure. The planning area is huge: it covers an area of sixty-two square kilometers, which is four and a half times the area of the existing city and twenty-nine times larger than the historic Baroque core. When we look closer, on the level of the legally binding subdivision plan, it is apparent that, compared to the planning documents of today, the plan is reduced to the bare essentials. We can identify the following elements: existing buildings and allotments, existing paths and topography, future streets, and squares with different dimensions. The objective of the plan was clear: to separate streets and building areas, and ultimately to separate the private areas from the public ones. On this point, we can see that this is an early example of a modern understanding of planning, as it attempts to deal with the two main sectors of modern urban development: the private and the public.

The ideas, logic, and elements of the expansion planning from 1859–1861 under the direction of James Hobrecht are the result of a planning process that involved several generations. The origins of this planning and the attendant discussion had been visible since 1812 in the undeveloped parts of the areas known as Köpenicker Feld and Stralauer Viertel, today parts of Kreuzberg and Friedrichshain. In their groundbreaking work "Das Berliner Mietshaus," Johannes Geist and Klaus Kürvers gave us a detailed description of how the preplans of Johann Carl Ludwig Schmid (1821–1830) and Peter Joseph Lenné (1840–1843), as well as the first terrain speculations like the "Waaren-Credit-Gesellschaft" were integrated into Hobrecht's planning.[4]

After the first development plan by Schmid (1830) was no longer able to match the explosive growth of the town, a building inspector was commissioned to revise Schmid's already outdated plans in 1852. Between 1852 and 1858, the original five departments for the development planning were reorganized into fifteen departments and expanded considerably.

At Trade Minister August von der Heydt's suggestion, based on preparations by Rothe and Köbicke in 1859, a "Commission for the Elaboration of the Development Plans for the Surroundings of Berlin" was set up. On April 1, 1859, James Hobrecht was appointed director of this commission. Hobrecht received some "Instructions for the Drafting of a Development Plan for Berlin and the Surroundings," with a detailed planning assignment from the minister. On one hand, the main task consisted of the "exact revision, completion, and, if necessary, conversion of the existing maps and, as far as necessary, new surveying and a complete mapping of all parts of the development plans still to be drawn up, with all existing buildings, plots, [and] waterways."[5] On the other, the drawing-up of the development plan was to be carried out "according to guidance"[6] from defined design and planning guidelines—partly with concrete

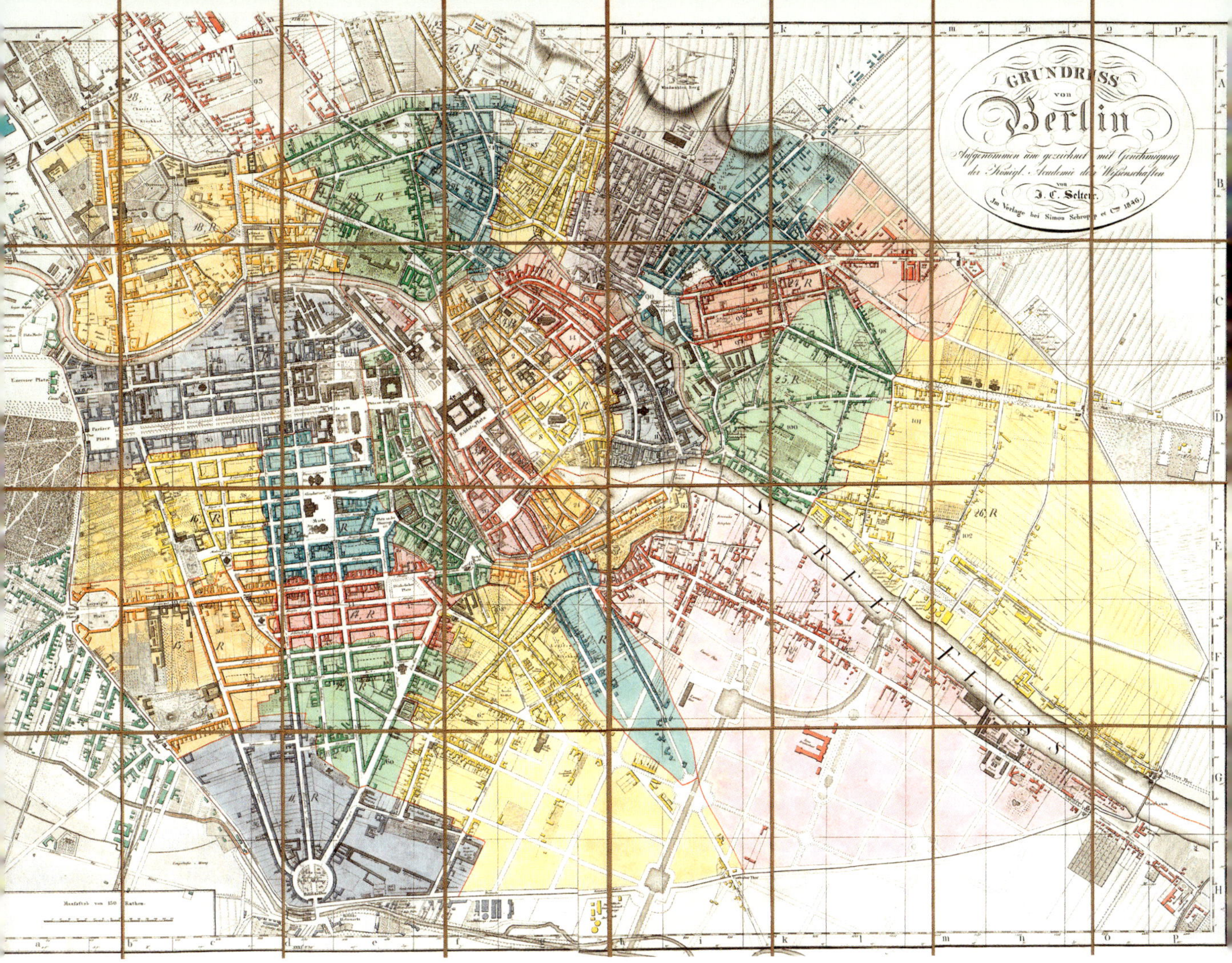

[2] J. C. Selter, Plan of Berlin, 1846.

Source: Zentral- und Landesbibliothek Berlin.

details on dimensions and with reference to specific examples, specifically the Baroque quarter of Friedrichstadt in the center of Berlin.

The process of Berlin's development planning from 1859–61 thus already began at the start of the nineteenth century and employed several planners before Hobrecht. He, as head of the commission, assimilated their ideas and intentions in the form of preliminary planning. Hobrecht was subject to ministerial instructions on the design of roads, parcels, and squares when compiling these early plans. Particular attention was to be given to existing land borders, buildings, and roads. Hobrecht's responsibilities included the coordination of surveying and mapping, the incorporation of the already extant partial plans, and the addition of the missing sections through his own designs.[7] In addition to the discussions and negotiations which had been held with the participating administrative commissions and authorities, the planning had to be coordinated with the land developers and other property owners.[8] We cannot know the extent to which Hobrecht conducted the negotiations himself, but according to his work instructions he was to weigh in on, argue, and decide on the planned urban grid. However, only one of the fourteen departments received a final approval during Hobrecht's time on the project. All the other departments were worked on further without Hobrecht's influence, and were not approved before 1862. This planning history leads to an understanding that the departments were influenced by many heads and hands. The complete plan had "at first only the negative meaning that the terrain defined for streets and squares must not be built [on].... The plan only shows the construction lines."[9]

As we can see, Hobrecht's work was embedded in an officially organized planning process. The focus of the plan was on the future city's ability to function, as the instructions from Minister von der Heydt show. Compared to other European cities, the expansion of the city of Berlin took place at an early stage, especially when we consider Schmid's plans as one of the precursors of the *Hobrechtplan*. This minimal objective for the plan contributes to a special relationship between stability and change. If we trace the development of the plan further, the flexibility of the Hobrechtian planning becomes clear in the revisions. The grid was adjusted several times, but without abandoning characteristic urban figures and attributes. Ultimately, the plan provided an ideal framework for the insertion of the characteristic urban elements: plots, houses (mixed residential or commercial, closed or open), and the free spaces of courtyards. But above all, it is certain that Hobrecht was not the only programmer of the new spatial code for Berlin.

The spatial impact of the plan

In the next section, we will take a look at the spatial impacts of the plan. It is important to see how Hobrecht translated the above-mentioned instructions into spatial settings and how these settings turned into an urban fabric. The comparison with predecessor and successor planning allows the positioning of the plan in the planning history of Berlin, and thus an evaluation of the nature of the work. When we look at Johann Christian Selter's[10] [2] plan of Berlin from 1846, around ten years before Hobrecht took over the job as planner, we can see a quite small city compared to today's dimensions [3]. But it becomes apparent that, urbanistically, every single element used later in the city expansion was already developed or defined at this point: a network of streets of different dimensions, boulevards, different squares for markets and fairs, rectangular blocks with smaller dimensions in the baroque structure of Friedrichstadt, or bigger ones in the extension area of Köpenicker Feld. This typical Berlin was of course the experiential space of the planners, the politicians, and the administration, all responsible together for the large project of steering the urban growth. And so it was for Hobrecht. We can assume, therefore, that the urban design figures and elements of the 1862 plan relate either to the topography of the area or to traditional Berlin motifs.

In our research project, we have analyzed in detail how the city planning elements are arranged in the Hobrecht plan using three sample spaces. One example is the Humannplatz in the large north-eastern city extension area, today Prenzlauer Berg. The area illustrates the extent to which predecessor plans

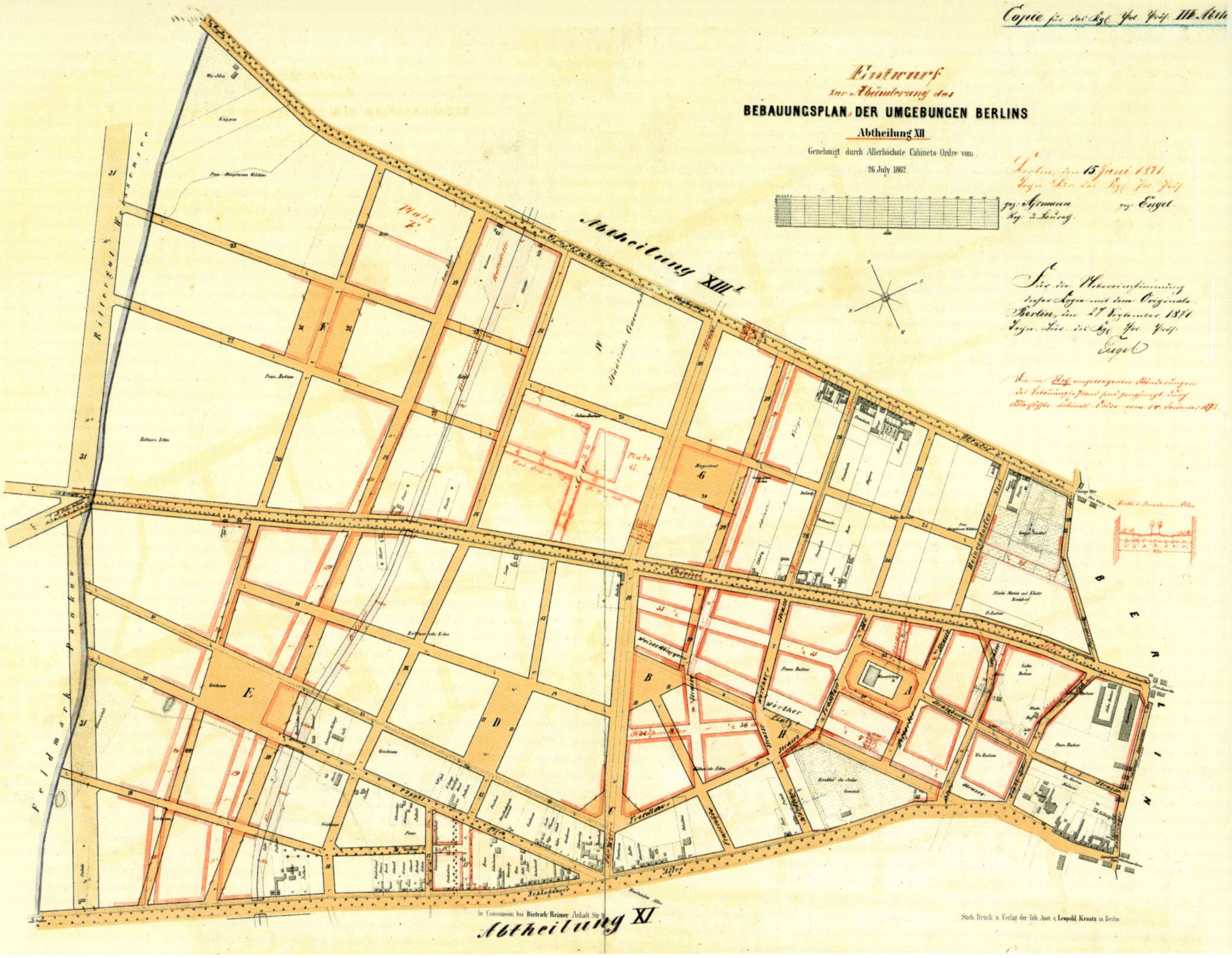

3 Section XII of the "Bebauungsplan" in a later version (1871). The older version supervised by Hobrecht in black, the later adaptions are marked in red.

Source: Landesarchiv Berlin

influenced the structure of the 1862 development plan. The Humannplatz perfectly embodies a space that has been implemented as a centerpiece for the new neighborhoods in the city extension.

In section XII of the development plan, between Schönhauser Allee and Prenzlauer Allee, Hobrecht plans one of the typical neighborhoods. What would later become the Humannplatz, *Square E* on the plan, is created by the omission of a smaller building block [1]. Despite the frequent occurrence of this simple urbanistic element in the plan, the Humannplatz is one of the few examples that were realized as shown in the plan version of 1862 and thus serve as an example of Hobrecht's own hand. Comparison of the surviving written explanatory reports with the later plan even shows that Hobrecht planned many more of such places. The criterion for the distribution was to maintain a "reasonable distance" between the several squares. Elsewhere, he explains more specifically the goal of distributing squares in the planning area at a distance of 100 to 150 Prussian rods, which corresponds to approximately 377 to 565 meters. The goal was probably the easy walking accessibility of the squares for the surrounding residents.

With this even distribution of squares over the entire expansion area, Hobrecht succeeded at the same time in satisfying one of the demands of Trade Minister von der Heydt, who demanded exactly this in his instructions from 1859.[11] However, the dense distribution of squares was later given up. The use originally planned for today's Humannplatz is not known due to the loss of the explanatory report for Division XII. The surviving explanatory reports attest to the fact that Hobrecht, also following von der Heydt's instructions, endeavored to make use of Berlin's rather flat topography by designing, for example, elevated places for the location of churches; that is, as *points-de-vue*.[12] In addition, von der Heydt also urges the establishment of marketplaces,[13] which according to contemporary planning theory should be present in every city quarter.[14] In its present form, the square is already a reduced version of the original plan. The original positioning of the square illustrates Hobrecht's approach in the preparation of his plans. He first accepted the specifications of the development plan drawn up in 1830 by Johann Carl Ludwig Schmid, who had integrated the adjacent *Pappelallee* into his plans as an existing road.

The surrounding road network in the *Hobrechtplan* is much smaller in scale than in the *Schmidplan* and is displaced in the northern area. While Schmid's predecessor planning had intended a straight course for today's Stargarder Straße and Diesterwegstraße (denoted by the number sixteen on the *Bebauungsplan*), the road slightly descends to the north in the 1862 plan. The reason for this change is to be found in the new buildings on Schönhauser Allee and Pappelallee, which would stand in the way of a straightforward continuation of the road. Hobrecht was encouraged to avoid conflicts with landowners as much as possible and to take account of existing buildings.[15] The fact that those principles were of high priority to him is shown not only by the change in the *Bebauungsplan*, but also in the explanatory reports.[16] The location of Humannplatz also makes this clear. The square is entirely on the property of the great land owner Griebenow, who was more easily able to cope with the loss of land value than the owners of the small plots of land south of it.[17]

The construction of the circular railway line, which was opened in 1871, necessitated another change in the plan, conceived by Assmann and Engel and approved in 1871 by cabinet order. In this amendment, all streets running east-west (today's Wichertstraße and Erich-Weinert-Straße) are shifted to the north. Both streets are slightly bent at the intersection with Greifenhagener Straße, which leads to a more charming urban development. With the displacement of these streets, the surface of the central square is also changed and reduced. The revision of 1871 also introduces the outer circular ring road (today Wisbyer Straße).

A glance at Straube's road map of 1910 shows how far urban development progressed over the next forty years. At this point, the urban development, marked by the last row of new tenement houses, ends at the circular railway line and at Greifenhagener Straße in the west. The area around the Humannplatz has not yet been built. This explains the low Wilhelminian-style block development in the district and the more mixed development structure. Most

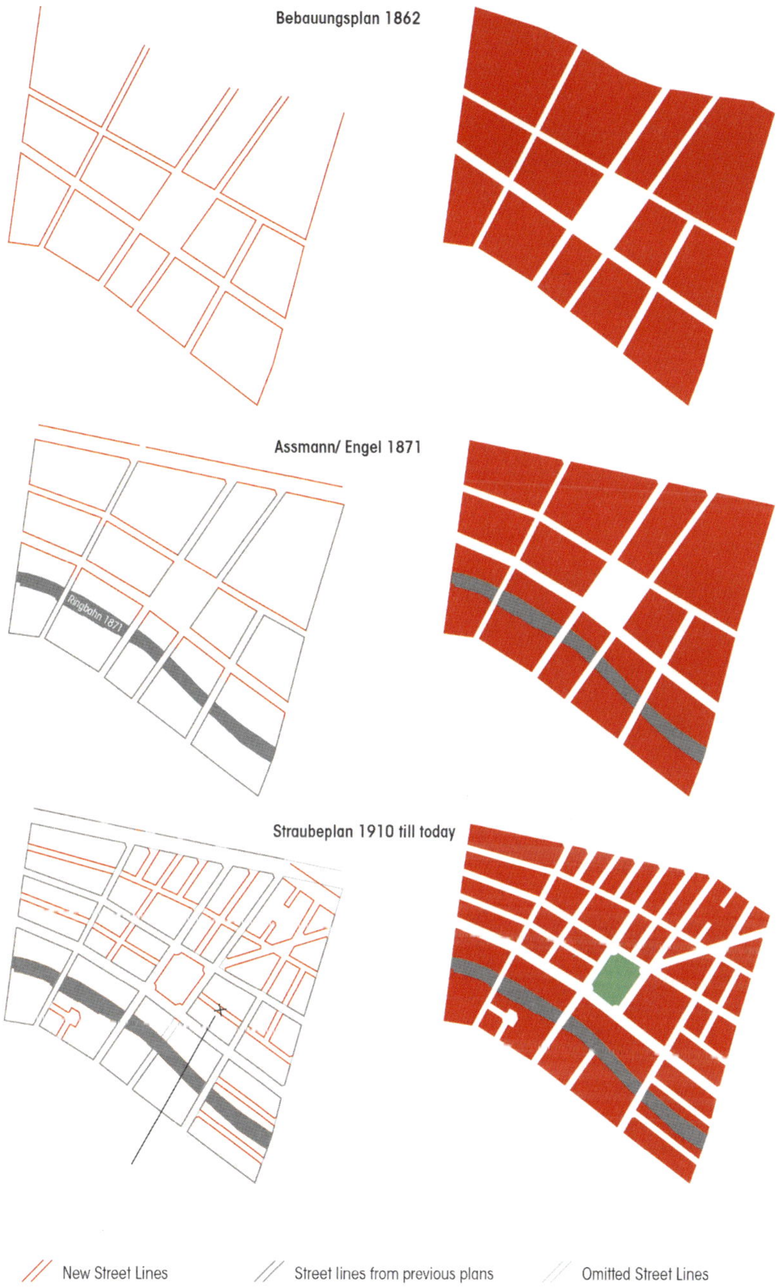

[4] Development of the street network and blocks around the Humannplatz.

Illustration by the author.

of the Wilhelminian houses follow the building regulations of 1897, which can be seen in the relatively large courtyards. Also striking is the regular parceling, with twenty-five-meter-wide plots of land and a regular development scheme consisting of a front house and two side wings, some also with rear houses. The road map of 1910 also shows the planned and subsequently constructed roads.

[5] Development of the buildings around the Humannplatz. It is remarkable that the grid could be adapted to integrate very different housing typologies.

Illustration by the author.

All original blocks are subdivided at least by a cross-street. This network still exists today, with the exception of minor changes [4].
In its formation and development, and thus also in its present state, the Humannplatz illustrates some of the features of *Hobrechtian Berlin*. In this urban area Hobrecht succeeded with the development plan by picking up and refining the original ideas from previous planning. Based on Schmid's schematic and rough planning, a consistent urbanistic image of a neighborhood could be developed through the addition of roads, the omission of a block, and the establishment of an urban square. The further development of the district illustrates the characteristic relationship between the flexibility and stability of the space and the shape of the space. Adaptations to changing conditions, in particular the construction of the circular railway line, were possible in a way that allowed the original idea to be retained. The development plan represents a framework, structuring and organizing the space into which various urban

functions—housing, work, recreation—could be inserted. The different periods of development and the addition or removal of roads do not interfere with the basic shape of the district designed by Hobrecht, but rather strengthen the character of the spatial framework. Depending on the requirements of the various building regulations, and working with very different property structures, customized solutions for different housing schemes could be found. Thus, the existing spatial structure of the Humannplatz becomes a stable element of the *Bebauungsplan*, which to this day expresses itself in its form and function as a neighborhood center. With reference to the idea of the plan as a genomic code, the *Bebauungsplan* of 1862 seems to be a specific occurrence in a series of mutations along strict genetic lines [5].

The transformation of the city

Until now, we have primarily considered the developments of the late nineteenth and early twentieth centuries. But the grid of the *Hobrechtplan* characterises even areas with newer developments in the building structure. The plan is capable of integrating nineteenth-century tenement houses, as well as the reform housing of the 1910s, the housing estates of classical modernism, post-war structures, modern social housing schemes in the urban renewal areas of the 1960s and 1970s [5], and projects of postmodernism. The implementation of changing conceptions of order has led to a particular disorder in the *Hobrechtian Berlin*. While formerly mixed-use neighborhoods have been converted into purely residential quarters, others have preserved their intended destination of use. Areas of purely new construction are contrasted with areas of exclusively old buildings. Areas of large-scale development compete with small-scale structured quarters. The *Hobrechtian Berlin*, which was never a uniform city area, has transformed itself into a multi-faceted neighborhood landscape that is typical of the whole of Berlin. This versatility shows the great adaptability of the spatial framework. The blocks are dimensioned in such a way that both the parcels and buildings of the start-up period and the large units of social housing can be inserted. The road network can be sufficiently differentiated by traffic calming and pedestrian zones without having to be completely changed. The change is not based on a unified scheme, but is carried out in certain spaces of urban change. Opportunities arise there because of conversions, aging processes, or demolition. Stability and change and order and disorder are equally decisive for development in *Hobrechtian Berlin* [6].

The fact that it is almost impossible to read the limits of the *Hobrechtplan* in the city's layout indicates additionally that the plan enforced more of a typical Berlin idea of the city than a particular urban design. This leads to the supposition that the development plans of the parts outside the *Hobrechtian Berlin* have been elaborated and refined with similar conceptions of urban structure. The areas that differ from the usual Berlin grid stand out even more as a result—areas in which the specific ideas of individual developers were enforced, such as the entrepreneur Johann Wilhelm von Carstenn's quarters in Wilmersdorf and Friedenau from the 1870s. Here we find curved roads and ring roads, round

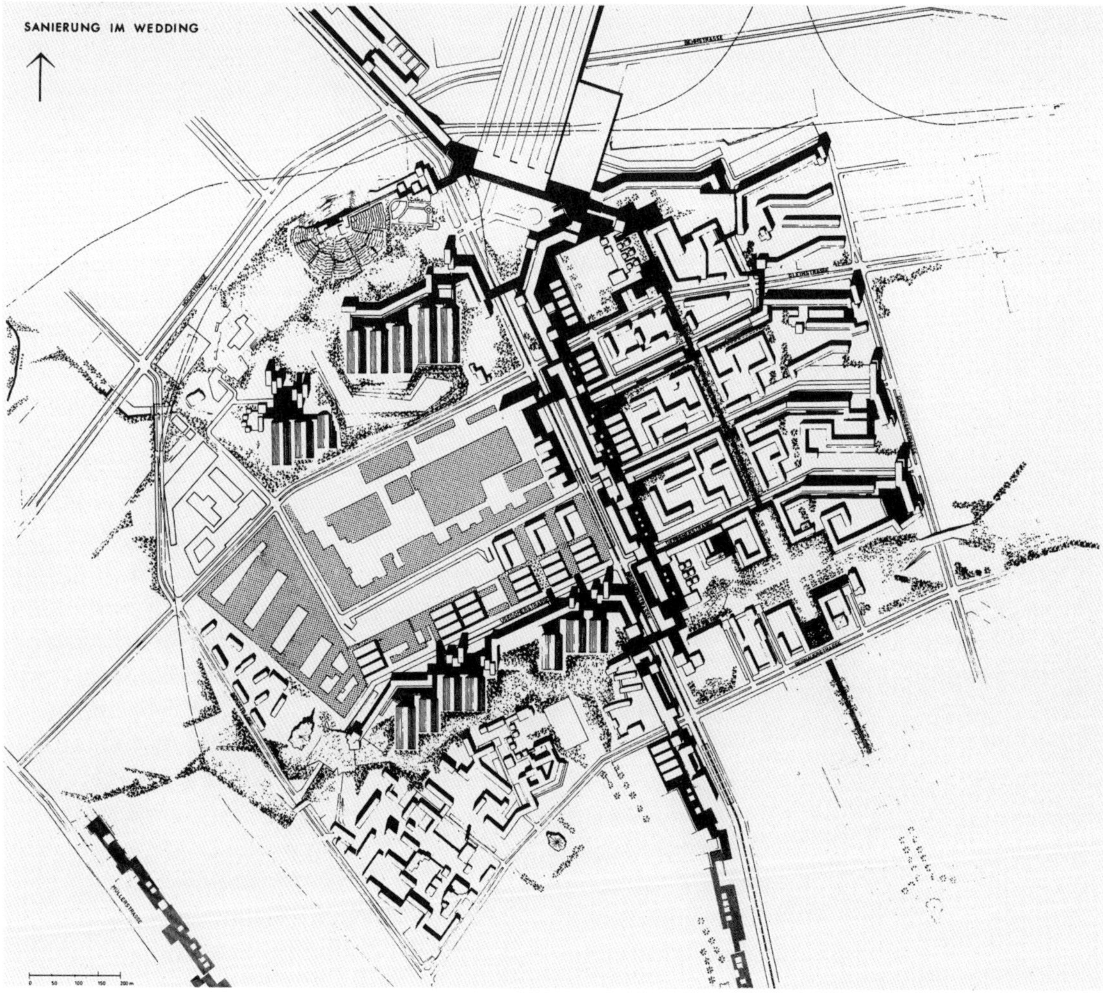

[6] Even in the most radical renewal concepts of the 1960s—such as in Wedding-Brunnenstraße, where the Berlin tenement house has been replaced by large meandering structures—the original grid of the *Bebauungsplan* from 1862 is still visible.

Source: TU Berlin Lehrstuhl für Städtebau und Siedlungswesen, Stadterneuerung von Berlin: Sanierung im Wedding (Berlin 1963).

plazas and squares, inspired by Baroque garden models in Versailles and Potsdam and based on an exaggerated cosmic concept (that is to say, the sun and its planets); motifs which did not matter to Hobrecht, who as an engineer was interested in the functionality of the city's expansion.

So in the end, what is the *Hobrechtplan*; what kind of code does it represent? First, the plan was not holistically invented by the person who lent his name to the document; we should therefore avoid using this name and refer to it by the older, technical title: *Bebauungsplan für die Umgebung Berlins*. What is certainly wrong is the image of the plan as a fixed programing code and of Hobrecht as the only programer. But what Hobrecht did was refine older ideas, add new parts, and combine them into a reasonable whole acting in the knowledge of the city's specific circumstances. The plan can be characterized as a summary of ideas which are adapted to the site, and which are based on traditional urbanistic concepts. As a result, highly recognizable urban areas with enormous potential for individual identification have emerged. The broad streets are a generous stage for urban life, the evenly distributed squares create a balance of greenery in the densely built city, and the modular structure of the network facilitates the formation of individual neighborhoods—known in Berlin as the *Kiez*. In that sense, both uses of the term "code" are relevant. The plan is part of an evolutionary development of urbanistic and land use plans. But in its urbanistic statements it is based on a very special programing code—and that code is Berlin.

Endnotes

1 Urban Development Plan for Berlin and its Surroundings
2 The project was jointly developed by the departments of Urban Design and Urban Development (Prof. Angela Million), Urban Renewal and Sustainable Development (Prof. Elke Pahl-Weber) and Heritage Conservation (Prof. Gabi Dolff-Bonekämper).
3 The text is based on the research results of the working group around Felix Bentlin, Stephanie Herold and Florian Hutterer.
4 Johann Friedrich Geist and Klaus Kürvers, *Das Berliner Mietshaus 1740–1862* (München: Prestel-Verlag, 1980), pp. 470–481.
5 Ibid., pp. 485–486.
6 Ibid.
7 Ibid., p. 468.
8 James Hobrecht, "Erläuterungsbericht zu dem Entwurf eines Straßennetzes auf den Abtheilungen XI und IX des Bebauungs-Planes von den Umgebungen Berlins," (unpublished, Landesarchiv Berlin, A Pr. Rep. 030-07, Nr. 188, Bl. 71–102, Berlin 01.06.1860).
9 Heinrich Wilhelm von Holzbrinck, "Begleitschreiben zur Übergabe der Pläne Sektion II, IV, V, VI, IX, X, XI, XII und XIII des Bebauungsplans," (unpublished, Geheimes Staatsarchiv Preußischer Kulturbesitz, I. HA Rep. 89, Nr. 28601, Bl. 177–190, Berlin 18.07.1862): pp. 186–190.
10 Johann Christian Selter, born in 1767, was a cartographer and editor of several ground plans of the city of Berlin in the first half of the nineteenth century.
11 Geist and Kürvers, *Das Berliner Mietshaus 1862–1945*, p. 485.
12 Hobrecht, "Erläuterungsbericht," p. 78.
13 August von der Heydt, " Anweisung für die Aufstellung und Ausführung städtischer Bau- und Retablissementspläne," *Zeitschrift für Bauwesen*, Nr. 5 (Berlin, 1855): pp. 440–444.
14 Johannes Andreas Romberg, *Der Stadtbau oder Anweisung zum Entwerfen von Gebäuden aller Art* (Darmstadt, 1836), pp. 118–120.
15 Geist and Kürvers, *Das Berliner Mietshaus 1862–1945*, p. 485.
16 Hobrecht, "Erläuterungsbericht," pp. 75–78.
17 Ibid., p. 94.

SHIFTING THE CORE AND SPINNING THE CITY
The Vittoriano and the Urban Recoding of Rome

Britta Hentschel

Rome, Coded by the Catholic Church

The conquest of Rome by Italian troops in September 1870 marked a drastic political and structural transformation of the Eternal City: the *Risorgimento* dream of a united Italy under the flag of monarchy with Rome as its capital had come true after almost ten years of struggle. Unfortunately, a peaceful agreement with the pope, as the former ruler of central Italy, turned out to be impossible. The requests for a modern nation-state were quashed by papal claims to power, and the use of force finally became inevitable.

But the conquest by the new regime under the elected King Vittorio Emanuele II (1820–1878) implied not only the end of papal dominance and a radical political change but also the beginning of an urban reorganization of the Eternal City. It led to the greatest urban shift that had taken place in Rome for centuries.

The old-fashioned city with its narrow streets, bad infrastructural and sanitary systems, and dense quarters at the bend of the Tiber was inadequate as a national capital seeking to compete with nineteenth-century metropolises such as Paris, Berlin or London. However, the major problem for the ambitious Italian government was the continuing presence of the pope and the Catholic Church within the city. Hundreds of churches, convents, and their wide urbanistic concepts of reception and self-representation had shaped the topography of Rome and proved the papacy's global and civic claims to power.

The new rulers had to battle with an old, ecclesiastically over-coded city fabric while Pope Pius IX (1792–1878) was unwilling to negotiate with the Italian state representatives and cloistered himself inside the Vatican. Italy had to wait until 1929 for the Lateran Pacts to pacify the tense relationship between the nation-state and the Papal States.[1]

[1] Michelangelo, Cupola of St. Peter, executed by Giacomo della Porta after Michelangelo's death in 1564.

Source: Christina Strunck, ed., *Rom, Meisterwerke der Baukunst von der Antike bis heute,* (Petersberg: Imhof Verlag, 2007), p. 215.

The most prominent symbol of the pope's continuous presence within the city was—and remains to this day—undoubtedly the cupola of Saint Peter conceived by Michelangelo (1475–1564) [1]. The vaulting over the apostle's tomb was commissioned under the terms of the Council of Trent as a visible sign of a reformed Catholic Church. Following Bramante, Raphael, Baldassare Peruzzi, and Antonio da Sangallo as master builders of Saint Peter, Michelangelo departed from the complicated ideas of his predecessor Sangallo and aimed at a fundamentally new concept. He returned to the idea of a centrally planned building, concentrating on the core area of the tomb, eliminating all of Sangallo's senseless galleries, and detesting the rich façade with its massive flanking towers.[2]

The double-shelled cupola with its enormous structuring pilaster strips was executed by Giacomo della Porta between 1588 and 1590, according to Michelangelo's drawings but after his death, and created a new ecclesiastical landmark within the cityscape and in the collective memory of millions of visitors, pilgrims, and travelers for centuries to come.

According to art historian Martin Warnke's essay "Bau und Gegenbau,"[3] large-scale monumental buildings of power always provoke a counter-reaction—especially in times of radical political change, as we see occurring in nineteenth-century Italy. The dome of Saint Peter by the architectural proponent of light Michelangelo challenged the young Italian nation-state to compete with and outdo the dome with its own works of art in order to inscribe itself into the ecclesiastically-coded urban texture.

This desire was closely connected to the urgent urban reorganization of the city and the death of Italy's first king Vittorio Emanuele II in January 1878.

Breaking the Code

Directly after coming to power in autumn 1870, the Italian government established a committee of experts to improve the city's networks. These improvements incorporated development trends from the 1860s, such as the construction of Rome's central train station Termini near the ancient thermal baths of Diocletian and city extension projects by the papal Minister of War Monsignore Frederic Françoise Xavier de Merode (1820–1874).

As a link between the new station that connected Rome with the Italian railroad network and the historic center of Rome next to the river Tiber, De Merode had designed a grid of streets flanking a principal axis but without a precise point of termination.[4]

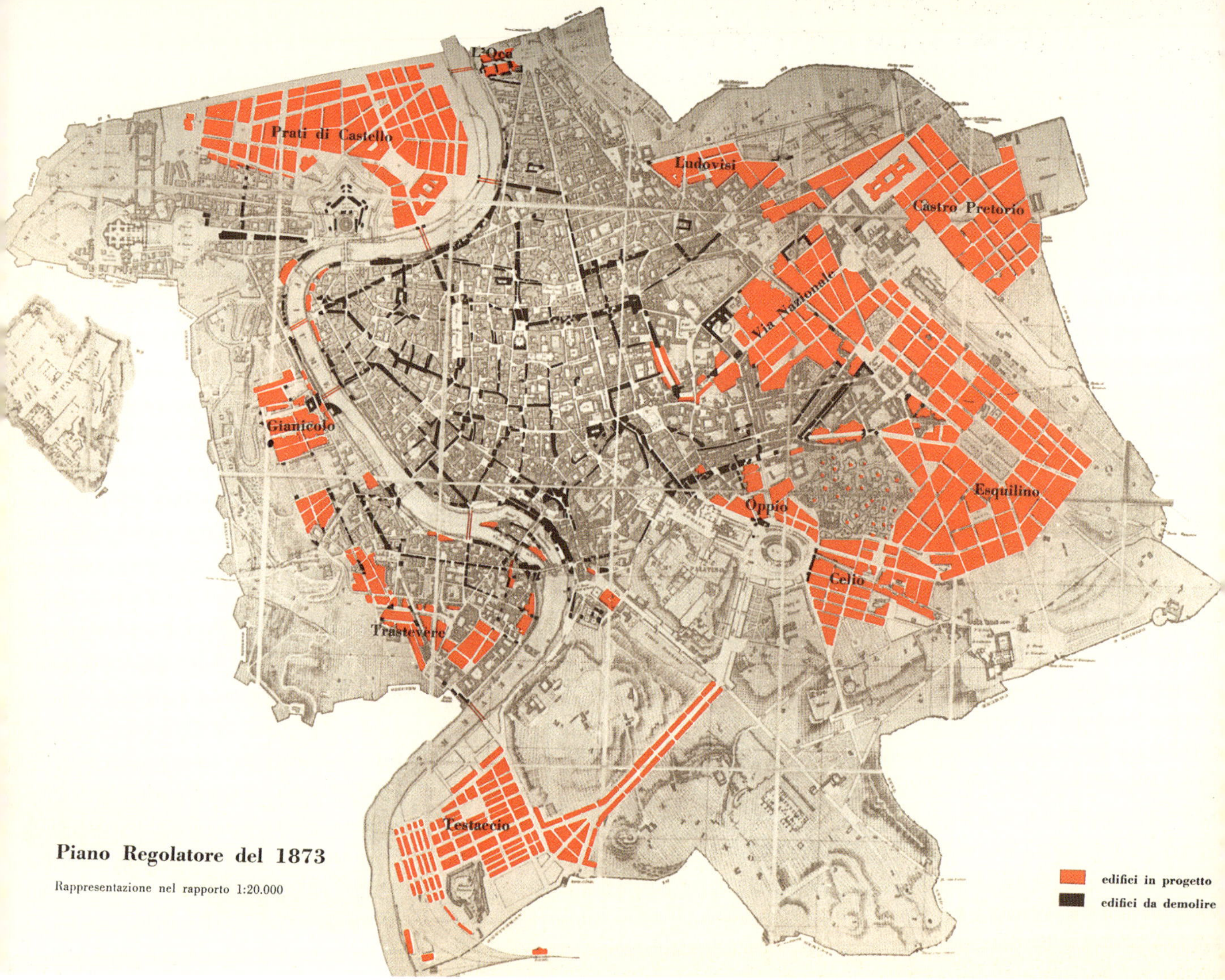

[2] Luigi Pianciani and Alessandro Viviani, *Piano regulatorio* of Rome, 1873.

Source: Italo Insolera, "Storia del Primo Piano Regolatore di Roma: 1870–1874," *Urbanistica*, no. 27 (1959), pp. 74–90, 83.

Under the aegis of Alessandro Viviani (1825–1905), head of the municipal *Ufficio tecnico*, the city planners incorporated these ideas into a much wider concept: the first master plan of Rome, called the *piano regolatore,* in 1873 [2].[5] De Merode's axis, known as Via Santa Maria degli Angeli, referring to the eponymous church incorporated into the imperial thermals baths by Michelangelo from 1561, or as Via Pia Nuova, referring to the ruling Pope Pius IX, was renamed Via Nazionale as part of the program. Besides other interventions, the master plan scheduled the extension of Via Nazionale toward Trajan's Market and its boundaries in a flowing curve to the Trevi Fountain. Crossing the central north-south interface Via del Corso south of Piazza Colonna, the new main road of the united Italy also included the Pantheon as the only fully intact building from antiquity in this new sequence of historic monumental buildings.[6]
Via Nazionale was intended to split in two at the forecourt of the Pantheon, the former temple of the gods, by that point rededicated as Santa Maria della Rotonda; one section was to lead towards the Piazza Navona, opening the square

at its northern end and running northward toward the river and the newly planned neighborhood of Prati di Castello next to the Castello Sant'Angelo, while the other strand joined the Pantheon in a direct connection with the tangential and extended Via dei Condotti.[7]

The aim of this axis was undoubtedly the creation of a terrific show-jumping course of the sights of the first Rome of antiquity, and the second Rome of the Popes, in honor of the prevailing third Rome of Italy the nation-state—as well as providing a fast connection between the city center and the train station at the far eastern end of Via Nazionale.

The layout of the nation's first *boulevard* was combined with the idea of creating a new secular center at Piazza Colonna, near the proposed crossing of Via Nazionale and Via del Corso and at the end of Via del Tritone, in opposition to the all-dominant Vatican. Succeeding various department stores, publishing houses, and a gallery based on its famous precursor in Milan, the National Bank of Italy intended to build its headquarters near the piazza.[8] The prime minister's seat of government and the chamber of deputies followed.

Next to the arrangement of a new urban hub and the creation of a sophisticated road network, Viviani's master plan also provided new radial quarters for housing and industry instead of the papal and cardinal belt of villas inside and outside the ancient Aurelian walls.

However, because of a lack of financing options, Viviani's proposals initially remained unexecuted and the development of modern Rome was opened to private housing speculation.[9]

Programing a New Code: the Vittoriano

The urban future of Rome was still uncertain when Italy's first king and self-styled *pater patriae* Vittorio Emanuele II died in Rome on January 8, 1878.

The people's grief brought the city to a halt for ten days and the government staged his burial as a triumphant funeral procession through the whole city. As the pope refused the use of the main basilicas for the exequies of his former enemy, the decision was made to inhume the king in the Pantheon, which then became the burial ground for the young Italian dynasty. Thus, the Pantheon was recoded as the "Basilica Palatina dei Re d'Italia"[10] and became a central urban anchor of the nation-state.

This decision accorded perfectly with the idea of a secular center at the nearby Piazza Colonna and the layout of Via Nazionale as stipulated in the master plan of 1873. But just a few days after the monarch's demise, a monument in honor of Vittorio Emanuele was demanded and an international competition followed in the autumn of 1880.[11]

It was Italy's long-awaited chance to create something distinctly and visibly opposed to the old regime of the Vatican and its towering cupola by Michelangelo, and to recode the city's fabric in order to implement the Third Rome's rewriting of the city's texture. Terry Kirk remarked that Vittorio Emanuele II served his nation best by his death, becoming the figurehead for the idea of an Italian nation that was to be expressed in the monument named after him.[12]

However, the call for proposals determined neither the character nor the location of the monument within the city. The Pantheon, the Capitoline Hill, Piazza Venezia at the southern end of Via del Corso, Piazza Esedra near the railway station, Porta Maggiore, and Piazza del Popolo were all mentioned as possible positions.[13]

The French architect Henri-Paul Nénot (1853–1934) emerged the winner with his project for an urban concept with triumphal arch for the Piazza Esedra, today's Piazza della Repubblica, as a modern entrance to Via Nazionale. But a foreigner winning first prize for the nation's most important construction was not considered desirable, and a second competition was announced in 1882.

This time the location of the monument was explicitly specified: the memorial in honor of Italy's father figure Vittorio Emanuele was to be situated at the Capitoline Hill, next to Michelangelo's Capitol and the ancient Roman Forum, facing the straight Via del Corso and the former entrance to Rome, the Piazza del Popolo.[14]

Selecting this position for the sculpture was an overtly political decision by the Italian government: the nearby Roman Forum guaranteed a direct link to ancient greatness and imperial claims to power and implied the capability and the validity of their succession as rulers over Italy. Furthermore, as one of the mythological seven founding hills of Rome, the Capitoline Hill was intimately connected with Rome's anti-clerical past in the modern age: from the eleventh century onward, it had been used as the residence of the civic government of Rome and was the site of numerous movements of urban resistance, such as the dramatic scenes of Cola di Rienzo's revived republic in the fourteenth century.[15]

Apart from its historical connotations of ancient grandeur and medieval disobedience against the pope, the Capitol was a prominent spot in the urban contest for Rome. The strategic decision to erect the nation's first large-scale building there caused the city to spin anew—a shifting of the urban Roman core.

A member of the jury, the art critic Camillo Boito (1836–1914), expressed the goals of the monument frankly: "immeddesimare la grandezza presente con la passata"—identify the greatness of the present with the greatness of the past—but "scindere dal passato il presente, portando il simbolo effetivo della nostra rigenerazione fuori delle memorie antiche"—sever the present from the past, bringing the actual symbol of our regeneration out of the ancient memories. Meanwhile, the president of the senate Domenico Farini (1834–1900) noted in his diary, in relation to the political importance of the monument, that "Italy had to do something big to show the Vatican".[17]

Ninety-eight artists and architects answered the call. Their submitted plaster models were exhibited in the recently built Palazzo delle Esposizioni located at the Via Nazionale beneath the Quirinal Hill.

On June 24, 1884, Giuseppe Sacconi (1854–1905), a young architect from the province of Ascoli Piceno in the Marche region, won the second competition of what was colloquially called the *Vittoriano*, referring to the first Christian

[3] The Vittoriano, 1920s.

Source: Maria Filomena Boemi and Carlo Travaglini, eds., *Roma dall'alto* Exhibition catalogue. (Rome: Università degli studi Roma tre, 2006), p. 109.

name of the dead king Vittorio Emanuele II. Sacconi's draft comprised a wide system of steps leading to an equestrian sculpture of the king. Executed by Enrico Chiaradia (1851–1901), the bronze statue formed the center of the composition and typologically tied in with the famous equestrian bronze of Marcus Aurelius that had survived since antiquity on the nearby Capitol [3]. The majestic staircase and the statue were surrounded and crested by a Corinthian colonnade ending in two pavilion wings with porticos and crowning quadrigas.

The construction work and demolition of the then surviving medieval quarter started a year later. While the medieval church of Santa Maria in Aracoeli was left untouched, its convent buildings and the famous tower of Pope Paul III were destroyed, obliterating the last traces of papal history on the site.

The erection of the Vittoriano took a long time—until 1927—and Sacconi died in 1905, well before the monument's completion. The construction management was taken over by his colleagues Pio Piacentini (1846–1928), Manfredo Manfredi (1859–1927), and Gaetano Koch (1849–1910).[18] Nominally already inaugurated on the occasion of the fiftieth anniversary of the foundation of Italy the nation-state in 1911, the monument was augmented with the function of the tomb of the unknown soldier following World War I.

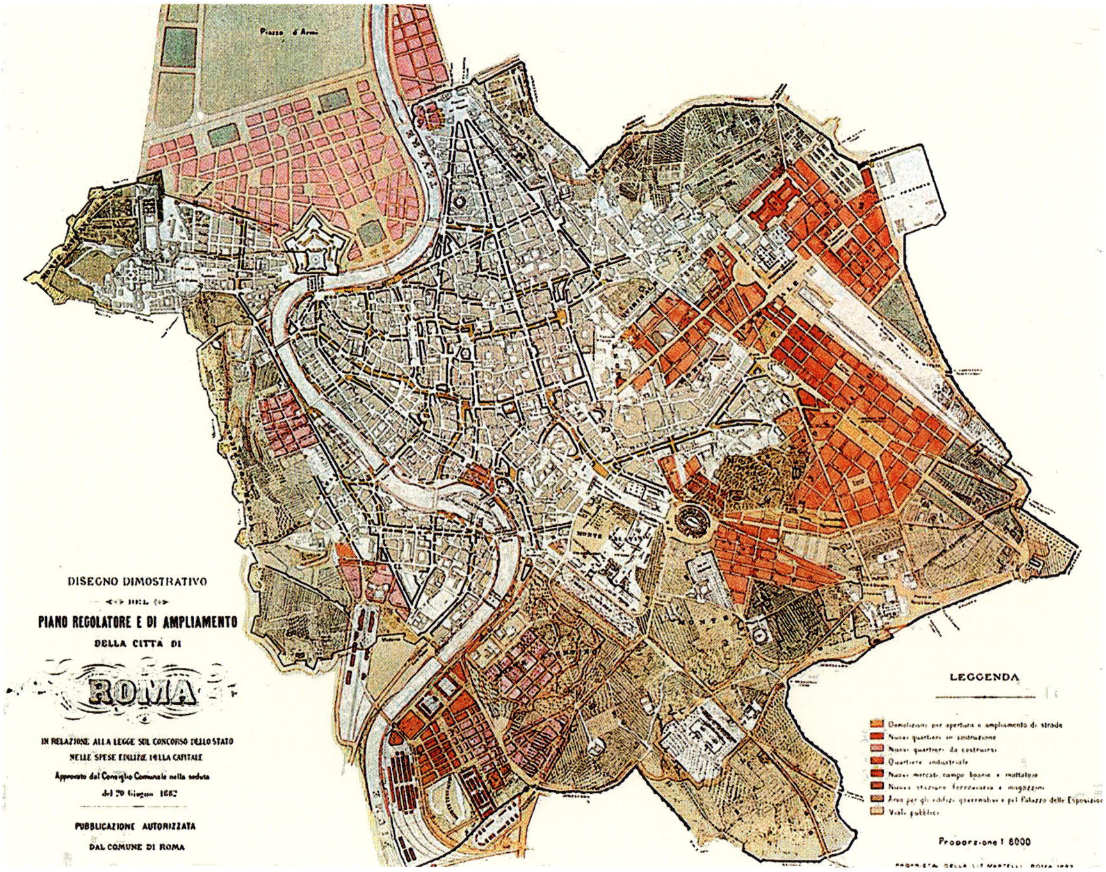

[4] Alessandro Viviani, Piano regulatore, Rome, 1883.

Source: Spiro Kostof, The Third Rome 1870–1950. *Traffic and Glory* (Berkeley: University Art Museum 1973), p. 44.

This examination seeks to focus on the spatial and urbanistic effects that the often architecturally and aesthetically criticized[19] Vittoriano had on the city's layout as a large-scale monument for the nation, recoding the existing urban layout.

Recoding the Urban Layout of Rome

Installing the Vittoriano—which praised Italy's first king at the Capitoline Hill on the southern flank of the until-then small and not very significant Piazza Venezia—as the new core of Rome caused a fundamental reorientation of the city [4].

The idea of a new secular center with governmental and shopping facilities at Piazza Colonna was pushed back in favor of an urbanistic concentration on an extended Piazza Venezia and the monument in honor of Vittorio Emanuele. Consequently, the course of the Via Nazionale was changed.

Instead of connecting the station with the Trevi Fountain, Via del Corso, the Pantheon as the new burial ground of Italy's constitutional monarchy, and Piazza Navona, the Via Nazionale now formed a steep double curve at the level of Trajan's Market leading into the Piazza Venezia, shifting the urban core southward toward the Vittoriano and the antique forums.[20] Thus the terminal point of the ancient Via del Corso, the former Via Lata, was accentuated and the ideological contiguousness of the two regimes highlighted.

But this significant change in the nineteenth-century urban planning of Rome is the product of a two-way process: already in 1876 the municipal policymakers had voted against Viviani's idea of elongating the Via Nazionale toward the Trevi Fountain, the Pantheon and the Piazza Navona. Even though this road configuration would have connected the sights of the city—evoking the significant interrelations of the buildings—it would at the same time have destroyed the unique shape of the historic squares. Traffic chaos in the narrow streets and alleys near Piazza Sciarra was also feared.

After taking into account various alternative projects by different architects, Viviani was forced to lead his axis through the aforementioned double bend into the enlarged Piazza Venezia.

This decision probably drew attention to the spot as a possible monumental site. But it was not until the construction of the royal monument at the edge of Piazza Venezia that the city layout was changed entirely: the updated *piano regolatore* of 1883 scheduled an extension of the Via Nazionale beyond the Piazza Venezia [5]. In a meandering course, the street later named Corso Vittorio Emanuele II connects the square and the adjacent Vittoriano with the monuments of the Renaissance and the Baroque at the bend of the Tiber such as the large Counterreformation churches of Il Gesù and San Andrea della Valle, the Palazzo Vidoni (at the time attributed to Raphael), Palazzo Massimo alle Colonne, and the famous Palazzo della Cancelleria. The Chiesa Nuova with the adjacent Oratorio dei Filippini by Francesco Borromini was also incorporated.[21] Therefore, the boulevard of Via Nazionale, elongated as Corso Vittorio Emanuele II, opened up new squares and connected architectural icons from the Second Rome of the Popes with the remains of antiquity such as the thermal baths of Deocletian, Trajan's Market, and the Roman Forum, and with the new landmarks of the Third Rome such as the Vittoriano, the Palazzo delle Esposizioni, and the National Bank of Italy.

Following the decision to rotate the city and to focus on Piazza Venezia and the Vittoriano, the bank's board decided to build its headquarters along Via Nazionale instead of Piazza Colonna, demonstrating this square's loss of importance.[22]

Furthermore, the construction of the king's monument—also colloquially known as the *wedding cake* or *typewriter*—had an impact on the silhouette of the city. Looking at Rome today, two giant buildings dominate the panorama: the dome of Saint Peter by Michelangelo and the Vittoriano by Giuseppe Sacconi [6]. The nation's monument is angled toward the Vatican, with the bronze king riding toward it on his horse [7]. This bellicose gesture from the statue is underlined by the bright white marble covering of the fabric, which, as the Italian historian Renato De Fusco remarked: "'spara,' per usare un termine fotografico, sul dominante ocra del panorama romano"—shoots, to use a term from photography, onto the dominant ochre of the Roman cityscape.[23]

[5] Corso Vittorio Emanuele II, 1970s.

Source: Leonardo Benevolo, *Roma oggi* (Rome: Ed. Laterza, 1977), p. 54.

As an architectural and material allegory for the new nineteenth century's civic and social order, the Vittoriano demonstrates its opposition to the old regime which was still alive within the city.

The Vittoriano, as an independent new landmark and symbol of Italy the nation-state, enabled the new rulers to establish something as dominant and as shaping of the city as Michelangelo's famous cupola: virtually a "counter-cupola"[6].[24] Whereas the sixteenth-century dome overarches the tomb of Saint Peter, the Vittoriano houses the memory of the king who united Italy and deprived the pope of his secular power, the altar of the fatherland, and the grave of the unknown Italian soldier.

The monument fulfilled its function as secular center of Rome perfectly—and appallingly, as the progression of history showed: Benito Mussolini (1883–1945) chose the Palazzo Venezia next to the Vittoriano as his office and established the Piazza Venezia as the starting point for his urbanistic revision of Rome in the 1920s and 1930s.[25] The main arteries of his endeavors to recode Rome again have their origin in Piazza Venezia. The Via dell'Impero—today's Via dei Fori Imperiali—connects the square with the forums and the Colosseum, and the new Via del Mare, also starting in Via Venezia, led toward the sea

6 Rome from Pincio with the Vittoriano crowning the city on the left and the cupola of Saint Peter on the right.

Photograph by the author.

7 The Statue of Vittorio Emanuele II (part of the Vittoriano) riding toward the dome of Saint Peter.

Photograph by the author.

and the site of the planned World's Fair or Esposizione universale (E'42) on the way to the ancient harbor of Ostia.[26] The construction and arrangement of these two new main boulevards isolated the Vittoriano and thereby served to accentuate it further.

The towering Vittoriano's successful establishment as a secular national center and counterbalance to the Vatican is not only attested to by the layout of the fascist-era avenues, but also underlined by diverse military parades, frequent public speeches by *Il Duce*, and memorial services and ceremonies, as well as today's national soccer celebrations.

Despite its ambivalent impact on the history of architecture, the Vittoriano must be valued as a strong national symbol in the urban context of Rome, squaring up to the dominating cupola of Saint Peter and giving the city's shape an entirely new east-west alignment, and as an attempt of the Italian nation-state to inscribe itself into the symbolically over-coded palimpsest of the Eternal City.

Given that the Vittoriano is listed among the most prominent buildings in Rome, it is paradoxical that it is one of the least researched and appreciated architectural monuments of the city, and has until the present day never been examined consequently in the context of its urbanistic significance and recoding value for the urban layout of Rome.

Endnotes

1 Concerning the historic events see, among others, Alberto Caracciolo, *Roma capitale dal Risorgimento alla crisi dello Stato liberale* (Rome: Rinascita, 1956); Denis Mack Smith, *Modern Italy. A Political History* (Ann Arbor: University of Michigan Press, 1997); and Gustav Seibt, *Rom oder Tod. Der Kampf um die italienische Hauptstadt* (Berlin: Siedler 2001), pp. 113–189. Regarding the transition of the Italian capital, see Taina Syrjämaa, *Constructing Unity, Living in Diversity. A Roman Decade* (Helsinki: Finnish Academy of Science and Letters, 2006) and Franz J. Bauer, *Rom im 19. und 20. Jahrhundert* (Regensburg: Pustet, 2009), pp. 76–87.

2 See Horst Bredekamp, *Sankt Peter in Rom und das Prinzip der produktiven Zerstörung: Bau und Abbau von Bramante bis Bernini* (Berlin: Wagenbach, 2008), pp. 97–112.

3 Martin Warnke, "Bau und Gegenbau" in *Architektur als politische Kultur*, eds. Hermann Hipp and Ernst Seidl (Berlin: Reimer, 1996), pp. 11–18.

4 Silvio Pasquarelli, "Via Nazionale. Le vicende urbanistiche e la sua architettura" in *Roma capitale 1870–1911. Architettura e urbanistica. Uso e trasformazione della citta storica* (exhibition catalogue Rome), eds. Giorgio Ciucci and Vanna Fraticelli (Venice: Marsilio Editore, 1984), pp. 295–324, and Mario Sanfilippo, *La costruzione di una capitale. Roma 1870–1911* (Cinisello Balsamo: Silvana Editore, 1992), pp. 82–87.

5 Regarding the first *piano regolatore* from 1873 see Italo Insolera, "Storia del Primo Piano Regolatore di Roma: 1870–1874," *Urbanistica*, no. 27 (1959): pp. 74–90; Spiro Kostof, *The Third Rome 1870–1950. Traffic and Glory* (Berkeley, CA: University Art Museum, 1973); and Giuseppe Cuccia, *Urbanistica edilizia infrastrutture di Roma Capitale 1870–1990. Una cronologia* (Rome: Ed. Laterza, 1991).

6 Manfedo Tafuri, "La prima strada di Roma moderna. Via Nazionale," *Urbanistica*, no. 29, 27 (1959): pp. 95–108.

7 Kostof, *Third Rome*, p. 42.

8 For further information, see Francesco Giovanetti, "Via del Corso rinnovata. La sistemazione di piazza Colonna," in *Roma capitale 1870–1911. Architettura e urbanistica. Uso e trasformazione della citta storica* (exhibition catalogue Rome), ed. Giorgio Ciucci and Vanna Fraticelli, (Venice: Marsilio, 1984), pp. 379–405.

9 Cuccia, *Urbanistica*, pp. 15–27.

10 Lorenzo Quilici, "La tutela archeologica nei piani regolatori e nella legislazione," in Roma Capitale 1870–1911. L'archeologia in *Roma capitale tra sterro e scavo* (exhibition catalogue Rome), ed. Assessorato alla Cultura di Roma (Venice: Marsilio Editore 1983), pp. 48–74, p. 54.

11 Thorsten Rodiek, *Das Monumento Nazionale Vittorio Emanuele II. in Rom* (Frankfurt am Main: Lang Verlag, 1983), pp. 34–42; Catherine Brice, "L'immaginario della Terza Roma: I Concorsi per il Monumento a Vittorio Emanuele II a Roma," in *Il Vittoriano. Materiali per una storia*, ed. Pierluigi Porzio (Rome: Palombi, 1986), vol. 1, pp. 11–24; see Lars Berggren and Lennart Sjöstedt, *L'ombra dei grandi. Monumenti e politica monumentale a Roma* (1870–1895) (Rome: Artemide Editore, 1996), pp. 56–62; Fabio Magone, Massimiliano Savorra and Maria Luisa Scalvini, eds. *Verso il Vittoriano. L'Italia unita e i concorsi di architettura. I disegni della Biblioteca Nazionale di Roma* (exhibition catalogue Rome), (Naples: Electa Napoli, 2002); Kathrin Mayer, "Im Kampf um die Geschichte. Die Nationaldenkmäler für Viktor Emanuel II. und Garibaldi" in *Kunst auf der Suche nach Nation. Das Problem der Identität in der italienischen Malerei, Skulptur und Architektur vom Risorgimento bis zum Faschismus*, ed. Damian Dombrowski (Berlin: Lukas-Verlag 2013), pp. 138–156, here pp. 142–144.

12 Terry Kirk, *The Architecture of Modern Italy. The Challenge of Tradition 1750–1900* (New York: Princeton Architectural Press 2005), pp. 231–233.

13 Pasquarelli, *Via Nazionale*, p. 318.

14 Rodiek, *Monumento Nazionale*, pp. 42–43.

15 Concerning further historical layers of the Capitoline Hill see Golo Maurer, "Nation building. Das Monument für Viktor Emanuel II." in *Kunst auf der Suche nach der Nation. Das Problem der Identität in der italienischen Malerei, Skulptur und Architektur vom Risorgimento bis zum Faschismus*, ed. Damian Dombrowski (Berlin: Lukas-Verlag 2013), pp. 157–183, here pp. 157–163.

16 Camillo Boito, *Questioni pratiche di belle arti. Restauri, concorsi, legislazione, professione, insegnamento* (Milan: Hoepli, 1893), 239. English translation by Britta Hentschel.

17 Hugh Petter, "Back to the Future. Archaeology and Innovation in the Building of Roma Capitale" in *Ancient Rome. The Archaeology of the Eternal City*, ed. Jon Coulston and Hazel Dodge (Oxford: Oxford University School of Archaeology, 2000), pp. 332–353, here p. 346.

18 See Britta Hentschel, *Gaetano Koch (1849–1910). Bauen für das Dritte Rom* (München: Hirmer Verlag, 2018).

19 See Maurer, *Nation building*, pp. 172–174.

20 Regarding the different projects of the routing and configuration of Via Nazionale between Largo Magnanapoli and Piazza Venezia see Tafuri, *Via Nazionale*, p. 98.

21 Britta Hentschel, "Der Corso Vittorio Emanuele II. Städtebau im Rom des 19. Jahrhunderts" in *Stadtformen. Die Architektur der Stadt zwischen Imagination und Konstruktion*, ed. Vittorio Magnago Lampugnani and Matthias Noell (Zürich: gta Verlag 2005), pp. 190–202.

22 Pasquarelli, *Via Nazionale*, p. 312, and Britta Hentschel, "Nationale Identitätsstiftung über Architektur und Städtebau in Rom. Gaetano Koch (1849–1910) und die italienische Stunde Null" in *Kunst auf der Suche nach der Nation. Das Problem der Identität in der italienischen Malerei, Skulptur und Architektur vom Risorgimento bis zum Faschismus*, ed. Damian Dombrowski (Berlin: Lukas-Verlag, 2013), pp. 120–137, here pp. 126–127.

23 Renato De Fusco, *L'architettura dell'Ottocento* (Torino: Utet, 1980), p. 147.

24 Arnold Esch, "Idealisierte Geister am Tarpejischen Felsen. Von Humboldt zu Wilhelm II. Eine Geschichte der deutsch-italienischen Nähe, dann der wachsenden Missverständnisse und Entfremdungen" in *Frankfurter Allgemeine Zeitung*, January 7, 2006. See also Golo Maurer, "Denkmal für König Viktor Emanuel II. (Monumento Vittorio Emanuele)" in *Rom. Meisterwerke der Baukunst von der Antike bis heute. Festgabe für Elisabeth Kieven*, ed. Christina Strunck (Petersberg: Imhof Verlag, 2007), pp. 497–499, here p. 499.

25 Ralph-Miklas Dobler, *Bilder der Achse. Hitler Empfang in Italien 1938 und die mediale Inszenierung des Staatsbesuchs in Fotobüchern* (Berlin: Deutscher Kunstverlag 2015), pp. 163–173.

26 See Harald Bodenschatz, *Städtebau für Mussolini. Auf der Suche nach der neuen Stadt im faschistischen Italien* (Berlin: Dom Publishers, 2011), pp. 128–129, 201–217, and Terry Kirk, *The Architecture of Modern Italy. Visions of utopia, 1900 – Present* (New York: Princeton Architectural Press, 2005), pp. 120–127.

URBAN AGENTS

2

NEW ACTORS AND OLD STRUCTURES
Vienna's Contested Space and the Strategies of Court, Aristocracy, and Bourgeoisie on the Ringstraße

Richard Kurdiovsky

In 1857, Emperor Francis Joseph I declared it his will that the inner city of Vienna, surrounded by its early modern city walls, should be united with its suburbs by demolishing the old city fortifications and rebuilding the whole area.[1] The result of this, the new city quarter along the Ringstraße, has become the symbol representing the newly emerging power and influence of the liberal bourgeoisie,[2] expressed not least by the enormous volume of new construction of bourgeois housing in this area. It was in this area of the city of Vienna that the members of the so-called second society, which consisted of especially wealthy bourgeois bankers, merchants, and industrialists who had just recently been ennobled, built their representative homes. And it was this area they used for their economic, political, cultural, and leisure activities.[3] However, this city extension project was not executed by the local municipality as the representative body of the bourgeois society of the city. Officially, it was a project initiated by the head of the Austrian state, the emperor himself, with his Interior Ministry responsible for preparing, developing, financing, and executing the city extension.[4] The intention was to guarantee the imperial character of the future Ringstraße and to ensure that nothing would escape the notice of state authorities. But however impressive and monumental the public buildings along the Ringstraße appeared, the mass of bourgeois houses started to characterize, if not dominate, the new city quarter. In what follows, I would like to present and analyze the tensions between the emerging group of bourgeois citizens and the imperial court at the hierarchical top of the Austrian Empire, including the high aristocracy which made up this court.[5] How did formerly dominant groups react to this city development project and to the new conditions which arose right in front of the imperial palace and the old palaces of the nobility? Changing circumstances started to redefine and recode the city which had been and was still intended to be the main seat of imperial power. For these formerly

[1] Rudolf von Alt, view on the inner city of Vienna from St. Charles' church, around 1841/1842.

Source: Wien Museum, inv. no. 31.096

dominant groups, the solution to this challenge was to retreat into tradition, into the legitimacy of their own history—a process which accompanied the general development of the Ringstraße right from the start.

The City of Vienna Encoded as Imperial

In the mid-nineteenth century, the city of Vienna was clearly encoded as an imperial city, as already signaled by the official name: k. k. Reichshaupt- und Residenzstadt, meaning the Imperial Royal Capital and City of Residence of the Austrian emperor. Visual signs existed which pointed toward this special characteristic of the city. The (inner) city of Vienna was separated from the surrounding suburbs by massive city walls [1] which helped to characterize Vienna as the seat of imperial power—not least by means of the Hofburg, the imperial palace which prominently overlooked the city walls, as did several other palaces belonging either to members of the Habsburg dynasty (as in the case of the Albertina palace, which belonged to Archduke Charles and his descendants,

among them the Archduke Albrecht) or to aristocratic families of the court (amongst the most prestigious examples were the Majoratshaus as the main palace of the princes of Liechtenstein, and the Coburg palace of the Viennese branch of the Saxe-Coburg and Gotha family). Whoever entered the city had to pass through city gates which were adorned with the Habsburg coat of arms or with inscriptions bearing the names of Habsburg emperors (on the Outer Hofburg Gate, for instance, the inscription bearing the name of Francis II/I is still visible, while the Stubentor and the Schottentor bore the name of his son Ferdinand I).[6] Once inside the city, the signs of imperial sovereignty continued. Apart from the Hofburg, there were the ancient baroque palaces of the *hoffähige* (presentable at court) families, the so-called first society, which made up the imperial court—and this court was considered the most exclusive of all European courts,[7] withholding access to court events from anyone without a sufficiently long line of aristocratic ancestors.[8] There were the buildings of official agencies and ministries which, in general, occupied former palaces of the

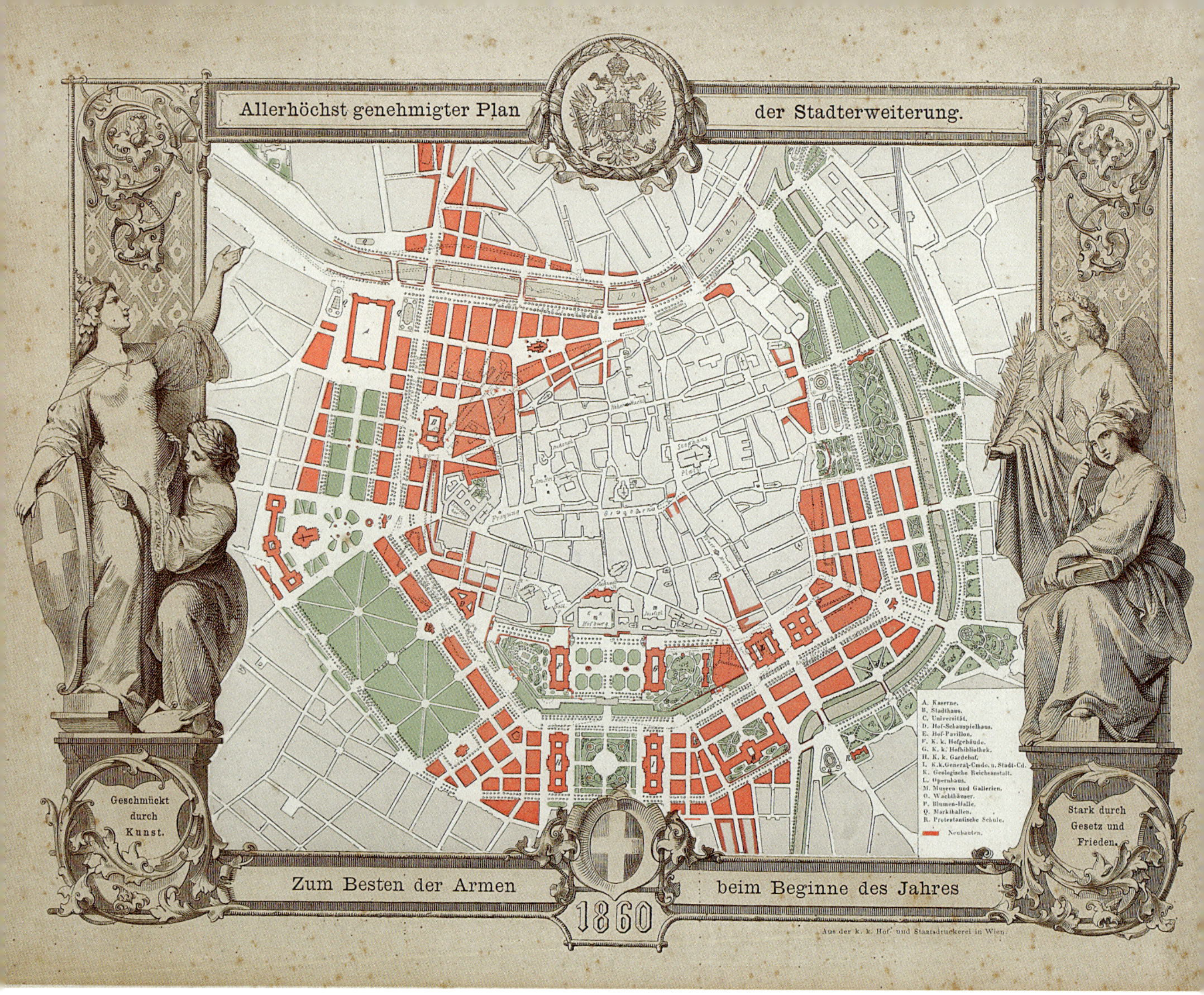

[2] k. k. Hof- und Staatsdruckerei (imperial royal court and state print office), greetings card for New Year's Day of 1860 with the Grundplan for the city extension from 1859.

Source: Wien Museum, inv. no. 8476.

nobility, such as the Ministry of Finance in the palace which had once belonged to Prince Eugene of Savoy, or the Ministry of War housed in one of the former Jesuit monasteries. Other courtly spheres such as the court theaters (the opera located in the Kärntnertortheater and the Burgtheater next to the Hofburg) were open to the public. And not least, there were the shop signs advertising the status of their owners as purveyors to the court, which indicated the general imperial character of the city.

Around the mid-nineteenth century, the city's appearance still reflected the status it had acquired in early modern times. Much too small for the increasing number of inhabitants, it lacked the essential infrastructure of a modern metropolis such as London and above all Paris.[9] To meet the new demands of a modern capital, a public competition was announced in 1857 to develop the so-called *Grundplan* [2], the plan for the general layout of the extension of the inner city of Vienna.[10] After the result of the competition had been approved by the emperor in October 1859, maps of the city extension were published by the imperial court and state printing office, symbolically expressing imperial hegemony within the city. This popular and widely distributed document did not show the city oriented toward the north, as was already usual at that time, but toward the north-east, which graphically turned the imperial palace into a kind of base upon which the whole city symbolically rested.[11] On the abstract graphic medium of a map which only highlighted public buildings, while individual private constructions formed a mass of unified rectangles, the city of Vienna could still look as imperially encoded as before.

According to the *Grundplan*, the number of buildings that were intended to serve either the imperial court, the military as one of its most important pillars,[12] or state agencies was significant, and covered a wide range of building types. It comprised the enlargement of the Hofburg complex, the construction of new court theaters, and included at least one religious building: the Votivkirche, a church promised by the emperor's younger brother Maximilian to commemorate the unsuccessful assassination attempt on the emperor, which was financed by donations from all the provinces of the Habsburg empire, turning the building into a symbol of the unity of the whole Habsburg state—in accordance with Francis Joseph's official motto, *viribus unitis*.[13] Military control over the whole new city extension was guaranteed by massive barracks and by a sequence of guard-houses at bends along the boulevard. In contrast to these buildings, the municipality of Vienna as the representative body of its bourgeois citizens was architecturally present only in a single building, the Stadthaus (literally: town house), which was to occupy a square on a rather remote section of the Ringstraße. Thus, the *Grundplan* gave visual expression to the traditional aim of subordinating the city of Vienna to the dominance of imperial power as the head of state.

The Rising Influence of the Bourgeois Element and the Lack of Aristocratic Presence on the Ringstraße

However, due to the way the city extension was financed, wealthy bourgeois circles could gain exceedingly strong influence. The area on which the new city quarter was to be developed (the demolished city walls and the leveled glacis) was in the possession of the state. In contrast to Haussmann's method in Paris,[14] building lots were sold to individuals who would build houses on their newly acquired property. The income from these sales went to the city extension fund (*Stadterweiterungsfonds*), out of which all public buildings were financed and which was managed by the Interior Ministry. Visually, the high number of private bourgeois buildings started to characterize the new boulevard—not least because they could be constructed in a shorter time than could the monumental public buildings, and were therefore able to react to the development of stylistic ideas more quickly. The imperial court opera, the very first public building erected on the Ringstraße, is a telling example of this: during the process of construction, the opera was already rivaled by its counterpart, the Heinrichshof, built for the bourgeois owner Heinrich Drasche [3] and completed years before the opera right across the street (1863 as against 1869).

[3] A. Wirth, view of Opernring, ca. 1873.

Source: Neue Illustrirte Zeitung from 23rd of November 1873.

While critics writing for in the daily press were able to praise the style of the Heinrichshof as the new paradigm for housebuilding in Vienna, the imperial court opera was strongly criticized for its mix of historical styles, which was regarded old-fashioned at the time, and for of its lack of monumentality, which resulted from the absence of a clear base for the opera to rest on.[15] Besides the arguments based on stylistic qualities, this quarrel pitted a construction ordered by imperial state authorities against a construction ordered by a bourgeois individual.

The bourgeois dominance as far as property along the Ringstraße was concerned becomes apparent when we consider the extent to which individual groups participated in the acquisition process of the new premises: from the 1850s to the 1870s, 43% of the owners of building lots were wealthy bourgeois individuals, most of them either industrialists or bankers and wholesalers, followed by a slightly smaller group of merchants and manufacturers. Nearly 20% were construction companies which would immediately sell the newly constructed buildings to individuals. Around 6% were architects and—notably—the same percentage were members of the high aristocracy.[16] This ostentatiously low number indicates that the location of the newly built Ringstraße did not offer attractive building sites for the long-established aristocratic families,[17] for whom there was no need to move out of their ancestral city palaces.

Accordingly, the number of noble palaces that were newly constructed in the area of the Ringstraße by families of the court aristocracy was correspondingly low. In many cases, these newly built palaces did not remain in the possession of the old, noble families for very long. The case of the Lützow family is telling, in that the need to construct the family palace in the Ringstraße area from 1869 to 1873 resulted from the loss of the old inherited palace in the inner city, which had to be torn down following the demolition of the city fortifications.[18] The palace, however, was sold only several years later, and in the early 1890s, the palace was named in an architecture magazine as the property of the recently ennobled bourgeois Richard Baron Drasche, the son of the client Heinrich Drasche mentioned above.[19] A similar parallel is seen in the neighboring premises, where Philipp Alexander, Duke of Württemberg, had his palace built between 1862 and 1865, which in 1870 was sold and turned into a hotel for the Vienna World's Fair of 1873.[20] Right from the beginning, the presence of aristocratic circles on the Ringstraße was rather small, and through sales to members of the so-called second society it diminished further. On the other hand, when members of the second society bought these properties they also acquired a certain amount of the prestige and aristocratic aura left by the former owners. Thus, members of the second society could distinguish themselves from the other bourgeois circles which resided along the Ringstraße but were not ennobled.

For bourgeois owners, questions of style and building type became important from the 1860s onward as the more-or-less anonymous apartment buildings which had been constructed in the first years of the new city quarter were gradually complemented by the so-called Zinspalais (literally: rental palace). In contrast to the traditional concept of aristocratic palaces, the Zinspalais was intended to house the owner's family on one floor and additional renters on the other floors. The style typically chosen for these Zinspalais was Neo-Renaissance, following the style of the historic epoch when the aristocratic city palace building type had been developed. The Lützow palace is again an illuminating example, as for this palace too the Neo-Renaissance building style was chosen. However, to make the new palace stand out from the neighboring (bourgeois) houses, the number of floors was reduced, the height of the ceiling of each floor was raised, and consequently the size of the windows was increased. Additionally, the amount of plain, undecorated wall surface remaining was much higher than on any other building of the Ringstraße area, calling to mind the clear models for the palace: the high-Renaissance palaces of Rome, which followed the model of the Farnese palace by Antonio da Sangallo and Michelangelo. Even if the Lützow family had to build on premises surrounded by bourgeois neighbors, the appearance of the palace clearly separated it from its environs.

Architectural Reactions by the Imperial Court

Now, how was the imperial decorum and the dignity of the imperial court to be maintained when things started to change? Concerning the Hofburg, described by the art historian and influential critic Rudolf von Eitelberger as

[4] Rudolf von Alt (watercolour) and Girard & Rehlender (perspective drawing), bird eye-view of the "Kaiserforum", 1872/1873.

Source: Burghauptmannschaft Vienna.

symbolically the central building of the Habsburg empire,[21] court authorities acted much more cautiously. According to the guidelines of the competition for the *Grundplan*, the space directly in front of the Hofburg was not to be developed in any architectural drafts. Without being explicitly stated, it was made clear that one day the emperor himself would decide how to shape the future enlargement of his palace—if not in person, then with his highest court officials in charge of all questions concerning construction activities.[22] On the final *Grundplan*, four buildings were planned in front of the Hofburg, two of which were for military use. In 1862, on his own initiative, the bourgeois architect Christian Ludwig Förster proposed to replace these military buildings with museums, and found support from the Viennese municipality. Of course, the court authorities responsible had to reject this plan from an outsider. At the same time, however, Moriz Löhr, an architect employed at the Interior Ministry, supported the idea of placing museum buildings in front of the imperial palace. He began the process of rethinking the *Grundplan* within the ministry, which finally led to the decision by the emperor, announced in 1864, to open a competition for two imperial museum buildings in front of the Hofburg.[23] In reality, it was not the imperial court around the person of the emperor that had developed the ideas on shaping the area in front of the imperial palace, as had been initially signaled in the program for the *Grundplan*. Innovative ideas came from outside this court, which remained remarkably passive throughout the formation process of the Ringstraße.

The two-part competition, which lasted until 1868, turned into a standoff as a result of the behavior of different parties, including members of the jury, the participating architects, and the public press.[24] To prevent the devastating loss of authority to the emperor that would result from his not being able to settle this dispute and declare his will regarding the outcome, the highest court functionaries decided to rely on the judgment of the renowned foreign architect Gottfried Semper. It was he who declared that the Hofburg itself should form the center of attention, with the museum buildings subordinated to the palace—an idea which the emperor accepted and which Semper developed together with Carl Hasenauer. The result was the so-called Kaiserforum[25] of 1869, a huge complex centered around an interior square which was never completed, but would have led from the court stables at one end to the Hofburg at the other, crossing the Ringstraße with giant triumphal arches which connected the two museum buildings to the two extension wings of the imperial palace with apartments for the imperial family and for their highest-ranking guests [4]. The centerpiece would have been the huge cupola over the throne room on the central axis of the whole complex, to which the two cupolas of the museum buildings were meant to be subordinate. This most impressive Kaiserforum, which was presented to the international public in a famous oversize watercolor by Rudolf von Alt at the 1873 World Fair in Vienna, would have definitively marked the spatial and architectural apex of the Ringstraße, subordinating the whole area to the imperial palace.

This artistic culmination works perfectly on plans, maps and drawings. It would have worked for everyone who entered the Kaiserforum by passing through the giant triumphal arches (although they were hidden in a recess between the museums and the wings of the Hofburg and were therefore out of sight of most of the Ringstraße). However, viewed from the outside and especially from the Ringstraße, the main parts of the Kaiserforum, such as the dominating throne-room cupola, would have disappeared from sight. Only the cupolas of the museums, which according to Semper were but subordinate parts of the Kaiserforum, work as a *point-de-vue* along certain sections of the Ringstraße, although they are pushed aside from the main axis of these streets. The Hofburg as extended by the Kaiserforum thus turned into a building complex invisible from the new city extension. Or to be more precise: only the outside facades of the Kaiserforum, which following Semper's architectural concept only form the rear of the palace complex, are visible. Although the Kaiserforum was the emperor's contribution to the new Ringstraße boulevard, it could dominate the new city quarter only symbolically (or on a graphic medium like a map), but not visually within the urban fabric.

However, there were other building—although significantly smaller ones—belonging to the imperial sphere which clearly acted as *points-de-vue* for a section of the Ringstraße, such as the palace of Archduke Ludwig Victor,[26] another of the emperor's brothers. But this palace was only one of four buildings equally framing the square of Schwarzenbergplatz, and the others again belonged to members of the second society. Only certain decorative motifs, such as free-standing columns and a different interior structure visible on the façade as a result of the extremely large windows and the reduced number of floors, could make the archducal palace stand out from its bourgeois neighborhood.

Architectural Reactions by the First Society

When the city fortifications were demolished, Archduke Albrecht lost the vast gardens, office, service and stable buildings in front of his palace. As compensation, the city extension fund ceded the new block between the court opera and the private imperial garden to Albrecht. Early plans for this area,[27] which have recently been discovered by Andreas Nierhaus,[28] show the whole block serving as an extension to the old palace, with a new façade in a palatial style facing the Ringstraße. Initially meant to serve as quarters for the archduke's horses and household staff, the new building was conceived so as to be easily turned into an extension of the living and reception rooms of the old palace. But the archduke decided differently, and in 1861 he had the area divided into several parcels which were sold to bankers, industrialists, and factory owners, who had their individual palaces erected on the lots. Archduke Albrecht obviously preferred to retreat to his historical palace and to profit economically from his newly acquired premises. However, he had to look out on newly constructed buildings directly opposite his palace, including a trivial beer-hall in the famous brewer Anton Dreher's palace. The Ringstraße was given over to new players while the traditional elite withdrew to their inherited historical building stock.

For the first society it was obviously especially important to keep undesirable neighbors (of any lower social class) at the furthest possible distance and to create a barrier which we might term a "buffer of respectability". In their arguments, at least, the beer hall in the neighborhood became an example of the vulgarity of lower-class social institutions, which had to be kept at a distance. In the case of John II, Prince of Liechtenstein, the family's main palace in Vienna was situated next to the city walls and overlooked the Volksgarten, the only public garden within the inner city. A small pavilion connected to the palace by a bridge and a gallery was situated on top of the ramparts. When the ramparts were torn down, a broad area became available for new construction, but the prince had to be given compensation from the city extension fund for the loss of his small pavilion. He claimed not only the parcels right in front of his palace, but also the option of purchasing the adjacent parcels to avoid a Zinskaserne, a massive tenement building, being built in front of his windows—by which he must have been alluding to the apartment buildings along the Ringstraße, which in their mass produced a certain quality of monotonous uniformity. And, by necessity, the prince's chancellery added that the prince would even buy all the buildings lots in question to be sure of not having a beer hall in front of his palace.[29]

The prince ordered a number of projects to be developed for the building lots in front of his palace. In the end, he chose not to struggle with building something new, but relied solely on his family's existing historical building stock, as it represented a unique value which no members of any lower class could acquire. The building lots in question, for their part, were turned into an extension of the public Volksgarten which the prince had no problem in accepting in front of his palace. As the property of the court and thus part of the Hofburg, the Volksgarten guaranteed a permanent unimpeded view from the Liechtenstein palace. Additionally, the public infrastructure of the Volksgarten (cafés and the museum for Canova's statue of *Theseus defeating the Centaur*) emphasized the garden's distinction as an elegant recreational ground mainly for the higher social stratum.[30]

The Rising Influence of Vienna's Municipality

Close to the Liechtenstein palace another remarkable change of use took place[31] which demonstrated the gradually increasing influence the municipality of Vienna could exercise on the city's most prestigious boulevard. In 1872, a committee consisting of members of the Interior Ministry and of court agents discussed plans for the future position of the Hofburgtheater,[32] as, in contrast to the original ideas of the *Grundplan*, the parade grounds had been redeveloped between 1868 and 1870. The result of this redevelopment was a huge square dominated by the city of Vienna's new town hall, which was prominently placed on the middle axis and flanked by two buildings—the new university and the parliament building—for which state authorities were responsible.[33] Nonetheless, the new court theater was still to be erected in this area as initially intended—however, as the whole urban situation had changed, the exact position of the theater had to be decided anew. Since new street lines had had to be approved by the municipal council of Vienna from 1868 onward,[34] the committee prepared two alternatives [5]: either beside the symmetry axis of the new town hall (plan A) or exactly on this axis (plan B).[35] The first plan of land would have offered a quite economical solution, as only minor expropriations of land would have been necessary. The second case, by contrast, would have resulted in considerably higher costs. The municipal council, however, approved neither of the two proposals, but submitted a third solution: plan C [6], with the theatre on the symmetry axis of the new town hall, but with different street lines.[36] And the council offered the sum of 250,000 gulden as an incentive for the committee to accept their proposal.[37] Although the committee reacted indignantly, as it regarded the city council's actions to be exceeding its remit,[38] the offer of a quarter million gulden was willingly accepted and the emperor Francis Joseph I ultimately gave his consent to the council's proposal.[39]

The result of this process can undoubtedly be regarded as a victory for Vienna's municipality. In the late 1850s and 1860s, the city could exercise no direct influence on the layout of the future city quarters. The responsibilities of the municipality were more or less restricted to street paving, street lighting, and the sewage system. However, approximately twelve years later, in 1872, the municipality could not only propose the position of court buildings like the court theatre within the new urban fabric, but could even play a significant role in turning the theater of the imperial court into an aesthetic counterpart to the new town hall of the bourgeoisie. On the most prominent street of the Habsburg capital, the urban community had succeeded in establishing a visual symbol to counter elitist court society and its state agencies. And,

Ring - Strasse
VOM K.K. MINISTERIUM

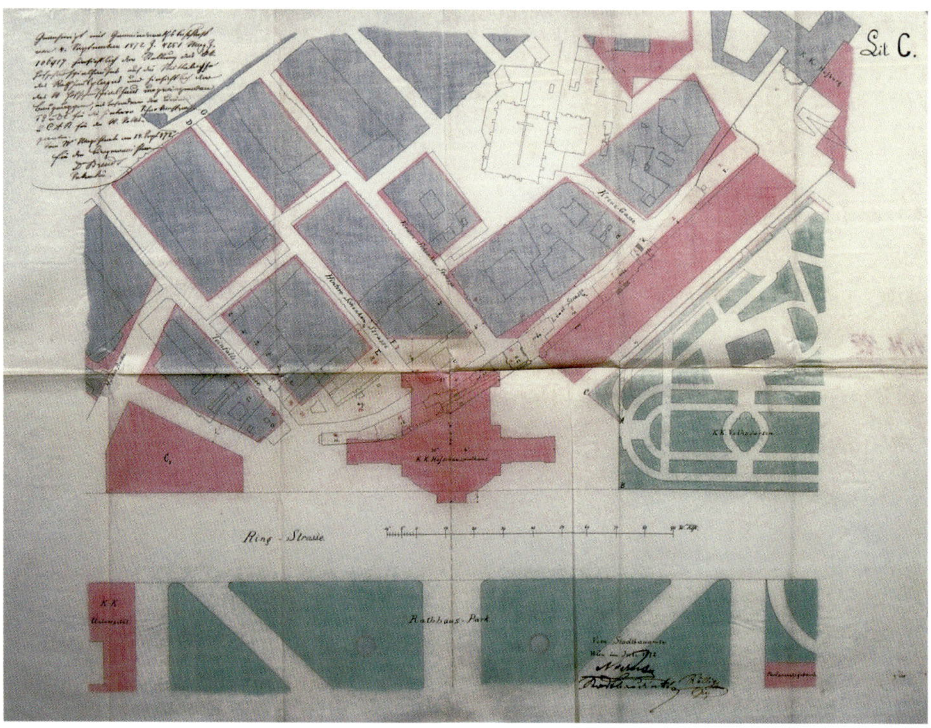
Lit C.
Ring - Strasse
Rathhaus - Park

[5] Draft A for the position of the new court theatre aside the symmetrical axis of the new town hall, ca. 1872.

Source: Austrian State Archive, attachement to HBC175.

most notably, it was a respectably large amount of money that convinced the state-sponsored committee to agree to the street lines as proposed by the local municipality.

The Habsburgs' Final Retreat into Tradition

There seems to be a correspondence between the retreat of the high nobility to its inherited family palaces, which had already started in the second half of the nineteenth century, and the steps that were undertaken by the imperial court after the turn of the century. In 1906, the heir to the throne Archduke Francis Ferdinand took over the responsibility for the imperial construction site, which was still unfinished due to constant conceptual changes in the function and architectural structure of the Kaiserforum as a result of the regular changing of the architects responsible. Francis Ferdinand immediately questioned the idea of completing the extension of the Hofburg—not least because the idea of the Kaiserforum was more than three decades old stylistically, and it no longer corresponded to the current situation of the imperial court functionally. The heir to the throne was successful in that several years later, in 1913, the emperor himself decided to abandon the Kaiserforum.[40] The budget was instead to be used for renovating the historical parts of the Hofburg, which was seen as a major means of expressing imperial power both visually and symbolically[41]. This was quite in accordance with the retreat of members of the aristocratic court society to their traditional architectural values as a means of legitimizing their position historically. This orientation toward their own history[42] was connected to criticism of the "usurpers" of the second society, who (as has been shown) could not only afford to build new constructions, but would also buy palaces which had been commissioned by members of the first society in the first place. In doing so, they ostentatiously pushed the former elite aside and replaced them, at least in the new representative zone of the Habsburg metropolis. For the old elites the greatest distinction lay in relying on family heritage and on every symbol of ancestry, and in not engaging in constructing something new. In oral records at least, Archduke Francis Ferdinand is said to have called the apartment wing of the Kaiserforum something "which every rich Jew can command to build,"[43] alluding to Jewish members of the second society who were insinuated to be able to afford anything.

[6] Draft C for the position of the new court theatre on the symmetrical axis of the new town hall, ca. 1872.

Source: Austrian State Archive, attachement to HBC175.

With the end of World War I and the fall of the monarchy the sociopolitical situation changed significantly. Still, it was decades before the newly founded republic could take possession of the former Habsburg palace and recode it as a place of public representation of democratic state authority (until that point, the Hofburg had only been used by cultural institutions such as museums and collections and as a venue for conferences, with large halls which could be rented for festivities and celebrations).[44] It was not until 1946 that the Office of the Federal President moved into the former state apartments of the Habsburg monarchy to use it as offices and reception rooms for the representation of the Second Republic of Austria.

Endnotes

1 *Wiener Zeitung*, December 25, 1857, 1–2. See also: Elisabeth Springer, "Geschichte und Kulturleben der Wiener Ringstraße" (= Renate Wagner-Rieger, ed. *Die Wiener Ringstraße. Bild einer Epoche. Die Erweiterung der Inneren Stadt Wien unter Kaiser Franz Joseph vol. 2*) (Wiesbaden: Franz Steiner Verlag GmbH, 1979), pp. 88–96.

2 Carl E. Schorske, *Fin-de-Siècle Vienna. Politics and Culture* (New York: Alfred A. Knopf, 1980), especially pp. 24–62.

3 Most recently: Alfred Fogarassy, ed. *Die Wiener Ringstraße. Das Buch* (Ostfildern: Hatje Cantz, 2014); Agnes-Husslein-Arco and Alexander Klee, eds. *Klimt und die Ringstraße. Klimt and the Ringstrasse* (Vienna: Belvedere Wien, 2015) Exhibition catalog; Gabriele Kohlbauer-Fritz, ed., *Ringstraße. Ein jüdischer Boulevard. Ringstrasse. A Jewish Boulevard*, (Vienna: Amalthea, 2015); Andreas Nierhaus, ed. *Der Ring. Pionierjahre einer Prachtstraße* (Vienna: Wien Museum, 2015); Exhibition catalog; Michaela Pfundner, ed. *Wien wird Weltstadt. Die Ringstraße und ihre Zeit* (Vienna: Metroverlag, 2015); Harald R. Stühlinger, ed. *Vom Werden der Wiener Ringstraße* (Vienna: Metroverlag 2015). Renate Wagner-Rieger, *Die Wiener Ringstraße. Bild einer Epoche. Die Erweiterung der Inneren Stadt Wien unter Kaiser Franz Joseph* (Wiesbaden: Franz Steiner Verlag GmbH, 1979).

4 Andreas Nierhaus, "Die Hauptstraße des 19. Jahrhunderts. Planung und Organisation der Wiener Stadterweiterung," in Alfred Fogarassy, ed., *Die Wiener Ringstraße* (Ostfildern: Hatje Cantz, 2014) pp.18–28, especially pp. 25–26; Christian Mertens, "Gegeneinander und miteinander. Die Rolle von Staat und Stadt bei der Entstehung von Neu-Wien," in Harald R. Stühlinger, ed. *Vom Werden der Wiener Ringstraße* (Vienna: Metroverlag 2015), pp. 41–67, especially pp. 53–60.

5 Victor von Fritsche, *Bilder aus dem österreichischen Hof- und Gesellschaftsleben* (Vienna: Gerlach & Wiedling, 1914), especially pp. 249–378 ("Der Hof und die Gesellschaft in alter und neuer Zeit 1914"). See also: Ivan Žolger, *Der Hofstaat des Hauses Österreich (Wiener staatswissenschaftliche Studien 14)* (Vienna: Deuticke, 1917); Martin Scheutz, *Der Wiener Hof und die Stadt Wien im 20. Jahrhundert. Die Internalisierung eines Fremdkörpers (Enzyklopädie des Wiener Wissens 10)* (Weitra: Bibliothek der Provinz, 2011); Karin Schneider, "Hofgesellschaft und Hofstaat," in Helmut Rumpler, ed. *Soziale Strukturen. Die Habsburgermonarchie 1848–1918 Band 9 1/2* (Vienna: Verlag der Österreichischen Akademie der Wissenschaften, 2010), pp. 1327–1348; Karin Schneider, "Das Wiener Zeremoniell im 19. Jahrhundert. Ein Ausblick," in Irmgard Pangerl, Martin Scheutz and Thomas Winkelbauer, eds. *Der Wiener Hof im Spiegel der Zeremonialprotokolle (1562–1800). Eine Annäherung* (Innsbruck-Vienna-Bozen: StudienVerlag, 2007), pp. 627–638.

6 Heike Krause, "Die Festung als Erholungs- und Wirtschaftsraum," in Sylvia Sakl-Oberthaler et al. eds. *Von der mittelalterlichen Stadtmauer zur neuzeitlichen Festung Wiens. Historisch-archäologische Auswertung der Grabungen in Wien 1, Wipplingerstraße 33–35* (Vienna: Phoibos Verlag, 2016), pp. 200–207, especially pp. 202–203.

7 von Fritsche, *Bilder aus dem österreichischen Hof- und Gesellschaftsleben*, p. 251: "Die Wiener Hofgesellschaft ist als die exklusivste bekannt."; Richard Kurdiovsky, "House Number 1: The Vienna Hofburg's Multiple Borders," in Carolyn Loeb and Andreas Luescher, ed. *The Design of Frontier Spaces: Control and Ambiguity* (Abingdon: Routledge, 2015), pp. 89–107, especially pp. 103–104.

8 Schneider, "Hofgesellschaft und Hofstaat," pp. 1327–1348, especially 1327–1329.

9 Bertrand Michael Buchmann, "Dynamik des Städtebaus," in Peter Csendes and Ferdinand Opll, eds. *Wien. Geschichte einer Stadt 3: Von 1790 bis zur Gegenwart* (Vienna-Cologne-Weimar: Böhlau, 2006), pp. 47–84, especially p. 68.

10 Harald R. Stühlinger, *Der Wettbewerb zur Wiener Ringstraße. Entstehung, Projekte, Auswirkungen* (Basel: Birkhäuser, 2015).

11 Nierhaus, *Der Ring. Pionierjahre einer Prachtstraße*, p. 122.

12 It should be remembered that eventually, the military (and more specifically the *Fortifikationsdistrikts-Direktion*) had exercised control over the former city fortification (see Walter Wagner "Die k. [u.] k. Armee—Gliederung und Aufgabenstellung," in Adam Wandruszka and Peter Urbanitsch, eds. *Die Habsburgermonarchie 1848–1918 Band 5: Die bewaffnete Macht* (Vienna: Verlag der Österreichischen Akademie der Wissenschaften, 1987), pp. 142–633, especially pp. 222–228 and pp. 452–460.

13 Werner Telesko, *Kulturraum Österreich. Die Identität der Regionen in der bildenden Kunst des 19. Jahrhunderts* (Vienna-Cologne-Weimar: Böhlau, 2008), pp. 95–96.

14 Alice Thomine-Berrada, "Der Ring und die Pastete. Parallelen zwischen dem Paris Hausmanns und der Wiener Ringstraße," in Andreas Nierhaus, ed. *Der Ring. Pionierjahre einer Prachtstraße*, Vienna: Wien Museum, 2015. Exhibition catalog, pp. 27–32.

15 Most recently: Andreas Nierhaus, "Bühne für Kaiserhaus und Bürgertum. Der Bau der Hofoper," in Andreas Nierhaus, ed. *Der Ring. Pionierjahre einer Prachtstraße*, Vienna: Wien Museum, 2015. Exhibition catalog, pp. 224–241. Concerning the critique on the architects see also: Elisabeth Springer, "Geschichte und Kulturleben der Wiener Ringstraße," pp. 319–333 and pp. 344–367.

16 Hannes Baltzarek, Franz Hoffmann, and Alfred Stekl, eds. *Wirtschaft und Gesellschaft der Wiener Stadterweiterung (= Renate Wagner-Rieger, Die Wiener Ringstrasse vol. 5)* (Wiesbaden: Franz Steiner Verlag GmbH, 1975), p. 260.

17 Andreas Nierhaus, "Wiener Paläste und die Repräsentation urbaner Eliten im Historismus," *Documenta Pragensia 28* (2009): pp. 713–736.

18 Peter Hohenbalken, ed. *Heinrich Graf von Lützow. Im diplomatischen Dienst der k. u. k. Monarchie* (Vienna: Oldenbourg R. Verlag GmbH, 1971), pp. 3–5; Baltzarek, Hoffmann, and Stekl, *Wirtschaft und Gesellschaft*, p. 274.

19 *Wiener Bauindustrie-Zeitung* 9, 1891/1892, p. 533.

20 Klaus Eggert, "Der Wohnbau der Wiener Ringstraße im Historismus 1855–1896," (= Renate Wagner-Rieger, *Wiener Ringstraße vol. 7*), (Wiesbaden: Franz Steiner Verlag GmbH, 1979), p. 169.

21 Rudolf Eitelberger, "Die preisgekrönten Entwürfe. Zur Erweiterung der inneren Stadt Wien," (Vienna 1859), p. 5: "Was Wien für die Monarchie ist, das ist die Hofburg für Wien, der eigentliche Mittelpunkt der Stadt."

22 Springer, "Geschichte und Kulturleben der Wiener Ringstraße," p. 306.

23 Ibid., p. 308–309.

24 Also for the following: Richard Kurdiovsky, "Wettbewerbs- und Planungsgeschichte (of the *Kaiserforum*)," in Werner Telesko, ed. *Die Wiener Hofburg 1835–1918. Der Ausbau der Residenz vom Vormärz bis zum Ende des "Kaiserforums" (Veröffentlichungen zur Bau- und Funktionsgeschichte der Wiener Hofburg 4)* (Vienna: Verlag der österreichischen Akademie der Wissenschaften, 2012), pp. 156–183.

25 In 1879, the philosopher of aesthetics Joseph Bayer was the first to compare Semper and Hasenauer's project with the imperial fora of ancient Rome (Joseph Bayer, "Gottfried Semper (1879)" in Joseph Bayer, *Baustudien und Baubilder. Schriften*

zur Kunst, aus dem Nachlass herausgegeben von Robert Stiassny (Jena: Eugen Diederichs 1919), pp. 86–128, especially p. 127) and in 1889, Camillo Sitte introduced the term "Kaiser-Forum" for the first time (Camillo Sitte, *Der Städte-Bau nach seinen künstlerischen Grundsätzen. Ein Beitrag zur Lösung modernster Fragen der Architektur und monumentalen Plastik unter besonderer Beziehung auf Wien* [Vienna: Graeser, 1889], p. 128); see Andreas Nierhaus, "Das Kaiserforum als Entwurf einer idealen Residenz," in Werner Telesko ed. *Die Wiener Hofburg 1835–1918. Der Ausbau der Residenz vom Vormärz bis zum Ende des "Kaiserforums" (Veröffentlichungen zur Bau- und Funktionsgeschichte der Wiener Hofburg 4)* (Vienna: Verlag der österreichischen Akademie der Wissenschaften, 2012), pp. 184–193, especially p. 184.

26 Andreas Nierhaus, "Urbane Öffentlichkeit. Schwarzenbergplatz und Stadtpark," in Andreas Nierhaus, ed. *Der Ring. Pionierjahre einer Prachtstraße*, Vienna: Wien Museum, 2015. Exhibition catalog, pp. 200–207.

27 Austrian National Library, Kartensammlung, inv.-no. K III, 112.450.

28 Andreas Nierhaus, ed., *Der Ring. Pionierjahre einer Prachtstraße*, Vienna: Wien Museum, 2015. Exhibition catalog, pp. 182–183.

29 Richard Kurdiovsky, "Carl von Hasenauer (1833–1894). Das architektonische und zeichnerische Werk des Miterbauers der Wiener Hofbauten und Gottfried Sempers Einfluß auf Hasenauers Stilentwicklung," (Diss. Phil. University of Vienna, 2008), p. 225.

30 Reingard Wittmann, "'Die Eröffnung des irdischen Paradieses.' Neue Lebenswelten auf der Wiener Bastei zwischen Josephinismus und Vormärz," *Österreichische Zeitschrift für Kunst und Denkmalpflege* 64 (2010), pp. 155–164, especially pp. 163–164.

31 Richard Kurdiovsky, "Carl von Hasenauer," pp. 221–227.

32 Minutes of the 1872 meetings of the *Hofbaucomité* (the court's committee on construction measures): fifteenth meeting from March 27 (Austrian State Archive, Allgemeines Verwaltungsarchiv, Stadterweiterungsfonds, HBC99), sixteenth meeting from April 3 (HBC100), seventeenth meeting from April 17 (HBC104) and eighteenth meeting from April 26 (HBC106).

33 Elisabeth Springer, "Geschichte und Kulturleben der Wiener Ringstraße," pp. 447–451; Kurt Mollik, Hermann Reining, and Rudolf Wurzer, "Planung und Verwirklichung der Wiener Ringstraßenzone" (= Renate Wagner-Rieger, *Die Wiener Ringstraße. Bild einer Epoche. Die Erweiterung der Inneren Stadt Wien unter Kaiser Franz Joseph, vol. 3*) (Wiesbaden: Franz Steiner Verlag GmbH, 1979), pp. 211–215, pp. 245–251.

34 New (third) building regulation for Vienna from December 2, 1868; compare Manfred Wehdorn, "Die Bautechnik der Wiener Ringstraße" (= Renate Wagner-Rieger *Die Wiener Ringstraße. Bild einer Epoche. Die Erweiterung der Inneren Stadt Wien unter Kaiser Franz Joseph, vol. 11*) (Wiesbaden: Franz Steiner Verlag GmbH, 1979), pp. 20–21.

35 Minutes of the twenty-seventh meeting of the *Hofbaucomité* from June 26, 1872 (HBC140) and plans as attachments to HBC 175.

36 Letter by the *Magistratsdirektion* (municipal authorities) to the *Obersthofmeisteramt* (Lord Stewart's Office) from September 14, 1872 (HBC175).

37 Magistrate of Vienna to the *Obersthofmeisteramt* from September 14, 1872 (Austrian State Archive, Haus-, Hof- und Staatsarchiv, Obersthofmeisteramt, Rubrik 89/3/j, no. 4476 ex 1872).

38 Undated and anonymous memo (HBC175).

39 Duplicate of an "allerunterthänigster" account by the minister of interior Eduard Lasser from December 23, 1872 and duplicate of a draft for the "allerhöchste" resolution from December 25, 1872 (HBC207 and 208).

40 Andreas Nierhaus, "Baumanns Gesamtplanung und das formelle Ende des Kaiserforums," in Werner Telesko ed. *Die Wiener Hofburg 1835–1918. Der Ausbau der Residenz vom Vormärz bis zum Ende des "Kaiserforums" (Veröffentlichungen zur Bau- und Funktionsgeschichte der Wiener Hofburg 4)* (Vienna: Verlag der österreichischen Akademie der Wissenschaften, 2012) pp. 330–332.

41 Andreas Nierhaus, "Die alte Burg im Schatten des Kaiserforums zwischen 1894 und 1918," in Werner Telesko ed. *Die Wiener Hofburg 1835–1918. Der Ausbau der Residenz vom Vormärz bis zum Ende des "Kaiserforums" (Veröffentlichungen zur Bau- und Funktionsgeschichte der Wiener Hofburg 4)* (Vienna: Verlag der österreichischen Akademie der Wissenschaften, 2012), pp. 278–283, especially pp. 281–283.

42 Richard Kurdiovsky et al., "Legitimacy through History and Architecture. The Vienna Hofburg as Dynastic Hub and Seat of Government between Tradition and Innovation," *The Court Historian. International Journal of Court Studies* 20 (2019), pp. 109–136.

43 Eduard Irmisch, *Beitrag zur Baugeschichte der Neuen Hofburg in Wien* (Vienna: M. Jank, 1932), p. 19.

44 Anna Stuhlpfarrer, "Residenz im Wandel. Die Hofburg nach 1918—Projekte und Planungen," in Anna Stuhlpfarrer and Maria Welzig, *Kulturquartiere in ehemaligen Residenzen: zwischen imperialer Kulisse und urbaner Neubesetzung. Das Wiener "Hofburg-Museums-Quartier" und der internationale Kontext* (Vienna-Cologne: Böhlau, 2014), pp. 17–38.

RECODING REFORM
Ideology and Urban Form in London's Early Housing Estates, 1865–1900

Irina Davidovici

An accelerated pace of change, as the consequence of laissez-faire capitalist development, underlined the recoding of London's residential environments during the nineteenth century. Urban migration, the displacement of poorer populations through the construction of the railways, and their regrouping near workplaces gave rise to infamous slums, known as rookeries, located throughout central London, Islington, and the East End. With these came the need to control, by way of law and philanthropy alike, the decay of the building stock, and to provide instead superior housing aimed at improving not only the physical living conditions but also the moral horizon of the working classes. These attempts supported the adoption in London of a housing type already well established in continental Europe: the multi-family tenement building.

Two key projects in the history of London housing—Peabody Square in Islington (1864–65) and the Boundary Street Estate in the East End (1895–1900) —illustrate a profound change in the conceptions of working-class housing at this time. One was undertaken by a charitable trust, the other by the local authorities, but both were animated by social conscience and responded to the same moral imperatives. Built on slum clearance, they adhered to the formula of the estate, understood as an ensemble of multi-storey residential blocks coordinated in terms of design, construction and administration. Where these estates diverged was in the scope of their urban and architectural strategies, pointing to two distinct ideological attitudes. The first in a series of similar developments, Peabody Square featured severe, standardized residential blocks oriented internally toward a central paved courtyard, defining a private, gated territory closed off from the surrounding neighborhood [1]. By contrast, the Boundary Street Estate was planned on a radial pattern, its blocks designed as distinctive, attractive, outward-looking townhouses, reinforcing the public spaces of the streets [2]. If the former embodied the idea of the estate as an

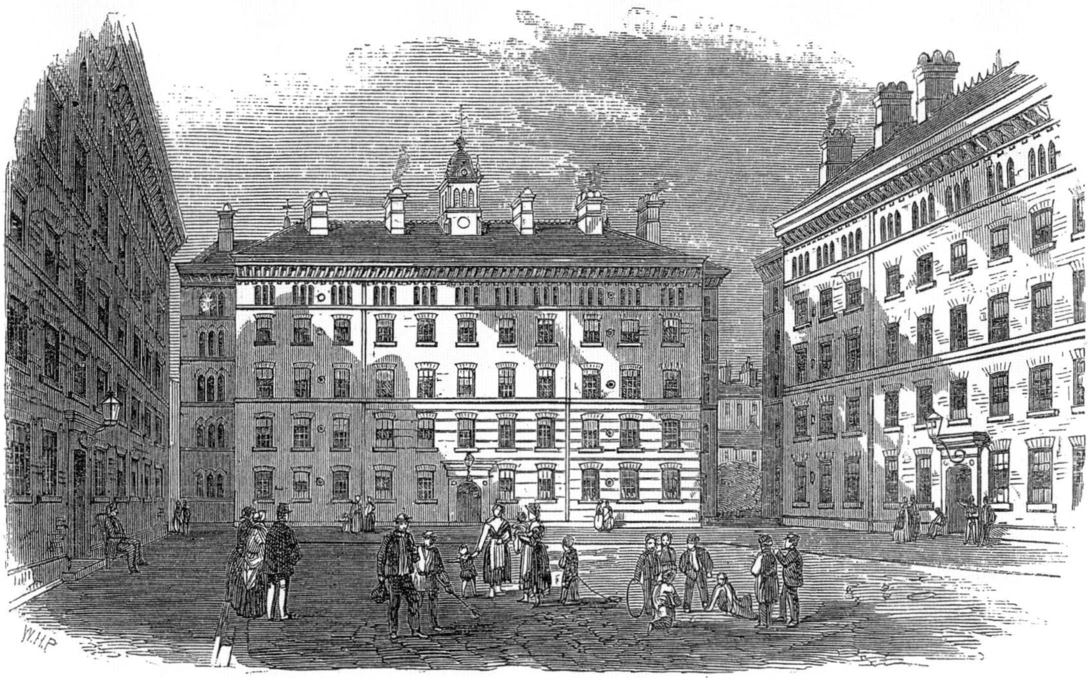

[1] H. A. Darbishire, Peabody Square, Islington, 1865. Image from *Illustrated London News*, 1865.

Source: Mary Evans / Peter Higginbotham Collection.

introverted, protected space for controlled habitation, the latter was conceived as an intrinsic part of the city, stitched into its fabric.

With their contrasting conceptions of what a housing estate might entail, these projects illustrate a two-stage recoding of the city as it occurred in the late nineteenth century. The first step was to reclaim urban territories from their casual, isanitary, and dysfunctional usage as inner city slums, thus marking the colonization of Victorian rookeries through bourgeois values. Overcrowding, crime, and disease were replaced by compartmentalized family dwellings, the normative maintenance of shared spaces, and centralized administration. In the second phase, the dichotomy of slum versus enclosed estate was supplanted by a more ambiguous, permeable territory, enabling a more dignified communal experience. These distinctions, perceptible in the urban configuration of the estates, are explained by the evolution of reform values at the end of the nineteenth century, moving from the regulatory and evangelical moralism of mid-Victorian reformers to a different kind of paternalism, touched by the enlightened rationalism of socialist ideals.

Peabody Trust: Corrective Reform

The ideological backdrop to the Peabody estates was a typically Victorian mixture of philanthropy and pragmatism, evangelical conscience and financial logic.[1] In 1862, *The Times* announced the donation by American banker and London resident George Peabody (1795–1869) of a gift of £150,000,

[2] London County Council. Boundary Street Estate, 1900. View of Arnold Circus, ca. 1903.

Source: London Metropolitan Archives.

intended to benefit "the poor and needy of this great city, and to promote their comfort and happiness."[2] The intended recipients were Londoners "by birth or residence," regardless of religious or political orientation, yet of proven "moral character and good conduct as a member of society."[3] This emphasis was consistent with Peabody's own circumstances as a self-made man of Puritan New England origins.[4] The Trustees, appointed from the uppermost echelons of Victorian society, used the funds to build housing for the working classes, a decision that Peabody supported by increasing his donation threefold over the following years. This initial capital was put to work: a clause of perpetuity was inscribed in the Trust's statutes, requiring the gift to be supplemented by rental profits of 3 percent so as to continue indefinitely. The moral stipulation for eligibility was translated into financial terms, benefiting those workmen and artisans who could afford the regular rents and were deemed "respectable" through income, as well as behavior.

Before the London County Council was founded in 1889, the Peabody Trust was London's largest provider of affordable housing. Between 1863 and 1887,

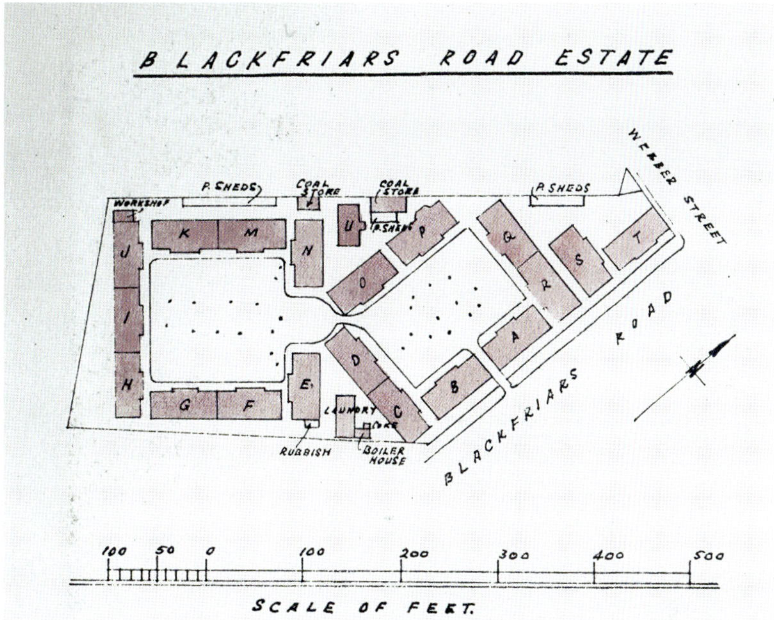

[3] H. A. Darbishire, Peabody Square, Islington, 1865. Bird eye's view from Appleton's Journal of Literature, Science and Art, 31st of July 1869.

Source: London Metropolitan Archives.

it had built eighteen estates, totaling over 5,000 dwellings, all designed by the Trust's Surveyor, architect Henry Astley Darbishire (1839–1908). Working within strict budgets, Darbishire defined a simple, economically sustainable formula (perimeter blocks placed around a central yard, spaced apart to ensure ventilation) that could be easily replicated and adapted to different sites.[5] First implemented in Islington in 1865, this pragmatic model was repeated, giving Darbishire the opportunity to improve it through trial and error. He thus arrived at a system in which investment costs and returns, in the form of rent, were carefully predetermined and tightly controlled.[6]

It was this serialized system that gave rise to the trademark appearance of Darbishire's Peabody estates: repetitive blocks of London yellow stock brick, four to six floors high, relieved at intervals by characteristic stripes of hard, cream-colored Suffolk bricks, with terracotta dressings up to first-floor height and around the entrance doors.[7] Construction materials were associated with a sense of solidity and permanence, even severity. Equally pragmatic were the internal finishes, chosen for considerations of hygiene and wear: painted brick walls, wooden floors, and tiling in wet areas.

Despite their visual dourness, Darbishire's systematized Peabody estates were easily capable of accommodating variations arising from site particularities and changing density requirements. The unusual configuration of the Blackfriars Road Estate (1871)—two quadrangles hinged at one corner, surrounded by four-story blocks—concealed the true innovation in the typology of these blocks. Following negative feedback from the previous estates at Islington and Shadwell (1866), Darbishire replaced the initial internal corridor access with a more compact arrangement, grouping five units per floor around one central

[4] Bird eye's view over Peabody Square, Islington, 1865. After *Appleton's Journal of Literature, Science and Art*, 31 July 1869.

Source: London Metropolitan Archives.

staircase. Derived from Henry Robert's Model Houses of 1851, this organization also resulted in greater external flexibility. From this point onward, blocks would abut side-to-side to form longer slabs, be spaced apart in sequential rows, or be crammed into smaller pockets of space [3].

Later, larger sites were acquired under the provision of the Artisans' and Labourers' Dwellings Improvement Act (1875) following the forced clearance of slums under the control of the Metropolitan Board of Works. The procedure freed up large central sites for redevelopment—on which, however, the Peabody Trust was obliged to house at least as many occupants as had been displaced. Under this statutory pressure, these larger estates became denser and higher, losing some of the ventilation, natural light and modest urban decorum that the earlier estates had enjoyed. The six-floor-high continuous blocks at the Wild Orchard Street estate in Covent Garden and at Apple Orchard Street in Victoria gave rise, for the first time, to higher infant mortality rates on the new estates than in the surrounding slums.

Peabody estates were frequently criticized for their grim sobriety. In 1870, a visitor to the Peabody blocks in Islington commented on their "prison-like appearance".[8] A few years later, the *Daily News* described them as "too much as barracks or workhouses, and too little like dwellings."[9] And yet, graphically, the Peabody estates were depicted as islands of order and light in the blackened mass of the city, presenting an idealized picture that abstracted their forbidding appearance. Liberties were taken with the proportion and scale of the buildings in drawings and prints, in order to convey them as civic and progressive propositions [4]. This manipulated representation was an accurate reflection of class prejudices, not only those of the bourgeoisie in relation to the working classes, but also within the poorer classes themselves.

The territorial delineation of the estates that was implied in the period prints was physically marked by perimeter railings and gates (to which resident families had keys) that were locked at night. The railings, a leitmotif of all the estates, separated two mutually distrusting urban realities: estate versus slum, working people versus non-working, domiciled 'settlers' versus 'nomads' of no fixed abode. The clause of morality included in the tenets of the Trust—intended, as we have seen, to benefit those of 'proven' character, which most often meant the families of working men and artisans—restricted tenancy of the Trust to those who could guarantee a regular income, and not to the poorest and most vulnerable. To be sure, this exclusivity reflected the strict social hierarchies already operating among the poor, dictated by the inflexible criterion of regular employment. Darbishire himself commented that the strictly reinforced social boundaries that separated the respectable from the destitute, and the employed from the unemployed, were reinforced by mutual suspicion on both sides of the social and economic divide.[10]

In order to encourage the continuity of the resident community, the estates provided a range of dwellings of different sizes, so that tenants and their families could move to smaller or larger units depending on their circumstances. In design and day-to-day running, the "improved dwellings" thus determined, almost physically, a limited, stable, controllable reality. Tenancy was governed by strict rules and the behavior of inhabitants closely observed by the resident superintendents, of whom a fair number had been selected from army backgrounds.[11] In their design, management, and selection of residents, these estates amounted to a social engineering project. The emphasis on social responsibility had a clear impact on the quality of life, which was sufficiently regulated to deflect the interest of less respectable and disruptive characters. Beyond mere shelter, the Peabody Trust thus provided oases of respectability guaranteeing, as Darbishire bluntly put it, contact with those "neighbours whose habits and appearance are superior to their own."[12]

LCC Housing: Reform Unbound

In 1889, the London County Council (LCC) took over from the Metropolitan Board of Works as London's municipal administrative body. Following the 1890 Housing of the Working Classes Act, the new organization added to its duties the provision of working-class housing, and in 1893 a dedicated unit, the Housing of the Working Classes Branch, was created in the LCC Architects' Department. The Boundary Street Estate (1893–1900) was its first project: the

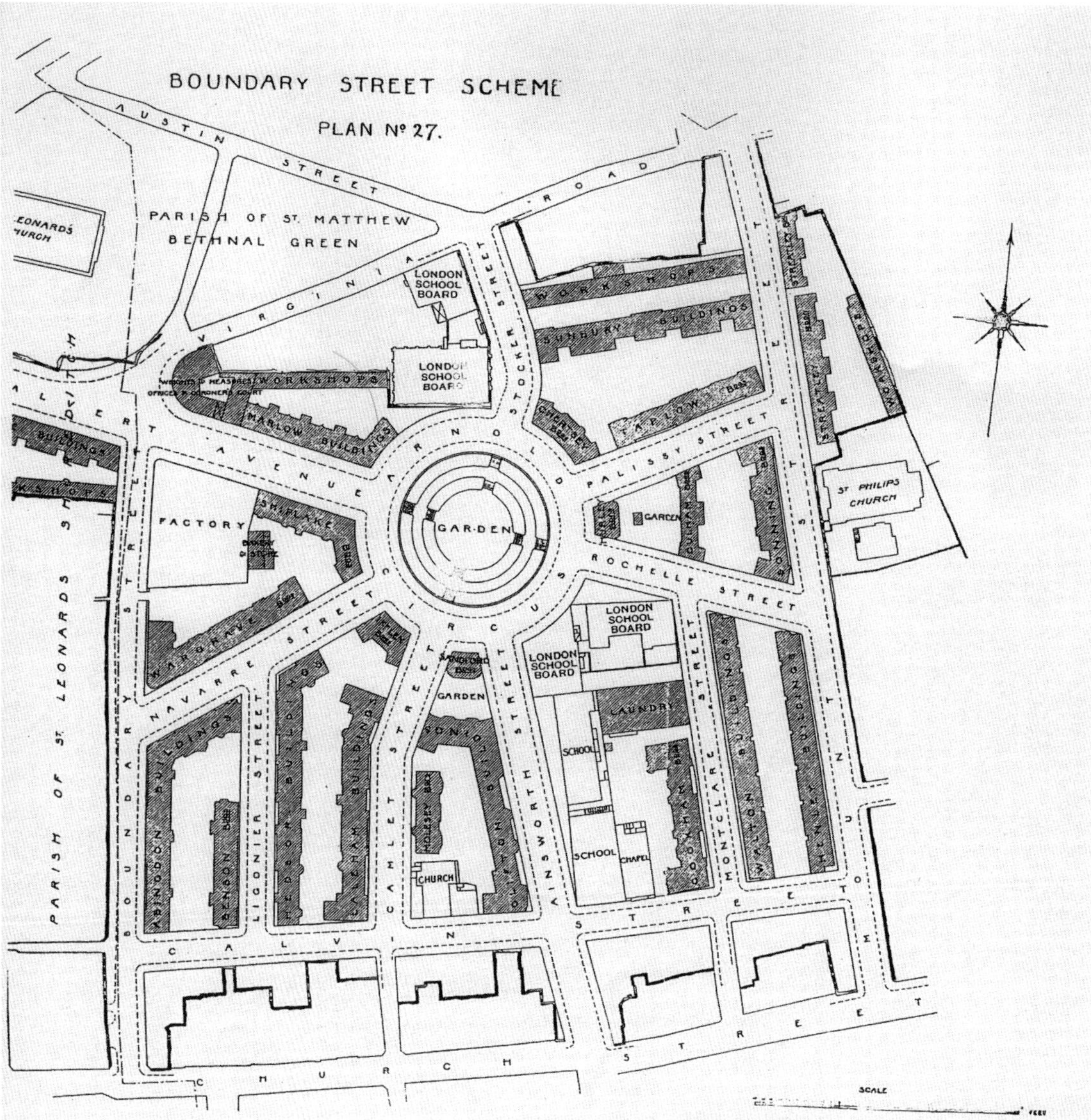

[5] London County Council, Boundary Street Estate, 1900.

Source: London Metropolitan Archives.

largest estate yet built on slum clearance in London, with thirty new blocks of five and six stories housing over five thousand inhabitants. Under the direction of Owen Fleming (1867–1955), the Branch's in-house design team consisted of young architects, most of them graduates of the Architectural Association (T. G. Charlton, R. Roberston, W. Hynam, C. C. Winmill, and A. M. Philips), as well as R. M. Taylor and H. R. Ward. While limited evidence exists ascribing certain buildings to certain authors, this collective endeavor represented the ethos of the LCC's Housing Branch, in turn shaped by William Morris's social reform ideals.[13]

Completed in 1900, the Boundary Street scheme replaced the Old Nichol rookery. In these fifteen hectares of slum between Shoreditch and Bethnal Green, more than five thousand people had lived in overcrowded speculative housing, built cheaply in masonry, without foundations, drainage, water supply, or ventilation. Following the compulsory purchase and clearance of the site, and the expulsion of its notoriously violent and disreputable inhabitants, the LCC planned to develop the estate on a rectangular grid of streets and plots.[14] At some point, however, a new vision of a centrally planned layout, with a hierarchy of streets of different widths converging upon an inner circus, emerged within the design team [5]. The most marked change from the Peabody precedents was the replacement of semi-enclosed private courtyards with this network of radial streets, culminating in the public park.

It was a requirement of LCC policy, caught between progressive idealism and a limited public budget, that this architectural concept had to be financially valid. Its economic justification as providing "more and pleasanter accommodation at a slightly smaller cost," covered, surely, a different motive: the creation of an urban community with its own identity.[15] This was an unprecedented approach in the design of working-class housing. The circus provided a symbolic landmark, "a unifying element in what was essentially a living community with a character of its own."[16] In a lecture to the RIBA in 1900, Fleming described an idyllic vision of couples walking around its bandstand on summer evenings, an ultimately bourgeois vision. In the event, the residents who could afford to live there turned out to be artisans and workers, whose economic means and ambitions of social mobility were matched by the architecture.

The architectural qualities of the estate reflected this ideological shift. As the project progressed, the designs became more sophisticated and expensive, the living standards of the dwellings higher.[17] All blocks were designed individually, emphasizing inventiveness and character, thus contrasting with the trademark monotony of standardized charitable trust housing. Their carefully calibrated appearance aimed to eliminate the previous connotation of working-class housing with prisons and army barracks. The adoption of the Queen Anne style, at the time normally associated with Norman Shaw's higher class of urban homes, signaled a social ascendancy toward the prosperous classes. Described as "Stripeland," the picturesque grouping around the central circus designed by Reginald Minton Taylor established a new standard in the placement of colors and motifs on the façade and the playful treatment of the gables.[18]

It is a mark of British pragmatism that the press, rather than commenting on its innovative architectural planning, tended to criticize the Boundary Street scheme for the increased cost of buildings and construction time. Appreciation came mostly from abroad, with the Cookham House (1897), also designed by Taylor, being one of few examples of lower-class housing to feature in Hermann Muthesius's *English House* of 1904.[19] Muthesius commended the estate's "simple distribution of masses, excellently balanced proportions, [and] pleasing grouping of buildings, combined with color in the shape of rich red brick walls and roofs."[20] The estate also constituted a model for affordable housing providers from abroad: one of the first actions of the Rothschild Foundation, established in Paris in 1904, was to visit the LCC's Boundary Street and Millbank Estates in London.[21]

The project was striking in its coordination of urban and architectural aspects: no longer a function of financial and legal pressures, but of aesthetic sensitivity, illustrating the combination of "the civic-societal with the aesthetic-artistic" in the realm of civic art.[22] In contrast to Darbishire's quasi-mechanical replication of standardized modules, here the blocks were envisaged primarily as "street architecture," responding to the site and to each other in the overall logic of the ensemble.[23] The radial structure predated Ebenezer Howard's Garden City sketch (1900) and its embodiment in Parker and Unwin's planning at Letchworth (1906) by only a few years. In Britain, the notion of civic art was connected to the Arts and Crafts movement, especially the central figures of William Morris and William Richard Lethaby. Openly critical of a technically, economically determined urban planning, Lethaby in particular held sway over the LCC architects[24]. Their architecture at Boundary Street and later the Millbank Estate in Pimlico (1905) shows its Arts and Crafts roots in terms not only of style, but of ideological content. Contrary to the idea of housing as a complement to industrial production, these blocks were conceived, detailed, and fashioned as lovingly as individual artefacts. At the layout stage, they were considered as part of a unique, personalized network of relationships within the urban ensemble. In the utopian tradition of circular and radial structures, the layout symbolized an open community, engaging the working classes in an implicit educational process complementary to everyday activities.

Disciplinary housing

The juxtaposition of Darbishire's work for the Peabody Trust with that of Owen Fleming and his colleagues for the LCC reveals a common concern with reforming the working classes through education. This social project is clearly encoded in the resulting spatial and urban configurations. Darbishire's simultaneously compassionate and patronizing observations regarding Peabody tenants summarized his ambivalence as bourgeois reformer. For him, the Peabody environment sought to induce "the gradual abandonment of injurious habits," without openly challenging the "jealously cherished prejudices" of the tenant working class.[25] The desire to improve living conditions and raise their socio-cultural standing was certainly genuine, yet the improvement was not at any point to undermine the status quo.[26] Workers could strive for social mobility, as long as middle-class values were emulated without trespass. The importance accorded to "respectability"—that rickety bridge between social classes—in Peabody's choice of tenants was significant, for it projected middle-class desiderata onto the background of working-class life.[27] The architecture had to perform an uneasy balancing act between lending decorum to working-class environments and reinforcing established class hierarchies. Darbishire's preference in the design of his blocks for the same indeterminate Italianate style that characterized Victorian industrial buildings was suitably ambivalent.[28]

The association between the early housing estates and industrial production was implicit, but palpable. Subject to the same currents of capital and demand, home and factory similarly dealt with the distribution of masses of people involved in manufacturing processes. Rather than a personal aesthetic agenda, the early Peabody estates emulated the principles of industrial manufacture, rendered efficient through serialization. The austere monotony of the resulting architecture became its most defining and controversial feature. In contemporary media, the Victorian Peabody estates were frequently likened to barracks, prisons and factories—building types in which Michel Foucault saw an architectural framework of the modern disciplinary apparatus. Articulated in the eighteenth century as a "general formula of social domination," discipline in Foucault's reading comprised "the meticulous control of the bodily operations" so as to force them into a relation of "docility-utility" and thus "dissociate power from the body."[29] In the case of workers' housing, the exercise of discipline placed the workforce under the control of the dominant classes through a mixture of architectural and surveillance means. The Peabody model revealed parallels with at least two of the constituents of Foucault's disciplinary apparatus: the gated enclosure, defining a "protected place of disciplinary monotony," and the spatial partitioning of living spaces into distinct cells, holding in check individual and group behavior. The third element, the imposition of a daily temporal rhythm, was in this case a consequence of the working day.[30]

The Ambivalence of Reform

The Boundary Street scheme moved away from these disciplinary undertones in several ways; most importantly by opening up the estate to the city, but also through the attention accorded to details, craftsmanship, and the odd decorative flourish. The two estates can be seen as successive steps in an evolutionary process. Two contrasting urban strategies were developed in reaction to the same problem of the slum—Peabody estates reverting to a closed order of quadrangles and standardized blocks, Boundary Street to an open one of decorative gabled blocks oriented outward, and of defining shared public space. Overall, the cost of the latter blocks was also greater, resulting from the designers' deliberate attempts to improve on the minimum standards of space, construction and facilities to which their Peabody predecessors adhered.[31]

Despite all efforts, the Peabody Trust and the LCC were equally criticized for their failure to address the needs of the most vulnerable members of society. For the liberals at LCC, the very poor presented a moral and educational problem, requiring a "kind of housing management which the council by its nature was totally unable to practice."[32] Rather than providing strict supervision and minimal accommodation, the estate targeted a class of artisans who could afford the rent for larger dwellings and who could more closely emulate, through their behavior and habitation needs, the values of the urban middle classes. The higher rent commanded by the new buildings amounted to an early bout of urban gentrification. Out of the 5,719 original evictees, only eleven returned to live on the estate, while others moved on to the surrounding slums.[33]

[6] The planned occupancy of the Boundary Estate, still under construction, as shown on Charles Booth's *Map Descriptive of London Poverty, 1898–1899, Sheet 5* (East Central District). The black and grey areas denote the poorest classes, the red and brown 'mixed' to 'fairly comfortable' inhabitants.

Source: Image in public domain.

In part, the displacement of slum dwellers was not simply the consequence of increased rents, but also of their own prejudices against disciplined tenement living. Arthur Morrison's popular novel *Child of the Jago* (1896), based on life in the Old Nichol, confirmed Darbishire's observations regarding the rigid, self-imposed social stratification of the urban poor. The new scheme represented for the old inhabitants of Old Nichol a perceived loss of individual freedom. Rather than submit themselves to the alien and demanding protocols of the new way of life, they preferred to move away. They would, in Morrison's words, infect the neighborhoods across the border, and crowd the people a little closer. They did not return to live in the new barrack buildings; which was a strange thing, for the County Council was charging very little more than double the rents which the [Old Nichol] landlords had charged. And so another Jago, teeming and villainous as the one displaced, was slowly growing, in the form of a ring, round about the great yellow houses.[34]

This ominous vision was confirmed by contemporary records. Charles Booth's *Maps Descriptive of London Poverty* (1889–90) used color coding to classify streets and blocks according to the residents' social and economic standing, resulting in what Robin Evans has called a "physical geography of moral conditions."[35] On Booth's map, the semi-transparent silhouette of the Boundary Street estate under construction, shown tentatively as inhabited by "fairly comfortable" tenants, is surrounded by streets hatched in grey and black, colors assigned to poverty and crime [6]. In a literal interpretation of its name, the area represented a boundary between social classes, transitioning from the "middle-class and well-to-do" along the main street to the "very poor, casual, chronic want" and "lower class—vicious, semi-criminal" to the east and north.[36] Thus, the LCC scheme introduced an equivocal element into the socioeconomic heterogeneity of the East End, relocating poverty rather than eradicating it. The ideological subtext of the Arts and Crafts architecture was colored by William Morris's *Socialist League Manifesto* (1885), maintaining that the industrial working classes, as potential agents of social revolution, required artistic instruction in order to "bring about a society where labor became dignified and its products beautiful."[37] If Morris could never really square his political views with the income he drew from producing expensive crafted items for the rich, a similar conflict was propagated in the LCC's ambiguity toward the working classes displayed at the Boundary Street estate. While the architecture boldly declared beauty not to be the prerogative of the rich, a certain class of the poor, considered beyond redemption, was excluded on primarily economic grounds. The amenities, detailing, and materiality of the Boundary Street Estate traded Morris's notion of aesthetic revolution for an anticipated social mobility, aiming at the wider adoption of middle class values and lifestyle.

Alison Ravetz has argued that "the proposition that people had to be educated into good taste before they were fit to spearhead social change ... had strongly authoritarian implications, for only after they had been taught how to live could they be trusted to make choices for themselves."[38] Similar authoritarian tendencies were inscribed in the eligibility clauses of the Peabody Trust, and the strict conduct it demanded of its tenants. Whether disciplinarian as in the Peabody estates or emancipatory as in those of the LCC, London's Victorian housing shows the impetus of social reform to be essentially paternalistic. While well intended and genuinely groundbreaking, these examples propagated the social stratification and innate passivity of the communities they had disrupted.[39] The urban recoding of late-nineteenth-century London permeated the private domain, imposing the top-down social order through the compartmentalization of the dwelling. By introducing their own values as desirable aspirations, the bourgeois reformers sought to reshape the working classes according to their own image, effectively inhibiting the explosive potential of inequality.

The research for this article was conducted with the support of a Swiss National Science Foundation Marie Heim Vögtlin Fellowship

Endnotes

1 For housing reform in working-class Victorian urban housing and the role of the Peabody Trust in particular, see John Burnett, *A Social History of Housing 1815–1970* (London: Methuen, 1980), pp. 140–187; Robin Evans, "Rookeries and Model Dwellings," *Translations from Drawing to Building and Other Essays* (London: Architectural Association, 1997), pp. 93–118; John Nelson Tarn, *Five per Cent Philanthropy: An Account of Housing in Urban Areas between 1840 and 1914* (Cambridge: Cambridge University Press, 1973); John Nelson Tarn, "The Peabody Donation Fund: The Role of a Housing Society in the Nineteenth Century," *Victorian Studies* (September 1966): pp. 7–38.

2 Quoted in Tarn, *Five per Cent Philanthropy*, p. 45.

3 Ibid.

4 Franklin Parker, *George Peabody—A Biography* (Nashville: Vanderbilt University Press, 1971), p. 3.

5 The Peabody Buildings in Commercial Road (1864) were the first development designed by Darbishire for the Peabody Trust. In contrast to the subsequent exclusively residential squares, this project had shops at street level. It was located on a triangular site on a sharp street corner, and comprised three connected wings enclosing a small courtyard. See Tarn, *Five Per Cent Philanthropy*, p. 45.

6 Tarn, *Five Per Cent Philanthropy*, p. 84.

7 Henry Astley Darbishire, "On Dwellings for the Poor," *The Builder* no. XXVI (1875), p. 53.

8 Quoted in P. Steadman, *Building Types and Built Forms* (Kibworth Beauchamp, UK: Matador, 2014), p. 16.

9 John Nelson Tarn, "The Peabody Donation Fund," p. 38.

10 The architect was aware of prejudices being "widely diffused through all sections of the poor. Those who consider that their wages entitled them to superiority ... will not compromise their dignity by condescension towards familiarity, and hold themselves aloof ... [the unemployed] acknowledge their disadvantage, and do not care to leave the shelter of their poverty". Darbishire, "On Dwellings for the Poor," p. 46.

11 This information was kindly provided by Christine Wagg, Peabody Trust historian and archivist, on 24 August 2015 in London.

12 Henry Astley Darbishire, "On the Construction of Dwellings for the Poor. Paper read at the Architectural Association, 13 November 1863," *The Builder* (21 November 1863), p. 822.

13 See Susan Beattie, *A Revolution in London Housing: LCC Housing Architects & Their Work 1893–1914* (London: Greater London Council; Architectural Press, 1980), pp. 9–54.

14 Tarn, *Five Per Cent Philanthropy*, p. 132.

15 London County Council, *Housing of the Working Classes in London. Notes on the Action Taken between the Years 1855 and 1912 for the Better Housing of the Working Classes in London, with Special Reference to the Action Taken by the London County Council between the Years 1889 and 1912* (London: London County Council, 1913), p. 36, https://archive.org/details/housingofworking00londrich.

16 Beattie, *A Revolution in London Housing*, p. 20.

17 Tarn, *Five Per Cent Philanthropy*, p. 134.

18 *British Architect*, vol. 47, 12 Feb. 1897, p. 110.

19 Hermann Muthesius, *Das englische Haus. Entwicklung, Bedingungen, Anlage, Aufbau, Einrichtung und Innenraum*, vol. 1–3, 1. Auflage, ([Wasmuth?]: Berlin, 1904–5).

20 Hermann Muthesius, *The English House: In Three Volumes*, trans. Dennis Sharp, (London: Frances Lincoln, 2007), vol. 1, p. 203.

21 Marie-Jeanne Dumont, *Le logement social à Paris 1850–1930: les habitations à bon marché* (Liège: Mardaga, 1991), pp. 32–33.

22 Wolfgang Sonne, "The Enduring Concept of Civic Art," in *Alternative Visions of Post-war Reconstruction: Creating the Modern Townscape*, ed. John Pendlebury et al. (London: Routledge, 2015), p. 21.

23 Tarn, *Five Per Cent Philanthropy*, p. 134.

24 Lethaby was directly involved in the LCC, acting as Art Inspector to its Technical Education Board, and set up the Central School of Arts and Crafts in 1896. Beattie, *A Revolution in London Housing*, p. 17.

25 Darbishire, "On the Construction of Dwellings for the Poor," p. 821.

26 See Eric Hobsbawm, "City, Industry, The Working Class," in *The Age of Capital, 1848–1875* (London: Abacus, 1975), p. 223.

27 "No term is harder to analyze than 'respectability' in the Victorian working class, for it expressed simultaneously the penetration of middle-class values and standards, and also the attitudes without which working-class self-respect would have been difficult to achieve such as sobriety, sacrifice, the postponement of gratification." Hobsbawm, "City, Industry, The Working Class," p. 224.

28 Edgar Jones, *Industrial Architecture in Britain, 1750–1939* (London: Facts on File, 1985), p. 54. For the relationship between Peabody estates and industrial architecture see Irina Davidovici, "The Depth of the Street," in *AA Files* no. 70, pp. 119–123.

29 Michel Foucault, *Discipline and Punish: The Birth of the Prison*, trans. Alan Sheridan (New York: Pantheon Books, 1977), pp. 141–142.

30 Foucault, *Discipline and Punish*, pp. 141–143.

31 For a comparison between the two approaches see Anthony S. Wohl, *The Eternal Slum, Housing and Social policy in Victorian London* (London: Arnold, 1977), pp. 264–265.

32 Tarn, *Five Per Cent Philanthropy*, p. 134.

33 Diana Maltz, "Introduction," in Arthur Morrison, *A Child of the Jago*, ed. Diana Maltz (Peterborough: Broadview, 2014), p. 18.

34 Arthur Morrison, *A Child of the Jago* (London: MacGibbon & Kee, 1969), p. 179.

35 Evans, "Rookeries and Model Dwellings," p. 99.

36 "Charles Booth's London. Poverty Maps and Police Notebooks," London School of Economics & Political Science, accessed February 20, 2017, https://booth.lse.ac.uk/map/16/-0.0744/51.5252/100/0.

37 Alison Ravetz, *Council Housing and Culture* (London: Routledge, 2001), p. 57.

38 Ibid., p. 58.

39 Ibid., p. 6.

RECODING BUDAPEST BY VISUAL RECORDS

György Klösz's Photographs as Evidence of Urban Development in Late-Nineteenth-Century Budapest

Ágnes Anna Sebestyén

Introduction

The Hungarian capital Budapest demonstrated a remarkable pace of urbanization and population growth during the last three decades of the nineteenth century. Following the Austro-Hungarian Compromise of 1867—the date marking the beginning of the Austro-Hungarian Monarchy and the relative independence of Hungary—Pest-Buda served as the second capital of the empire after Vienna. In 1873, the cities Pest, Buda, and Óbuda were unified, and under the name of Budapest this city became the fastest-growing metropolis in Europe after Berlin.[1] The urban fabric changed increasingly; new buildings and urban ensembles emerged, new architectural styles prevailed, and industrial as well as technological progress began to proliferate. This unprecedented improvement was extensively communicated via different media. Stability and prosperity were reflected in the arts, national exhibitions, the press, and through the architecture which itself served as a medium of communication.

One of the most important means of publicizing the renewed built environment was through the printed image, which increasingly came to mean the photograph. Before the introduction of half-tone printing in the 1880s, which enabled the printing of type and photographs together in a single operation,[2] the nineteenth-century illustrated press mostly used engravings due to the technical limitations of the printing process. Photography, however, started to dominate architectural imagery well before the invention of half-tone printing, as photographs were frequently put into circulation as engraved images. Architectural periodicals and illustrated magazines in Hungary also followed this practice.

The urban development of Budapest in the late nineteenth century was a favorite subject of photographers such as György Klösz, Antal Weinwurm, Károly Divald, and Mór Erdélyi, among others. The German-born Klösz (1844–1913) was one of the first and most influential photographers to record the growing Hungarian capital, beginning to produce his topographical series of photographs in the 1870s and following the growth of the city until the turn of the century.

The Growth of Budapest into a Metropolis

Count Gyula Andrássy (1823–1890), who served as prime minister between 1867 and 1871, was the major supporter of the new capital's urbanization. During his years as an émigré following his participation in the Hungarian revolution of 1848, he spent time in London and in Paris where he witnessed the transformation of the French capital under Georges Eugène Haussmann. In 1870, the Municipal Council of Public Works was established to execute and finance urban planning.[3] Guided by the models of Paris and Vienna, the core idea conceived the future urban fabric as a network of avenues and boulevards.

The first and paramount undertaking was the Radial Avenue, which was built between 1871 and 1885 and renamed Andrássy Avenue after its great advocate in 1885.[4] The main idea was to connect the inner city and the City Park with a representative road that replaced the old city fabric, which was regarded as poor, unhealthy, and dusty. The new radial road followed a straight and unbroken line, flanked by buildings largely comprised of immense apartment blocks, as well as villas and a few cultural institutions. The Radial Road demonstrated the emerging power of the bourgeoisie with a spectacular row of new buildings, while creating an appropriate setting for their social life.[5] The Avenue was also characterized by its Neo-Renaissance style, which best expressed the image of Budapest as an aspiring metropolis. Italian Neo-Renaissance represented a universal, cosmopolitan style without national connotations.[6] This image was also formulated parallel to the enhancement of national consciousness and the proportional increase of the Hungarian ethnic population compared to the German and Slavic ethnicities in the city. Other examples soon followed Andrássy Avenue, but with a different character and function; for example, the Grand Boulevard and the extension of what was then Kerepesi Street toward the Danube in the late nineteenth century.

Recoding Budapest: Urbanization, Photography, and the Press

The new urban fabric and built environment represented a significant change in itself, but it is important to highlight how the process of recoding was communicated. The photographer György Klösz is the key example with which to demonstrate the visual strategies in publicizing urban growth.

Klösz was born in Darmstadt in Germany as Georg Kloess in 1844, and after studying chemistry he joined the photographers Dr. Hermann Heid and F. Ronniger in Vienna as an aspiring photographer.[7] Around 1866–67 they arrived in Pest, where they opened a studio. Within a short time, Klösz started to work independently and soon became one of the most well-known photographers in Hungary. His career successfully covered the period of prosperity and the building boom in Budapest. In the early 1870s, Klösz began to take outdoor photographs in the newly unified Hungarian capital, which was the beginning of the production of several photographic series of the old and new urban ensembles in Budapest.[8] In addition to recording Budapest (regularly commissioned by the municipality) he also took pictures of country houses, artworks,[9] exhibitions, social events, and illustrious people. He was a commercial photographer and entrepreneur who led a studio with a growing staff and also pursued his career as the head of a printing house.

Although he did not monopolize urban photography, he remained a firm reference point in the mainstream due to his up-to-the-minute reports, broad coverage of the period between 1870 and 1900, and the circulation of his photographic images in albums or as individual photographs, stereoscopic photographs, and reproductions. He insistently followed urban growth while becoming both an observer and a chronicler of change. His pictures entered into mass circulation, which defined the ways the contemporary viewer perceived the city. The images still fulfill this role, as Klösz's photographs today are considered as *vedute* of Budapest's past. Klösz's referential status was perhaps not very evident in his time, but, with regard to his position in both the scholarly literature and journalism in Hungary, it is indisputable today. Klösz systematically recorded Budapest as a metropolis under the process of recoding, while—owing to the technological progress of photography and the changing urban environment—being himself the subject of recoding. These changes required different attitudes, to which Klösz easily adapted his vision.

Throughout his long-term endeavor, he believed in the importance of visual records and their potential for preserving the different stages of urban development. Thus, similarly to many of his contemporaries, he placed his trust in the documentary function of photography. In the 1870s, Klösz pursued the tradition, then a few decades old, of documenting urban development. He might have been familiar with other photographic projects of urban documentation in Europe. It is probable, for instance, that he was aware of the photographic campaign that recorded the city walls of Vienna, which had been earmarked for demolition. Klösz had direct links with Vienna as a result of his involvement with the Wiener Photographen Association and its systematic documentation of the Vienna World's Fair in 1873.[10] Thanks to a remarkable invitation to participate in the association's work, Klösz was in the right place at the right time to hone his skills in commercial photography. He and his colleagues had six months to document the exhibition, make reproductions, and carry out mass distribution. Klösz's work at the Vienna World's Fair must have had a great impact on his work as a photographer, especially in relation to the promotion of photography as a means of documentation. Klösz continued this systematic work in Budapest, capturing, for example, the 1885 National Exhibition, the 1896 Millennium Exhibition, and urban growth.

In the 1870s, due to the demands of the wet-collodion process, he was required to carry a darkroom with him. He overcame this inconvenience by taking photographs from a carriage which housed his darkroom. In addition to containing his darkroom, Klösz also used the carriage to stand on in order to take pictures from an elevated point of view. In addition to the elevated viewpoint, the different results of long exposure times—static or blurred figures, or the total lack of people—contributed to particularly idealized images that documented a pristine, novel state of architecture and the urban environment. From the beginning of the 1880s, he used dry plates, which he also started distributing in Hungary. This process freed photographers from the pressure of developing images on the spot and allowed for shorter exposure times. This development precipitated new visual strategies which were closer to realistic urban records than idealized images. Using dry plates, Klösz began to make a new series of Budapest in the 1880s, which he continued into the 1890s. He called this series "Pictures of the New Budapest," naming his series from the 1870s "Pictures of the Old Budapest".[11]

Klösz's urban photographs were published in the press, which interpreted Klösz's images using different narrative patterns. *Vasárnapi Ujság (Sunday Journal)* was one of the leading illustrated magazines of the time in Hungary, and was published weekly in Hungarian between 1854 and 1921—a remarkably long time.[12] In order to overcome the people's significant lack of visual knowledge, it included illustrations from its very first issue and featured photographs from the mid-1880s. Aimed at defining public taste and educating people, it addressed the broad spectrum of contemporary society. Its audience was comprised mostly of the gentry, the educated middle-class, and the urban intelligentsia. The magazine incorporated a wide array of different subjects, such as current events (festivities, social life, coronations, funerals, exhibitions, world fairs, and so on), travel, disasters, science, history, archaeology, ethnology, literature, technology, culture, and the urban environment. It began a campaign to disseminate architectural knowledge from its very first issue. In the 1850s, the Neo-Classical Pest and then the erection of new public buildings were emphasized, and after the 1867 Compromise the magazine followed the building boom in Budapest. It is therefore crucial to analyze *Vasárnapi Ujság* and the visual strategies with which the urban transformation was communicated to its readers, who represented a broad, popular, and Hungarian-speaking audience.[13]

There are three distinctive topics in Klösz's oeuvre and its dissemination in the journal *Vasárnapi Ujság*: contemporary architecture, paradigms of progress, and the "old city" to be demolished for urban renewal projects.[14] The journal was very consistent in praising the urban development of Budapest, constantly accentuating its aspiring and later actual status as a European metropolis. The regulation of the Danube riverbanks, the expansion of the new road network (especially the highly acclaimed Andrássy Avenue), the emergence of new buildings, the demolition of the old city fabric, and the construction of transport systems all received extensive coverage. The journal firmly insisted on a positivist approach, maintaining the image of the city as the epitome of uninterrupted progress. Recurring narrative schemes included the disparagement of some old and allegedly "dirty" parts of the city like Terézváros (the site for

[1] György Klösz, *The People's Theatre in Budapest, circa 1875.*

Source: Fortepan/Budapest City Archives.

[2] Lajos Elischer, *Engraving after György Klösz's photograph of the People's Theatre in Budapest.*

Source: *Vasárnapi Ujság* 22, no. 51 (1875): p. 812.

Andrássy Avenue), the persistent endeavor to equal and even surpass big cities, especially the eternal rival Vienna, and the recognition of civic pride. Klösz's photographs proved to be ideal illustrations for such narratives as a result of his matter-of-fact recording of new buildings in their pristine state.

Klösz's photographs began to appear as engravings in *Vasárnapi Ujság* in the mid-1870s. In the 1870s, his pictures depicted prominent new buildings in the former outskirts of Pest, which became the site of rapid urban growth.

[3] György Klösz, *Clinic in Üllői Road in Budapest, circa 1978.*

Source: Fortepan/Budapest City Archives.

[4] Engraving after György Klösz's photograph, *Clinic in Üllői Road, Budapest.*

Source: *Vasárnapi Ujság* 25, no. 43 (1878): p. 681.

Usually his authorship is credited, or it is at least indicated that the engravings were "based on a photograph." Although this kind of caption strengthened the images' status as visual evidence, the engraver had the freedom to alter certain details in the pictures. For instance, in the case of the People's Theater, known later as the National Theater (designed by Ferdinand Fellner and Hermann Helmer, 1874–75), the engraver Lajos Elischer enlivened the desolate streets surrounding the building in the original photograph in order to make readers imagine the audience arriving for a performance.[15] Editing consciously, he also replaced some of the neighboring one-story buildings with an impressive urban palace. In this way, the engraver illustrated the accompanying text, which highlighted the planned alterations to the immediate surroundings of the theater. The print created an ideal image that the matter-of-fact photograph could not communicate, firstly because exposure time was too long to capture strolling passers-by in the 1870s, and secondly because the photograph could not conceal the inadequate neighborhood of the brand-new theater. [1], [2]

Similar virtual landscaping can be traced in other images, such as in the picture depicting one of the clinics in Üllői Road (designed by Ferenc Kolbenheyer, 1874–79).[16] Klösz's photograph shows the finished exterior of the building, but construction work on the roads was still ongoing. The published engraving, however, perfected the view by including paved streets, alleys, and elegant passers-by. [3], [4]

Klösz almost monopolized Andrássy Avenue as a photographer, taking a large number of photographs of its development. In 1884, immediately before the completion of Andrássy Avenue, *Vasárnapi Ujság* published an article about the representative avenue and its landmark building, the Foncière Palace (designed by Adolf Feszty, 1881–82).[17] With its impressive facades and dominant spire, the palace highlighted the start of the avenue. It was a recurring subject of Klösz. He recorded the building while showing the beginning of the avenue in a striking perspective, on a stereograph, and at the time of Lajos Kossuth's grand funeral in 1894. In *Vasárnapi Ujság,* Klösz's photograph appears in print and is accompanied by lengthy praise of the avenue's magnificence, endorsing the idea of new construction as the epitome of progress. [5]

In 1896, coinciding with the Millennial Celebrations in Hungary, mainland Europe's first underground railway was opened. Klösz returned to Andrássy Avenue at the time of its construction in order to record the different stages of the work. His systematic records of the construction of the underground received extensive coverage in *Vasárnapi Ujság,* belonging to the series of reports on the Millennial Celebrations and Budapest's progress.[18] Klösz provided new views of the avenue, which became a construction site for several months. Scaffolding, building materials, bare structures, and workers were all included in the pictures, which totally altered the idealized impression of the Avenue previously published. However, the accompanying text reassured readers of its enduring representative function, which was being enriched with a new structure that communicated technological progress and modernization. These images, while maintaining the dominant concept of progress, represented new visual strategies, closer to reportage than idealized image-making. [6]

At the end of the nineteenth century, two new road bridges were constructed across the Danube, which were ordered by an act of Parliament in 1893.[19] The first bridge to be built was referred to as the Fővám Square Bridge, after completion named the Franz Joseph Bridge and later the Liberty Bridge (designed by János Feketeházy and Virgil Nagy, 1894–96), and the other as the Eskü Square Bridge, later the Elizabeth Bridge (designed by Antal Kherndl,

[5] György Klösz, *Andrássy Avenue with the Foncière Palace on the left in Budapest, circa 1890–1893.*

Source: Fortepan/Budapest City Archives.

Aurél Czekelius and Virgil Nagy, 1898–1903). Like the underground railway, the Fővám Square Bridge was opened during the Millennial Celebrations in a ceremony attended by Emperor Franz Joseph himself. Largely because of the construction of the Eskü Square Bridge, significant parts of the old Pest and Buda were earmarked for demolition.[20] The old, mostly late-Baroque and Neo-Classical inner city of Pest and the Tabán district of Buda blocked the traffic heading toward the planned new bridge. According to the traffic regulation scheme, Kerepesi Street was extended toward the bridgehead, Kossuth Lajos Street was widened, and the small squares and buildings of the inner city were pulled down. Klösz, as well as other notable photographers, started to record these urban ensembles in order to document the changes for future generations.[21] In 1895, he wrote a letter to the Budapest city council asking for a commission to document the parts of Tabán intended for demolition.[22] He highlighted his intention to produce visual records of an urban environment soon to disappear. [7]

[6] György Klösz, *The construction of the underground railway in Budapest, 1895.*

Source: Fortepan

[7] György Klösz, *Rózsa Square and Lipót Street in Budapest, 1892.*

Source: Fortepan.

In 1897, *Vasárnapi Ujság* published a lengthy report on the demolition of the inner city of Pest (1894–97), which was illustrated by a large number of photographs.[23] The images were taken by various photographers including György Klösz, Mór Erdélyi, and Antal Weinwurm at various stages of the demolition and construction works during the 1890s. Klösz's pictures from 1892 represent the last moments of the lively streets full of passers-by, traders, and carriages, which were soon replaced by workers, load-carrying wagons, and the remains of the old buildings as they were recorded in 1897. In 1898, the journal featured an account of similar works in the Tabán area with an accompanying

[8] György Klösz, *Lajos Kossuth's funeral procession in the Grand Boulevard in in Budapest, 1892.*

Source: Fortepan/Budapest City Archives.

image, again by Klösz, which depicted the pulling down of old buildings in Döbrentei Street.[24] Although *Vasárnapi Ujság* contributed to the visual survival of these urban ensembles via these reports, it ultimately returned to the praise of urban development. However, it is important to point out the difference in attitude compared to the 1870s, when not a single image of the destruction of Terézváros was published as it gave way to the majestic Andrássy Avenue.[25] Recoding by visual means is thus more perceptible in the 1890s, when the old urban fabric—evoking the onset of nostalgia—and the construction works were marked as appealing subjects for contemporary photographers.

Staging the Metropolis

The new urban ensembles like Andrássy Avenue, the Grand Boulevard, and the adjoining renewed areas became the perfect stage for bourgeois self-representation, including social events, celebrations, and commemorations.[26] Communicating the metropolitan status of Budapest, the Historicist building facades provided an ideal background for such ceremonies. Klösz was one of the major chroniclers of these events in Budapest: he recorded, among other celebrations, the Hungarian statesman Lajos Kossuth's grand funeral in 1894[27] and the visits of the German Emperor Wilhelm II[28] and the Romanian royal couple in 1897,[29] all of which appeared in the pages of *Vasárnapi Ujság*. Like the visual report on the construction of the underground railway in 1896, where Andrássy Avenue was recoded as a construction site as well as a location of technological progress, Klösz's accounts embraced the city as a setting worthy of hosting meaningful events of national and international importance. Through Klösz's photographs, the recoding of Budapest as a metropolis was visually evident. However, the new road system, means of transportation, and ornate facades did not communicate the social problems emerging parallel to urban growth. Photographs of the streets including records of poverty only appeared in the early twentieth century. Thus, the loyal readers of *Vasárnapi Ujság* were shown only a completely new metropolis and a positivist belief in progress. [8]

Conclusion

György Klösz's systematic documentary work in the last three decades of the nineteenth century coincided with the building boom in Budapest. Signaled by rapid urbanization, landmark buildings, and technological advancement, the Hungarian capital was recoded as a European metropolis during this period. Performing the work he was commissioned—usually by the municipality—and satisfying commercial demands, Klösz documented the patterns of progress that nourished civic pride. When recording new constructions, he supported a positivist approach that was also communicated by journals such as *Vasárnapi Ujság*. The last years of the 1890s, however, witnessed emerging nostalgia for the good old days as the old inner city was replaced with new urban ensembles. Although this shift was palpable among contemporary photographers, the concept of progress still prevailed—especially in the daily news, which also covered events of national and international importance and used the image of the metropolis as an impressive backdrop. Klösz was a conscious observer and chronicler who engaged with commercial needs and undertook the campaign to publicize Budapest's development. The media found an ideal contributor in Klösz as a tireless agent whose work still continues to shape our perception of the late-nineteenth-century urban environment.

Acknowledgements

Sincere thanks are owed to Pál Ritoók, who provided invaluable insights for this paper.

Endnotes

1 At the time of the unification of Budapest in 1873, the population of the city was about 300,000 and it exceeded 700,000 in 1900.

2 Robert Elwall, *Building with Light: The International History of Architectural Photography* (London and New York: Merrell Publishers, 2004), pp. 87–88.

3 Attila Déry, "A Fővárosi Közmunkák Tanácsa (1870–1948): Egy független városrendező hatóság" (The Municipal Council of Public Works [1870–1948]: An Independent Authority for Urban Planning), *Budapesti Negyed* 3, no. 3 (1995): pp. 77–96; József Sisa, ed., *Motherland and Progress: Hungarian Architecture and Design 1800–1900* (Basel: Birkhäuser, 2016), pp. 574–84.

4 For more on Andrássy Avenue in the English-language literature, see: Ákos Moravánszky, *Competing Visions: Aesthetic Invention and Social Imagination in Central European Architecture, 1867–1918* (Cambridge, Mass. and London, England: The MIT Press, 1998), pp. 43–50; Sisa, *Motherland and Progress*, pp. 590–95.

5 Károly Vörös, "Városépítészeti modell Kelet-Európában" (Urban Planning Scheme in Eastern Europe), *Budapesti Negyed* 1, no. 1 (1993): pp. 33–42; Moravánszky, *Competing Visions*, pp. 46–50.

6 Sisa, *Motherland and Progress*, p. 435; for more on the Neo-Renaissance architecture in Budapest, see: Tamás Csáki, Violetta Hidvégi, and Pál Ritoók, eds, *Neoreneszánsz építészet Budapesten / Neo-Renaissance Architecture in Budapest* (Budapest: BFL, 2008).

7 László Lugosi Lugo, *Klösz György 1844–1913 fényképek / photographs* (Budapest: PolgART, 2002), pp. 259–61.

8 Lugosi Lugo, *Klösz photographs*, pp. 261–62.

9 Júlia Papp, "Artwork Photography in Hungary: The Early Years (1859–1885)," *Visual Resources* 25, no. 3 (2009): pp. 193–238.

10 László Lugosi Lugo, *Klösz György élete és munkássága 1844–1913* (György Klösz's Life and Oeuvre 1844–1913) (Budapest: PolgART, 2002), pp. 16–20.

11 Ibid., pp. 264–65.

12 For more on the popular press of the time in Hungary, see: Dorottya Lipták, "A családi lapoktól a társasági lapokig: Újságok és újságolvasók a századvégen" (From Family Periodicals to the Popular Magazines: Journals and Readers in the Late Nineteenth Century), *Budapesti Negyed* 5, no. 2–3 (1997): pp. 45–70.

13 In the 1870s, the greater part of the educated middle class read the German-language magazines. This changed during the 1880s and 1890s, when the Hungarian-language press gained predominance due to the gradual decrease in the German ethnic population, assimilation, and the Hungarian rural population's increasing migration to Budapest. (See Lipták, "Journals and Readers," pp. 45–70.)

14 Decisive topics as they are grouped and examined in Micheline Nilsen, *Architecture in Nineteenth-Century Photographs: Essays on Reading a Collection* (Farnham: Ashgate, 2011).

15 *Vasárnapi Ujság* 22, no. 51 (1875): pp. 812, 814.

16 *Vasárnapi Ujság* 25, no. 43 (1878): pp. 681–82.

17 *Vasárnapi Ujság* 31, no. 7 (1884): pp. 108–10.

18 *Vasárnapi Ujság* 43, no. 17 (1896): pp. 260–63.

19 Sisa, *Motherland and Progress*, pp. 604–5.

20 The inner city of Pest's transformation, demolition, photographic records, and the reception of the changes are the main topics of Emőke Tomsics's PhD dissertation and her following publications: Emőke Tomsics, "A láthatatlan Belváros: A Belváros mentális képének változása a fényképek tükrében, a 19. század második felében" (The Invisible Inner City: The Transformation of the Mental Image of the Inner City of Pest in the Light of Photographs in the Second Half of the Nineteenth Century), *Tanulmányok Budapest múltjából* 36 (2012): pp. 207–52; Emőke Tomsics, *Budapest Atlantisza: A pesti Belváros átalakulása a 19. század végén* (Atlantis of Budapest: The Transformation of Pest's Inner City in the Late Nineteenth Century) (Budapest: Városháza Kiadó, 2015).

21 Lugosi Lugo, *Klösz's Life and Oeuvre*, pp. 60–65; Lugosi Lugo, *Klösz photographs*, pp. 268–69.

22 Lugosi Lugo, *Klösz's Life and Oeuvre*, pp. 62–63.

23 *Vasárnapi Ujság* 44, no. 28 (1897): pp. 449–56.

24 *Vasárnapi Ujság* 45, no. 6 (1898): pp. 88–89.

25 Emőke Tomsics points out that, contrary to Terézváros, the inner city of Pest was once Pest's most urbanized area (see Tomsics, "The Invisible Inner City," p. 231.). Thus, in addition to the changing attitude, it was also the different status of these two city parts that was taken into account.

26 For more on different interpretations and representations of Andrássy Avenue, see: Zita Nagy, "A berendezett város—Fotográfusok az Andrássy úton (1875–1925)" (The Furnished City—Photographers in Andrássy Avenue [1875–1925]), in *Budapest neoreneszánsz építészete* (Neo-Renaissance Architecture in Budapest), ed. Tamás Csáki, Violetta Hidvégi, and Pál Ritoók (Budapest: BFL, 2009), pp. 99–120.

27 *Vasárnapi Ujság* 41, no. 14 (1894): pp. 228, 234–35.

28 *Vasárnapi Ujság* 44, no. 39 (1897): pp. 636, 638.

29 *Vasárnapi Ujság* 44, no. 40 (1897): pp. 658–59.

ROME OR BABYLON
Cosmopolitics in Second-Empire Paris

Bradley Fratello

[1] Adolphe Yvon (1817–1893), *Baron Georges-Eugène Haussmann meeting with Napoleon III to discuss the annexation by Paris of its suburbs*, 1865.

Source: Musée de la Ville de Paris, Musée Carnavalet.
Photo credit: Scala/Art Resource, NY.

Introduction

Textual and visual sources from the Second Empire demonstrate that recasting the French capital as a new Rome—a cosmopolitan utopia capable of embracing and organizing the Empire's global reach—served as a key strategy for legitimizing the ambitions of the restored Bonapartists. This essay explores both the official coding of second empire Paris as a new Rome and a simultaneous, opposing discourse that sought to undercut the regime's idealizing vision with one that recast the newly cosmopolitan Paris as disorganized, chaotic, and incomplete. Detractors of the Empire called Haussmann's new city a modern Babylon.

Official Coding: Paris as a Modern Rome

In *Baron Georges-Eugène Haussmann meeting with Napoleon III to discuss the annexation by Paris of its suburbs*, Adolphe Yvon staged an opulent tableau in which Napoleon III and his council move forward with expanding Paris's modernization to the ring of suburbs immediately surrounding the capital: today, the city's outer arrondissements. [1] Presiding over the scene from the wall behind, Jacques-Louis David's *Emperor Napoleon in his Study at the Tuileries* suggests the long shadow that the first Bonaparte's reign cast over the aspirations of his nephew. Humbled by his uncle's overwhelming military achievements, Louis-Napoleon wrote in 1842 that his ambitions would be more akin to those of Augustus Caesar than to Julius,

[2] Perspective view of the Boulevard de Sebastopol, taken from the bank of the Seine toward the East railway station, 1858.

Source: *L'Illustration, Journal Universel*, vol. 31 (June 19, 1858), pp. 392-393. Courtesy of the Library of the University of California, Berkeley.

focused on glorifying the capital. "I want to be a second Augustus, because Augustus … made Rome a city of marble."[1]

Rome served as the obvious model for an imperial capital, and Napoleonic monuments like the Arc de Triomphe, the Vendôme column and La Madeleine had already begun remaking Paris in the image of the Eternal City. Rome's capacity to bear the legacy of the classical tradition notwithstanding, it also stood as an ideal of cosmopolitanism. Nineteenth-century French writers understood ancient Rome to have been the center of a culturally diverse empire: a dynamic capital that had spread a unifying *lingua franca* to the furthest reaches of civilization, and into which the resources of the known world had poured. It was the cosmopolitan city *par excellence*, capable of accommodating and reconciling diverse energies. The culinary historian Jean-Anthelme Brillat-Savarin asserted that the breadth of their empire's territory had made even the Romans' palates cosmopolitan. At table, the world they had conquered was served up on platters:

All the wealth of the universe flowed into her treasury, and the luxury of the table was increased to a height almost incredible. The Romans ate of everything, from the grasshopper to the ostrich, from the dormouse to the wild boar … They brought African guinea fowl and truffles, Spanish rabbits, Greek pheasants and peacocks from the extremity of Asia.[2]

Baron Haussmann seized every opportunity to massage the Emperor's ego by reinforcing the link between second empire Paris and imperial Rome, suggesting that the French capital, too, could embrace a diversity of creative and intellectual talents.

This beloved city of letters, of the sciences and the arts, which knows how to reconcile this cult with the industrial and commercial instincts of our time, the political center which has given the Empire its prestige and its leadership: is this not truly the Rome of modern times?[3]

At the dedication of the Boulevard de Sebastopol, the city's major north-south axis on the right bank, Haussmann declared, "Sire, it is our descendants who will reap the fruits of Your Majesty's constant solicitude as regards the administration of Paris, who will find that among us, the nephew of Caesar renewed the Imperial City."[4] The Empire's official journal, the *Moniteur Universel*, similarly described the Boulevard de Sebastopol by comparing it, and finding it superior, to an ancient Roman predecessor, calling it an "endless perspective … beside which the Via Sacra of Rome pales."[5]

An illustration of that newly opened boulevard visualizes its "endless perspective". [2]

Viewed from above the Place du Châtelet looking north, the lithograph depicts a well-peopled (but not crowded) space filled with bourgeois Parisians moving briskly about the wide thoroughfare. To the right, the Tour St. Jacques draws the eye up and away from a construction site that offers only the slightest evidence of the messy, traumatizing demolition and displacement that Haussmannization wrought. While the off-center tower lends energy to the composition, a conveniently arranged cloudscape precisely follows the line of vision from the tower's apex to the rooflines of Haussmann's new edifices, mitigating any sense of imbalance. Declarative horizontal, vertical and orthogonal lines define the Classically inspired new apartment buildings, the broad sidewalks, and the shop awnings in this symmetrical, centralized view. The lithograph visualizes the Boulevard de Sebastopol in the manner of late-quattrocento and early-cinquecento paintings of imagined Italian piazzas, albeit peppered with visual incident like the tower's Gothic fretwork, the dense foliage, and the scattered figures that soften the declaratively linear composition. Through its combination of Italian and northern visual idioms, the image mirrors the stylistically and geographically nimble attitude of eclecticism in the arts.

First presented as a philosophical school in the 1810s by Victor Cousin, eclecticism's influence on politics, aesthetics, history, art, and architecture made it a critical touchstone for French cultural discourse in the mid-nineteenth century. Its principles laid the foundation, too, for linking Paris's cosmopolitan complexion to Rome's. The influential historian Jules Michelet offered an account of the French past that described the national character in these same eclectic, transnational terms.[6] He rejected the notion that French identity could be reduced to a single principle as earlier constructions that traced the nation's roots

[3] Gare du Nord, circa 1900.

Source: Image in the public domain (author's collection).

to either Celtic, northern or southern Latin origins had, condemning those attempts as divisive and exhausted. For Michelet, France was the child of both the north and the south, her identity at once dual and indivisible. "France … is not composed of two principles. In her, the Celtic element has combined with the Roman, and makes but one with it."[7] Thomas Couture, eclecticism's chief proponent in the arts, founded his teaching studio on precisely these terms, declaring that his instruction would be "based above all on the great art of ancient Greece, the Renaissance masters and the admirable Flemish School".[8]

Jacques Hittorff's design for the Gare du Nord, completed in 1865 as the second, expanded version of the station, typifies eclecticism in architecture. [3] While its glass and iron rail hangar borrowed from contemporary English design, the Gare presented an ornate, classicizing façade with Ionic pilasters and a Romanizing triple arch to the city.[9] Gautier romantically lauded train stations for their cosmopolitan potential, celebrating them as "palaces of modern industry where the religion of the century is displayed ... these cathedrals of the new humanity are the meeting points of nations, the center where all converges, the nucleus of huge stars whose iron rays stretch out to the ends of the earth".[10]

In his introduction to the official catalog for the Universal Exposition of 1855, which served to debut the first phase of Haussmannization to the world, Gautier lauded the rapidly expanding French rail system for its culturally unifying promise.

This is the first time that the fine arts of all peoples will come face to face on the peaceful battlefield of the Universal Exhibition: the great idea of our century which we can realize through its prodigious means of communication, before which neither seas nor mountains nor distances nor obstacles any longer exist. "The Pyrenees are no more" is a phrase now applicable to every frontier, overriding the fictitious blue, green and red lines of maps that countries have typically put between them from one end of the world to the other.[11]

Instead of the kings, saints and prophets found adorning cathedrals, Hittorff ordered statues symbolizing the destinations that the "Compagnie du chemin de fer du nord" served. Allegories of French cities adorn the lower colonnade, and perched above them, atop the raking cornice, are evocations of destinations further afield: Amsterdam, Brussels, Berlin, Cologne, Frankfurt, London, Vienna, and Warsaw. And at the pinnacle of the central pediment, a crowned, toga-draped personification of Paris herself lords it over the rest at this, the busiest terminus not just in France, but in all of Europe.[12]

Alternate Coding: Paris as a Modern Babylon

The February 2, 1868 issue of *L'Eclipse* featured on its cover caricature of Eugène Pelletan by Gill. It was Pelletan's fifty-fourth birthday, and the journal honored the left-wing writer and politician by picturing him as a hawk with a club between his talons and a statue of Athena tucked under his right wing. [4] Pelletan keeps a watchful eye over Paris, which stretches across the background. Gill pictured the author standing on a copy of *La Nouvelle Babylone, Lettres d'un provincial en tournée a Paris*, a scathing indictment of Haussmannization that he had published in 1862. The book's apparent notoriety, even six years after its debut, merited its inclusion as the best symbol for its author. Pelletan's central thesis amounted to declaring that the Emperor's cosmopolitan ambitions were a failure. "It is obvious that the memory of Babylon and the Seven Wonders of the World ... were not without influence on the embellishments of Paris."[13] Babylon's usefulness as a metaphor for a disorganized, chaotic brand of cultural pluralism derives from God's curse upon the city during the construction of the Tower of Babel:

Behold, the people is one, and they have all one language; and this they begin to do: and now nothing will be restrained from them, which they have imagined to do. Go to, let us go down, and there confound their language, that they may not understand one another's speech. (Genesis 11: 6–9)

La Nouvelle Babylone offered a view on train stations and their consequences for Paris that directly contradicted Gautier's. Not "cathedrals of the new humanity" in which the world came together, Pelletan argued instead that they had transformed Paris into the crowded, confused terminus of the world: a sort of French Ellis Island fueling the fire of Paris's chaotic globalization.

Trains pour into this new Babylon ceaselessly, wave after wave of English, Russians, Germans, Norwegians, Swedes, Danes, Dutch, Serbs, Bedouins, Croat, Moldavians. And there was such a clogging of the sidewalk because of this foreign invasion that pedestrians had to queue up in the street as if for a show.[14]

[4] André Gill, "Eugene Peletan", 1868.

Source: *L'Eclipse: Journal Hebdomadaire Politique, Satirique et Illustré*, February 2, 1868. Reproduced with permission from the Eberly Family Special Collections Library, Penn State University Libraries.

In 1860, the Goncourt brothers had described Paris in their private journals as "some American Babylon of the future," and Victor Fournel adopted the metaphor in his own book two years after Pelletan:

Confusion of languages has presided over these ambitious undertakings, and the great modern Babel as professors of rhetoric call it, the city where all ideas, all beliefs and all passions clash in a contradictory melee, seems complacently mirrored in the chaos of disparate monuments.[15]

The hybrid structure of the Gare also lent itself to recoding. While proponents of the Empire characterized the two components of the Gare du Nord as a synthesis of old and new, north and south, the structure could be recast as a disparate combination of elements lacking cohesion or purpose.

What strikes us immediately about this building is the lack of any relationship between its exterior and interior… If we examine the interior, we see clearly that the purpose was to satisfy bare necessities... As for the design of the façade, it would seem to have had an entirely different rationale; necessity has had little influence on it; neither the nature of the materials nor their function governed the thickness of the walls; it is not the discipline of necessity which dictated the forms... [but] wild imaginativeness.[16]

Babylon, then, connoted not simply the ostentatious decadence of Paris's high-flown courtesans and rampant financial speculation, but a different type of global city. Instead of a stable cultural center like the imperial Rome described by eclectics, one that would be enriched through the controlled assimilation of certain outsiders, the modern Babylon's cosmopolitan ambitions would lack cohesion. Babylon signified a decentralized, disorganized brand of cultural mixing, less a hub or nucleus like Rome than simply a crowded, urban intersection into which foreigners poured without system or logic. It would be buffeted by foreign influence to the point of cultural annihilation. Babylon offered critics of the Empire and its works an alternative code that, instead of rejecting cosmopolitanism for a national or provincial model of Frenchness, acknowledged the cultural diversity of the city but denigrated its consequences. It established the terms for a nineteenth-century French "cosmopolitics."[17]

Edouard Manet's *Dejeuner sur l'herbe*, completed a year after Pelletan's *La Nouvelle Babylone* was published, embeds the notion of a culturally fragmented city in its style. [5]

Like his eclectic master Thomas Couture, Manet suggested with *Dejeuner sur l'herbe* that French painting was cosmopolitan; but the range of sources the younger artist acknowledged was broader, and his manner of combining them abrupt and incomplete.[18] At its center, Manet's decidedly French figures have adopted a pose based on a figure group in an engraving by Marcantonio Raimondi after a lost Raphael painting of *The Judgment of Paris*. The leftmost nude woman, posed by Victorine Meurent, exhibits the stark pallor of Francisco Goya's *Nude Maja*. The overturned basket of fruits and brioche at the bottom left derives from the still-life tradition of seventeenth-century Dutch painting, and the verdant landscape speaks to the rise of the English informal style taking hold in Paris. Critically, each area of the canvas exhibits a distinct facture, each distinct and unblended with the others. Smoothly painted figures, the chalky pallor used to depict Victorine's skin, thickly impastoed fruits in the still life, and a lush, feathery range of brushstrokes in the landscape fail to read as a synthetic, coherently painted surface. Instead, Manet's painting results in a stylistic confusion of tongues that vexed conservative critics when *Dejeuner sur l'herbe* debuted at the notorious Salon des refusés.

One can't really designate this product of Manet's labors as an *esquisse* or an *ébauche*. In an *esquisse* properly understood and properly executed, all the parts are rendered to the same degree. Nothing explains or justifies Manet's incoherence, his inequality of execution.[19]

Manet's *Judgment of Paris*—for certainly the painting is that if nothing else—and its rejection from the Salon of 1863 suggests the difficulty that the Second Empire's institutions had in accommodating this cultural critique.[20]

[5] Edouard Manet, *Dejeuner sur l'herbe,* 1863.

Source: Musée d'Orsay. Photo: Benoit Touchard/Mathier Rabeau. Photo credit: RMN-Grand Palais/ Art Resource, NY.

While so many of Paris's medieval, crooked streets gave way to rationalized boulevards that lent themselves easily to the rules of linear perspective in art and illustration, its new parks and squares took on the appearance of irregular English gardens, as per the Emperor's wishes. Adolphe Alphand, the designer of the newly planted Bois de Boulogne, wrote explicitly of the trend's cultural geography. "Irregular gardens are rapidly propagating in France. The climate is favorable to them, but they must struggle against the classical art, which is not well-accommodated to the surroundings."[21]

Unlike its designer, however, the Comtesse d'Agoult found in the newly designed Bois not a naturally ordered sylvan retreat, but a rude destination in which the Second Empire's tacky opulence unabashedly paraded itself. She found in the Bois, which is perhaps the setting for Manet's *Dejeuner sur l'herbe*, a microcosm of the gauche new Babylon that the French capital had become:

Mingled with all languages, all the slang of Europe … English by its turf, Italian by its trails, German by its music, Dutch by its skates, Chinese by its lanterns, French by its ladies and gendarmes, the once quiet, rarely frequented Bois ... is now the favorite meeting point of vanities, effronteries, pell-mell cosmopolitans.[22]

Conclusion

Government-sponsored journals, illustrations, monumental architecture and imperial celebrations loudly proclaimed that second empire Paris had become a modern Rome. Dissenting voices like those of the Goncourt and of the Comtesse d'Agoult were relatively private, and Manet's *Dejeuner sur l'herbe* earned a marginal position in Paris's art world at the notorious Salon des refusés. Nonetheless, Pelletan's *La Nouvelle Babylone* appears to have brought the author lasting notoriety and suggests that the city's alternative coding had a salient, if unofficial, currency.

Endnotes

1 Napoleon III (1842), quoted and translated in Robert Cole, *A Traveler's History of Paris*, 4th edn. (Northampton, MA: Interlink Publishing, 2008), p. 165.

2 "...affluer à Rome toutes les richesses de l'univers, le luxe de la table fut poussé à un point presque incroyable. On goûta de tout, depuis la cigale jusqu'à l'autruche, depuis le loir jusqu'au sanglier ; tout ce qui put piquer le goût fut essayé comme assaisonnement ; on employa comme tel, des substances dont nous ne pouvons pas concevoir l'usage, comme l'assafetida, la rue, etc. ... On apporta d'Afrique les pintades et les truffes, les lapins d'Espagne, les faisans de la Grèce ... et les paons de l'extrémité de l'Asie." J.A. Brillat-Savarin, *Physiologie du gout: A Handbook of Gastronomy* (New York: J.W. Bouton, 1884), pp. 361–363.

3 "cette ville aimée des lettres, des sciences et des arts, qui sait en concilier le culte avec les instincts industriels et commerciaux de notre époque, ce centre politique auquel l'Empire a rendu son prestige et sa preponderance, n'est-ce pas en vérité la Rome des temps Modernes?" Haussmann, June 6, 1861. Transcribed in André Morizet, *Du Vieux Paris au Paris Moderne: Haussmann et ses prédécesseurs* (Paris: Hachette, 1932), p. 249.

4 "Sire, nos descendants, qui recueilleront les fruits de la constante sollicitude de Votre Majesté pour tout ce qui se rapporte à l'édilité parisienne, constateront que chez nous aussi, le neveu de César a renouvelé la Ville Impériale." Haussmann (August 14, 1861). Transcribed in Morizet, *Du Vieux Paris*, p. 220.

5 Unnamed author, *Moniteur Universel* (March 30, 1858). Quoted and translated in David van Zanten, *Building Paris: Architectural Institutions and the Transformation of the French Capital, 1830-1870* (Cambridge: Cambridge University Press, 1994), p. 205. See also Micheline Nilsen, *Railways and the Western European Capitals: Studies of Implantation in London, Paris, Berlin and Brussels* (Basingstoke: Palgrave Macmillan, 2008), p. 75.

6 Arthur Mitzman, *Michelet, Historian: Rebirth and Romanticism in Nineteenth-Century France* (New Haven & London: Yale University Press, 1990), pp. 8–10; Steven A. Kippur, *Jules Michelet: A Study of Mind and Sensibility* (Albany: SUNY Press, 1981), pp. 26–30.

7 Jules Michelet, *The People*, trans. C. Cocks (London: Longman, Brown, Green and Longmans, 1846), p. 149.

8 Thomas Couture, advertisement for the opening of his art school, 1847. Reprinted and translated in Albert Boime, *Thomas Couture and the Eclectic Vision* (New Haven & London: Yale University Press, 1980), p. 135.

9 Wolfgang Schivelbusch, *The Railway Journey: Trains and Travel in the 19th Century*, trans. Anselm Hollo, (New York: Urizen Books, 1979), p. 162–163.

10 Théophile Gautier (1868), quoted and translated in Jean Dethier, "The Station: a modern-day Tower of Babel," in *All Stations: A Journey through 150 Years of Railway History*, trans. Richard Foxcroft (London: Thames & Hudson, 1981), p. 6.

11 "C'est le première fois que les beaux-arts de tous les peuples vont se voir face à face sur ce pacifique champ de bataille de l'Exposition universelle. – Grande idée que notre siècle pouvait réaliser avec ses prodigieux moyens de communication, devant lesquels il n'existe pas ni mers, ni montagne, ni distances, ni obstacles. – 'Il n'y a plus de Pyrénées' est un mot applicable maintenant à toute frontière, et par-dessus les fictives lignes bleues, vertes et rouges des cartes géographiques, les pays causent familièrement entre eux d'un bout du monde à l'autre." Théophile Gautier, *Les Beaux-arts en Europe, 1855* (Paris: Michel Lévy Frères, 1857), 1, pp. 1–2.

12 Michel Ragon, *L'architecture des gares* (Paris: éditions Denoel, 1984), pp. 5-50; Marie-Laure Crosnier Leconte, *La naissance des gares* (Paris: Hachette, 1990), pp. 2–6 & pp. 30–35; Claudine Cartier and Emmanuel de Roux, *Patrimoin Ferroviaire* (Paris: Scala, 2007), pp. 62–71; Stéphanie Sauget, *À la recherche des pas perdus: Une histoire des gares parisiennes au XIXe siècle* (Paris: Tallandier, 2009).

13 "Il est évident que le souvenir de Babylone et des sept merveilles du monde ... n'a pas été sans influence sur les embellissements de Paris." Eugène Pelletan, *La Nouvelle Babylone, Lettes d'un provincial en tournee à Paris*, 3rd ed. (Paris: Pagnerre, 1863), p. 32.

14 "Les trains des chemins de fer versent sans cesse, dans cette nouvelle Babylone, des flots et des flots d'Anglais, de Russes, d'Allemands, de Norvégiens, se Suédois, de Danois, de Hollandais, de Serbes, de Bédouins, de Croates, de Moldaves. Il y avait, du fait de l'invasion étrangère, un tel encombrement sur le pavé, que le passant devait prendre la file dans la rue, comme à une queue de spectacle." Pelletan, *La Nouvelle Babylone*, p. 32.

15 "La confusion des langues a présidé à ces entreprises ambitieuses, et la grande Babel modern comme disent les professeurs de rhétorique, la ville où toutes les idées, toutes les croyances et toutes les passions se heurtent en une mêlée contradictoire,

semble se mirer avec complaisance dans ce chaos de monuments disparates." Victor Fournel, *Paris nouveau et Paris futur* (Paris: Jacques Lecoffre, 1865), p. 227.

16 Thomas von Joest, "Hittorff et la Nouvelle Gare du Nord," in *Hittorff un architecte du XIXème* (Paris: Musée Carnavalet, 1986), p. 275.

17 Pheng Cheah, *Cosmopolitics: Thinking and Feeling beyond the Nation* (Minneapolis: University of Minnesota Press, 1998).

18 Michael Fried, *Manet's Modernism or, the Face of Painting in the 1860's* (Chicago: University of Chicago Press, 1996).

19 Pelloquet, "L'Exposition" (Paris, 1863). Translated in Fried, *Manet's Modernism*, p. 305.

20 This correspondence of spatial incongruity and mixed national idioms is also evident in Manet's *The Old Musician* (1862) and *Mlle. V. in the Costume of an Espada* (1862), further suggesting that cultural mixing played a significant role in Manet's implementation of fractured space.

21 "Les jardins irréguliers se sont assez rapidement propagés en France. Le climat leur était favorable; mais ils on eu à lutter contre l'art classique, qui s'accommode mal de leur voisinage." Adolphe Alphand, *Les Promenades de Paris* (Paris: J. Rothschild, 1869 ; repr., Paris: Connaissance et Mémoires, 2002), p. xxxi.

22 "mêlés de toutes les langues, de tous les argots de l'Europe.... Anglais par son turf, italien par son corso, allemande par ses musiques, hollandaise par ses patins, chinois par ses lanterns, français par ses demoiselles et ses gendarmes, le bois de Boulogne autrefois infréquenté, silencieux... est à cette heure le retentissant rendez-vous des vanités, des effroneteries, du pêle-mêle cosmopolite." Comtesse d'Agoult, quoted in Morizet, *Du Vieux Paris*, p. 195.

DESIGNING THE CITY

3

BETWEEN DECODING AND RECODING
Raymond Unwin's *Town Planning in Practice* and Rudolf Eberstadt's *Handbuch des Wohnungswesens* as Means of Reflection and Regulation

Katrin Albrecht, Lukas Zurfluh

Handbooks for Urban Planning and Design

In 1928, the art historian Joseph Gantner stated that, in contrast to the impressive literary evolution of art history, the questions of its new sub-discipline "civic art" had their origins in the needs and necessities of the present.[1] And, indeed, the issues initially dealt with in modern town planning literature revolved around hygiene and sanitary aspects, the improvement of widespread dreadful housing conditions, and the relief of serious housing shortages caused by rapid population growth. They were accompanied by demands for mandatory regulation of building activity and for the establishment of means with which to control urban development. Economic considerations were closely linked to these claims, particularly the questions of land ownership, the rights and duties of landholders, and the possibilities of land expropriation and financing. In his book *Stadt-Erweiterungen*, published in 1876, the civil engineer Reinhard Baumeister placed the main emphasis on precisely these issues.[2] His writing was the first handbook on modern urban planning to meet the requirement of describing its wide range of issues and tasks in detail—or, in other words, which summarized them systematically and offered methodical instructions for contemporary practice.

In 1890, Josef Stübben edited his comprehensive volume *Der Städtebau*, which was included in the series *Handbuch der Architektur*.[3] It was to become the classic handbook of urban planning and design *par excellence*, and managed—along with Camillo Sitte's epochal treatise, released only a year earlier[4]—to draw attention to typological and artistic aspects, and to what became known as civic art. Social concerns were increasingly focused on after the turn of the century, encouraged by Ebenezer Howard's edition of *Garden Cities of Tomorrow* and the British Garden City movement.[5] They were comprehensively addressed in the handbooks of Raymond Unwin and Rudolf Eberstadt, which

[1] Commissioners and speakers of the "Town Planning Conference" in London, 1910. Among them Raymond Unwin (top row 3rd left) and Rudolf Eberstadt (middle row 3rd right).

Source: *The Transactions of the Royal Institute of British Architects Town Planning Conference, London, 10–15 October 1910* (London: RIBA, 1911), pp. 14b, 108c.

will be introduced in this essay.[6] The range of key topics was further expanded by the issue of park and landscape planning, essentially influenced by the North American discourse of the City Beautiful movement as well as by the publications of Charles Mulford Robinson and of the British landscape architect Thomas H. Mawson.[7] With regard to the unbridled urban growth of the major European cities, attention was also directed at the preservation of historic sites, centers, and monuments.[8]

In the genre of handbooks, the theory, practice, and history of urban planning and design were brought together. The books provided an important means of compiling theoretical and practical knowledge of the new discipline; they aimed to classify, arrange, and codify it, and to make it accessible for the education of future town planners, as well as for practical implementation and for the work of public authorities. Handbooks consequently always accomplished a twofold aim: the systematization of knowledge and the communication of methodical concepts by means of a manual. Thus, they represented both the conclusions of scientific studies and an educational tool for the regulation and planning of future building projects. Although the authors usually intended to present views and statements in the most unbiased and universally applicable way possible, they were unable to avoid formulating ideal concepts of urban planning. That is why their works inevitably also reflect contemporary urbanistic theories and ideologies.

The publication of specialized literature such as handbooks was strongly related to the establishment of educational institutions, the foundation of professional associations, the release of urban planning journals, town planning legislations and the emergence of specialized publishing houses. In this regard, Germany had undoubtedly assumed a pioneering role by the end of the nineteenth century. This is confirmed by a closer look at German town planning literature, as well as by statements published in contemporary English and French journals.[9] Great Britain considered itself to have reached its apex around 1909; this was the year that Unwin's handbook was published, the British Town Planning Institute was founded, the first issues of *The Town Planning Review* came out, and the significant Housing, Town Planning etc. Act was passed. A similar set of circumstances was to be found in France a few years later, as well as in Italy around the 1930s.[10]

This essay highlights two key works of town planning literature: Raymond Unwin's *Town Planning in Practice* and Rudolf Eberstadt's *Handbuch des Wohnungswesens*, both published in 1909. They are in many respects revealing with regard to the urban planning debate at the turn of the century. On the one hand, they summarized the subject matter of the preceding first phase of handbook literature, which was brought to an end by the World War I. On the other hand, they opened up a new range of topics and offered new methodical approaches. The books were reprinted in numerous editions and were well received within the European, transatlantic, and Russian context, and therefore had a significant impact on the contemporary urbanistic discourse. The two authors, at the time already well known, read and reviewed each other's work and papers, and even met personally—possibly as early as at the International Housing Congresses in Liège and London in 1905 and 1907 respectively, and certainly at the renowned "Town Planning Conference" in London in 1910. [1] On the latter occasion, they both spoke in the session "City development and extension" alongside other contributors such as Stübben, William E. Riley and Augustin Rey.[11] Beyond that, Unwin put together the exhibition that accompanied the conference. He had gathered the greater part of the exhibits from the Berlin exhibition held a few months earlier, where Eberstadt had presented his prize-winning entry in the "Greater Berlin Competition". In their home countries, Unwin and Eberstadt were both heavily involved in social housing issues, active members of the Garden City movement, and engaged in legislative matters. However, their studies and conceptions of urbanistic issues were based on very disparate positions resulting from their diverse personal, educational, professional, and cultural backgrounds.

Raymond Unwin's *Town Planning in Practice*

Raymond Unwin's sociopolitical and artistic attitudes were closely connected to his personal and professional career. Born in 1863 in Whiston, Rotherham, he had been brought up in a rural area of Oxford and was educated as a draughtsman of machines and company buildings in the industrial district of Derbyshire during the 1880s. There he became acquainted with the philanthropic ideas of the early social reformers, the Arts and Craft movement, the Fabian Society, and the Labour Church. His way of thinking was highly influenced by encounters with extraordinary individuals such as John Ruskin, William Morris, Edward Carpenter, Walter Crane, and Samuel Barnett. As a result of his desire to improve the poor housing conditions in British industrial cities, Unwin became more and more engaged in matters of town planning and building law after the turn of the century. He played a key role in the Garden City Association, which was founded by Ebenezer Howard in 1899. Together with his partner Barry Parker, Unwin was entrusted with the planning of Letchworth, the first Garden City, from 1904 onward, and with the Hampstead Garden Suburb from 1906 onward. Their planning projects provided the first genuine results of the international and swiftly expanding Garden City movement, and laid the foundations for the practical implementation of a new and until that point only theoretical type of town. The programmatic and artistic setup of the two model towns made them a unique key reference, which enormously inspired the international urban planning discourse. Unwin belonged to the leading circle of closely connected, proactive, and socially minded British town planners.[12] He continually published articles, participated in conferences and exhibitions, gave lectures to experts and students, and involved himself with professional and political associations. In 1914, he disbanded his collaboration with Parker and became employed in public administration in order to address the housing problems and urban development of London on a less practical but more political and public level.[13]

The publication of his main theoretical work *Town Planning in Practice* coincided with the passing of the Housing, Town Planning etc. Act in 1909. Along with the writings of Howard, Thomas C. Horsfall, and Patrick Geddes, Unwin's handbook marked the beginning of an independent British town planning literature.[14] As its subtitle *An Introduction to the Art of Designing Cities and Suburbs* suggests, it established the building of towns as an artistic discipline, and town planning as a social commitment in Great Britain. Only a year after its release it was translated into German, and a few years later into French as well; it was continually reprinted until the 1930s.[15] The reviews by Glenn Brown, Henry V. Lanchester, Stübben, and Eberstadt, as well as the publications of other town planners, reveal that Unwin's book had a significant impact far beyond its time and the country's borders. It was quoted countless times and its characteristic images found their way into Russian, Belgian, French, Romanian, Italian, and American literature. Although it suffered from loss of interest due to the modernist town planning theories propagated by the CIAM

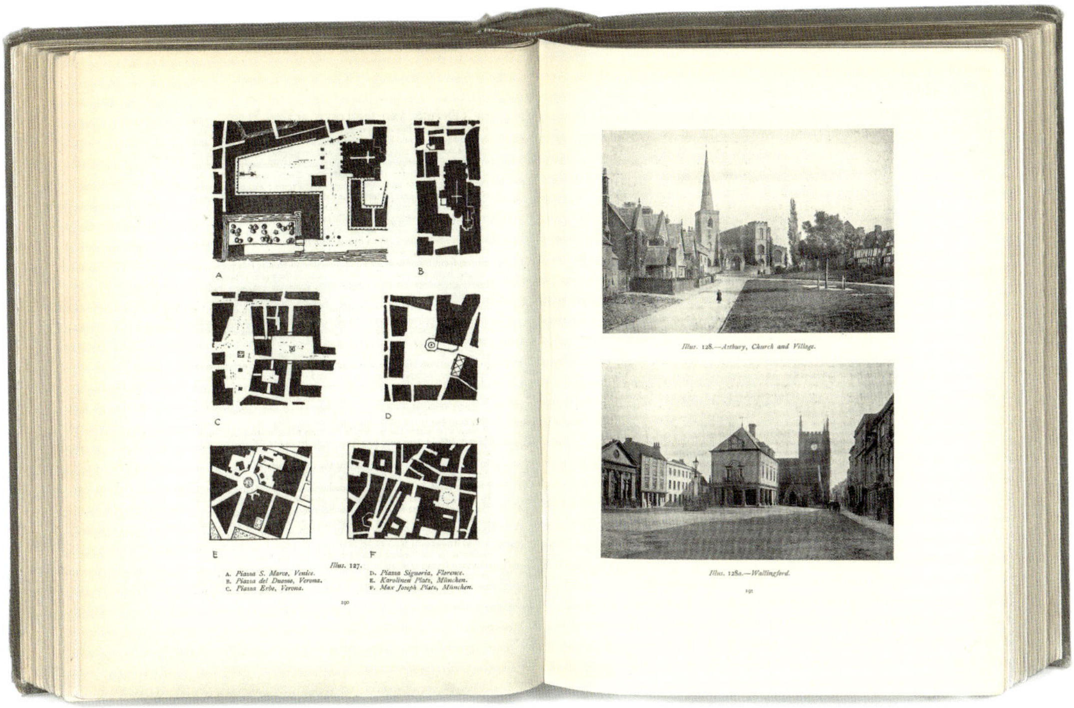

[2] Raymond Unwin, "Of Centres and Enclosed Places", 1909.

Source: Raymond Unwin, *Town Planning in Practice* (London/ Leipzig: T. Fisher Unwin, 1909), pp. 190–191.

from the 1930s onward, it has been regularly reissued and translated into other languages since the 1970s.[16] [2]

Unwin divided the book into twelve chapters. The first three introduce his general conception of town planning and the history of urban design, discussing basic subjects such as the meaning of civic life, formal and informal design, and planning itself. After a chapter on survey methods, the actual planning work is laid out in six chapters, systematically arranged around the topics of boundaries, centers, streets and planting, site planning, plots, and buildings. In conclusion, he added two chapters commenting on cooperation in planning and the improvement of the criticized practice of planning through building bye-laws.

Unwin tied the spatial and artistic design of towns tightly to social ambitions, ideological positions, and a specific planning procedure. To him, town planning served in a dual sense to control the development of cities as well as the establishment of society. A core issue of his manual, which legitimizes the act of planning, concerns the question of whether the design of new districts and towns should be built to a definite plan or whether it could be the result of gradual growth. Unwin thereby differentiated between conscious and unconscious design, between planned and instinctive order. Bearing in mind the historical development of towns, he fundamentally considered both ways to be reasonable. However, he was convinced that an instinctive approach was no longer possible because the "fine and all-pervading tradition" of building had gone and the instinct, therefore, was lost: "Modern conditions require, undoubtedly, that the new districts of our towns should be built to a definite plan. They must lose the unconscious and accidental character and come under the rules of conscious and ordered design."[17] And so, he concluded, planning was the only way to continue in the present: planning was the means by which to achieve order and beauty and to create relationships, harmony, and consistency; planning defined the design of the urban pattern, but it also, furthermore, implied a form of collaboration, financial strategy, and the regulation of ownership; and the planner had to be conscious that its implementation would involve a very dynamic and long-term process.[18]

Unwin's notion of the town was fundamentally affected by his experience of the radical contrasts between traditional medieval town structures and the uncontrolled industrial urbanization of Great Britain on the threshold of the twentieth century. His ideal corresponded to the Garden City type, which had been defined by Howard for the first time in 1898, and which would evolve into the idea of satellite towns in the 1920s when the Garden City movement became a vast international undertaking.[19] The Garden City is characterized by its limited size, its low density, the integration of housing and workplaces, and its close relationship to the countryside. It doesn't refer to a specific formal design, but is an ideal conception based on corporate ownership and planning criteria.

Consequently, Unwin's handbook deals exclusively with planning on the scale of small towns. It comments specifically on certain issues, and in doing so expresses the author's views on urban planning and his objections to current conditions as well as his practical approach. To begin with, he identifies a disordered, haphazard building practice and a fundamental deficit generated by the loss of art. Unlike his colleague Eberstadt, Unwin focused on art as an essential human need and expression; analogously, he declared civic art to be "the expression of the life of the community."[20]

His objections to the current situation were threefold. Firstly, he criticized the unsatisfying technical and regulatory preparation for controlling city development, especially the existing building bye-law practices which led to the schematic, unthinking layout of new districts. Unwin promoted a classification of road types, which should be adapted to their use and traffic, and the legal foundation of planning as a tool for public authorities. A liberalization of the bye-laws had already been achieved for the planning of the Hampstead Garden Suburb. From 1909 on, the Housing, Town Planning etc. Act finally allowed local authorities to prepare town planning schemes for their land and for neighboring lands.[21] The publication of Unwin's handbook was clearly linked to this act of legislation, enabling the instruction of town planners in their future assignments.

Secondly, Unwin criticized the low quality of life in many locations, particularly the poor housing conditions of the working class caused by overcrowding, the devastating influence of individual interests, and the lack of careful design of buildings, streets, and open spaces. He wanted to reduce costs (reducing, for example, unnecessary expenses in road construction by adjusting the width

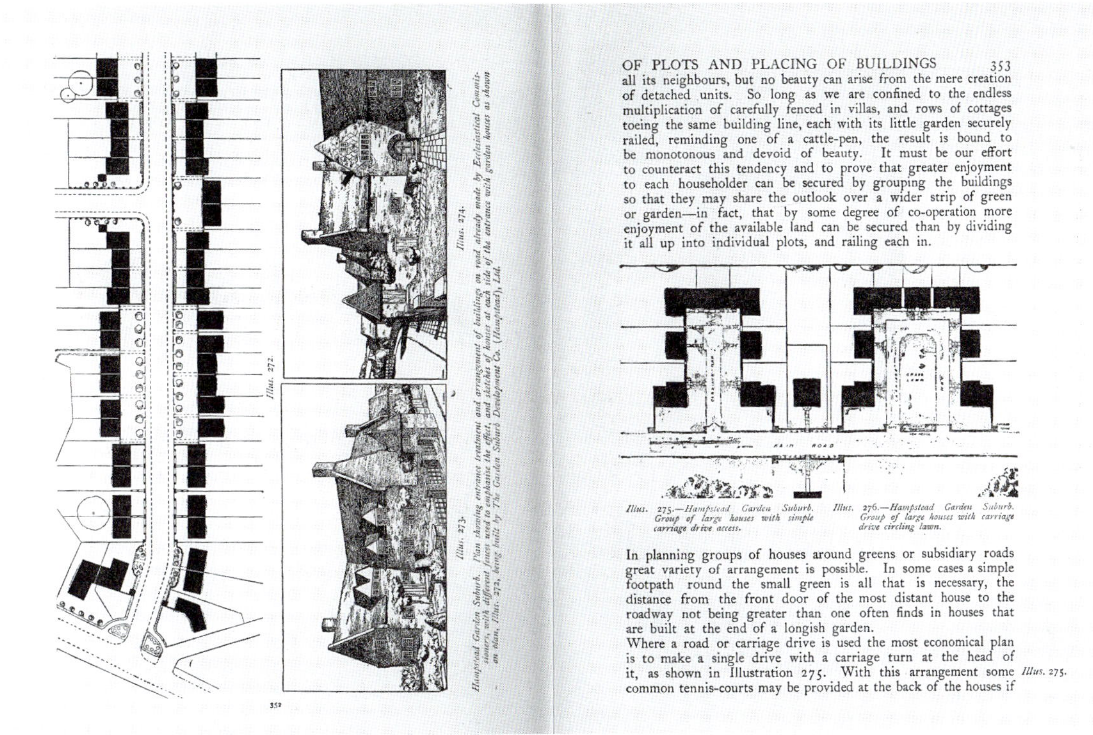

Illus. 272.

Illus. 273. Illus. 274. Hampstead Garden Suburb. Plan showing entrance treatment and arrangement of buildings on road already made by Ecclesiastical Commissioners, with different fences used to emphasise the effect, and sketches of houses at each side of the entrance with garden houses as shown on plan, Illus. 272, being built by The Garden Suburb Development Co. (Hampstead), Ltd.

352

OF PLOTS AND PLACING OF BUILDINGS 353

all its neighbours, but no beauty can arise from the mere creation of detached units. So long as we are confined to the endless multiplication of carefully fenced in villas, and rows of cottages toeing the same building line, each with its little garden securely railed, reminding one of a cattle-pen, the result is bound to be monotonous and devoid of beauty. It must be our effort to counteract this tendency and to prove that greater enjoyment to each householder can be secured by grouping the buildings so that they may share the outlook over a wider strip of green or garden—in fact, that by some degree of co-operation more enjoyment of the available land can be secured than by dividing it all up into individual plots, and railing each in.

Illus. 275.—Hampstead Garden Suburb. Group of large houses with simple carriage drive access.

Illus. 276.—Hampstead Garden Suburb. Group of large houses with carriage drive circling lawn.

In planning groups of houses around greens or subsidiary roads great variety of arrangement is possible. In some cases a simple footpath round the small green is all that is necessary, the distance from the front door of the most distant house to the roadway not being greater than one often finds in houses that are built at the end of a longish garden.
Where a road or carriage drive is used the most economical plan is to make a single drive with a carriage turn at the head of it, as shown in Illustration 275. With this arrangement some common tennis-courts may be provided at the back of the houses if Illus. 275.

[3] Raymond Unwin, "Of Plots and Placing of Buildings", 1909.

Source: Raymond Unwin, *Town Planning in Practice* (London/Leipzig: T. Fisher Unwin, 1909), pp. 353–354.

of the streets to meet only their actual requirements) in order to lower the cost pressure on land returns, allowing the density in residential areas to be decreased. He further anticipated that cooperative planning could help to preserve both individual freedom and the interests of the community, and therefore be for the benefit of all.[22]

Thirdly, in terms of design, Unwin criticized the haphazard order of new town extensions created by *laissez-faire* policies, the general lack of awareness in planning matters, and the unthinking application of formal principles. He made a large number of practical proposals presenting subtle solutions for the spacing and placing of buildings along roads and intersections, for the introduction of primary, secondary, and access roads, and for the varied arrangement of buildings in groups. From his point of view, the distinction between main and secondary roads was not only necessary because of the financial benefits, but might well also reduce the undesirable contrast between a well-presented front and unattractive backyards, improve the quality of open spaces, and evoke delightful relationships between buildings and the surrounding landscape.[23] [3]

In addition to the streetscape, to which Eberstadt also directed his consideration, Unwin treated the square as another urban element of vital importance. He consistently used the French term *place* for it:

The English word "square," besides limiting the shape to a regular form, denotes something often quite different. We must, therefore, be content with the

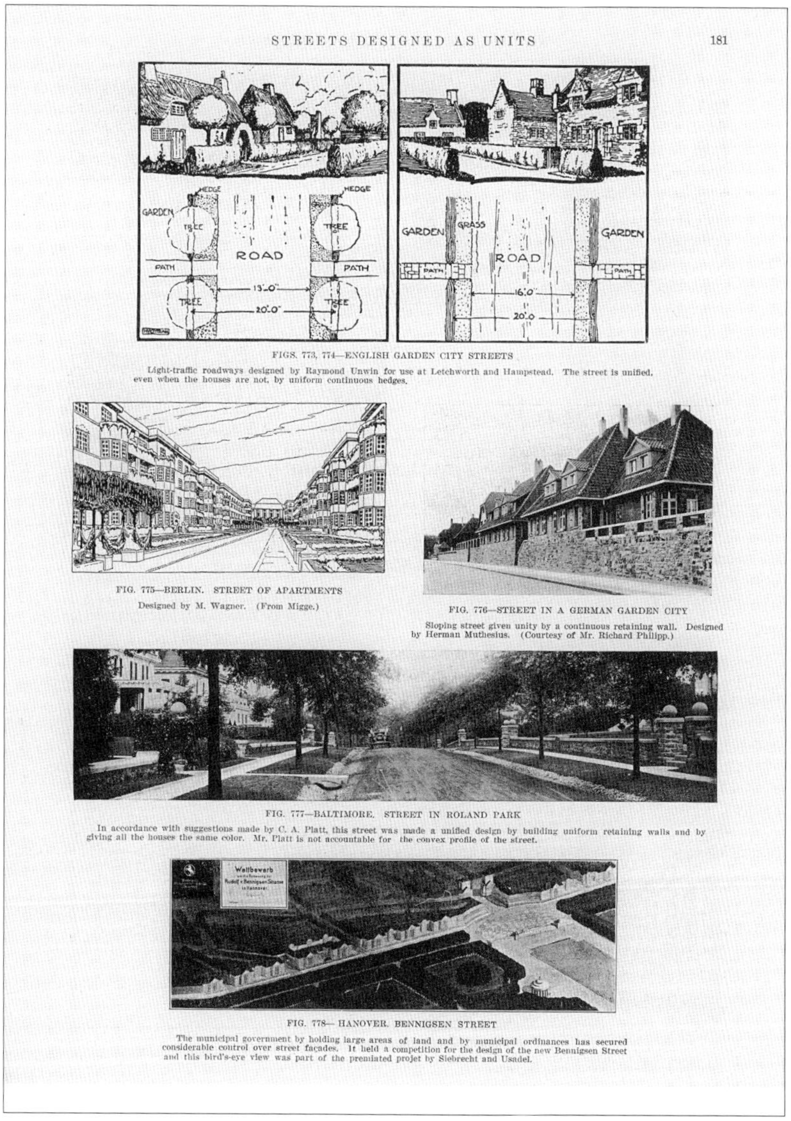
STREETS DESIGNED AS UNITS 181

FIGS. 773, 774—ENGLISH GARDEN CITY STREETS

Light-traffic roadways designed by Raymond Unwin for use at Letchworth and Hampstead. The street is unified, even when the houses are not, by uniform continuous hedges.

FIG. 775—BERLIN. STREET OF APARTMENTS

Designed by M. Wagner. (From Migge.)

FIG. 776—STREET IN A GERMAN GARDEN CITY

Sloping street given unity by a continuous retaining wall. Designed by Herman Muthesius. (Courtesy of Mr. Richard Philipp.)

FIG. 777—BALTIMORE. STREET IN ROLAND PARK

In accordance with suggestions made by C. A. Platt, this street was made a unified design by building uniform retaining walls and by giving all the houses the same color. Mr. Platt is not accountable for the convex profile of the street.

FIG. 778— HANOVER. BENNIGSEN STREET

The municipal government by holding large areas of land and by municipal ordinances has secured considerable control over street façades. It held a competition for the design of the new Bennigsen Street and this bird's-eye view was part of the premiated projet by Siebrecht and Usadel.

[4] Werner Hegemann and Elbert Peets, chapter "Streets Design as Units", 1922. With Raymond Unwin's street sections of an English Garden City.

Source: Werner Hegemann and Elbert Peets, *The American Vitruvius: An Architect's Handbook of Civic Art* (New York: Architectural Book Pub. Co., 1922), p. 181.

French word *place*; it has the advantage of being essentially the same word as the Italian *piazza* and the German *Platz*; and if at present it does not convey a sufficiently definite idea, perhaps it may be possible for us to pack more meaning into it. A *place*, then, in the sense in which we wish to use the word, should be an enclosed space.[24]

For Unwin, *place* represented the center—a modern form of the Greek *agora* and the Roman *forum*. As such, it played an important role in the public life of a community: in its civic life. Like the street and the whole city, *place* should be characterized by its enclosure, not in a hermetic sense, but rather offering attractive views of the landscape, and being varied in shape and form.

In Unwin's opinion, the visual effects of spaces and streets were of central importance, something which is apparent from the large number and quality of images used in his handbook. Examples of this are the street sections of Garden Cities, which combine diagrammatic street plans with perspective street views, as well as the numerous photographs and perspective drawings often accompanied by little ground plans to relate the perspective view to the technical drawing of the plan. The figures of the German town of Buttstädt, drawn by Unwin's young assistant Charles Wade, are characteristic for the type of illustrations, sources, references, and content of imagery generally used in the book: the image sequence shows scenic views of a picturesque German townscape and leads the reader's eye on an urbanistic promenade through the streets and places of the small medieval town.[25] Along with other similar drawings, the images of Buttstädt are strangely anachronistic and have been held responsible for Unwin's reputation as a romantic and medievalist. Beyond that, they document his distinctive personal perception of German town planning, German literature, and German towns. However, Unwin also used many other references; for example, American Park Reports, the French planning concepts for traffic, gardens, and green spaces (mainly tracing back to the writings of Eugène Hénard), and particularly Unwin and Parker's own designs for Letchworth Garden City and the Hampstead Garden Suburb, which themselves were widely accepted in the international planning literature. [4]

The outstanding success of Unwin's handbook at both the national and international level is certainly due to the convincing connection of idealistic ambitions to pragmatic solutions. His statements remain general and therefore also applicable to other times and places. He presented precise proposals for handling specific tasks in current practice and was very much concerned with providing a balanced view. Nonetheless, he took a clear position regarding artistic, social, legal, and educational issues. At a more personal level, his significant activities in theory, practice, teaching, institutions, and politics, his vast international network, his engagement for the Garden City movement as well as his exemplary planning for Letchworth and the Hampstead Garden Suburb, must also be considered—which altogether made him a key figure of urban planning.

Rudolf Eberstadt's *Handbuch des Wohnungswesens und der Wohnungsfrage*

A rather different background and professional career can be pointed to for Rudolf Eberstadt. Born in Worms in 1856 and dying in Berlin in 1922, he originally completed his training as a banker. After having worked for several years in the profession abroad, he began to study economics in Zurich in 1894, and graduated in Berlin in 1897. In 1902, he received his habilitation under Gustav Schmoller, doyen of the historical school of economics. During those years, Eberstadt developed a large body of written work, which can be roughly grouped into three thematic phases: the first, early stage was devoted to purely economic matters,[26] the second and longest phase introduced economic issues relating to questions of urban development,[27] and the third, somewhat later

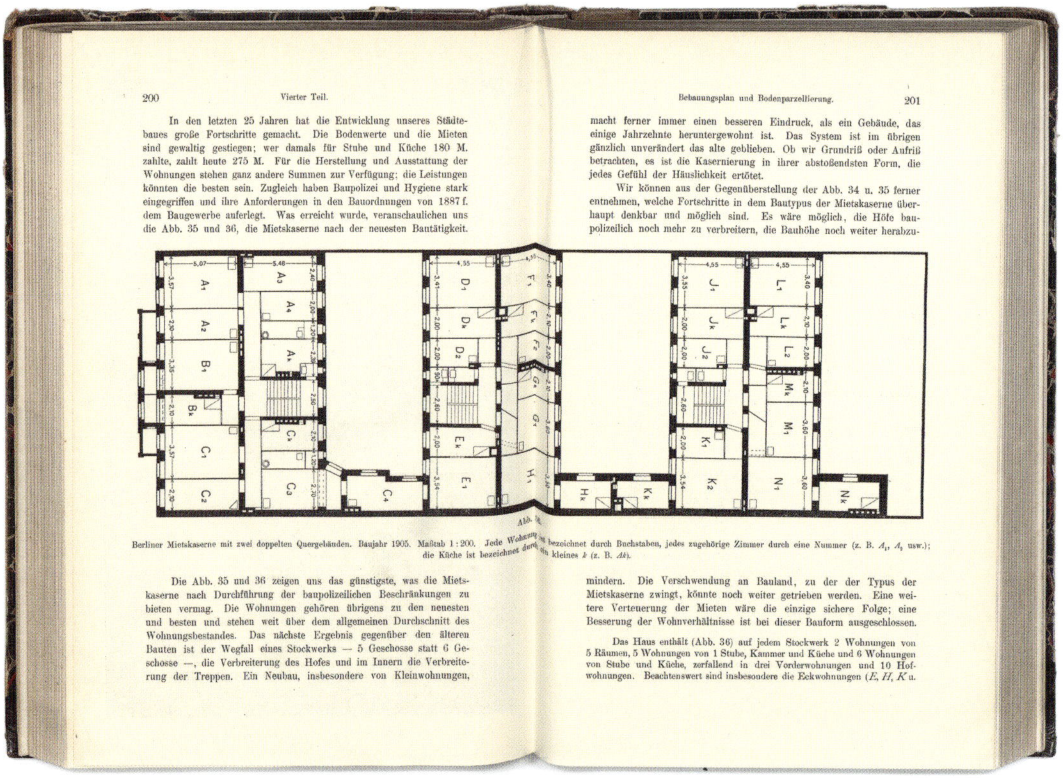
200 Vierter Teil.

In den letzten 25 Jahren hat die Entwicklung unseres Städtebaues große Fortschritte gemacht. Die Bodenwerte und die Mieten sind gewaltig gestiegen; wer damals für Stube und Küche 180 M. zahlte, zahlt heute 275 M. Für die Herstellung und Ausstattung der Wohnungen stehen ganz andere Summen zur Verfügung; die Leistungen könnten die besten sein. Zugleich haben Baupolizei und Hygiene stark eingegriffen und ihre Anforderungen in den Bauordnungen von 1887 f. dem Baugewerbe auferlegt. Was erreicht wurde, veranschaulichen uns die Abb. 35 und 36, die Mietskaserne nach der neuesten Bautätigkeit.

Abb. 36.

Berliner Mietskaserne mit zwei doppelten Quergebäuden. Baujahr 1905. Maßtab 1 : 200. Jede Wohnung ist bezeichnet durch Buchstaben, jedes zugehörige Zimmer durch eine Nummer (z. B. A_1, A_2 usw.); die Küche ist bezeichnet durch ein kleines *k* (z. B. *Ak*).

Die Abb. 35 und 36 zeigen uns das günstigste, was die Mietskaserne nach Durchführung der baupolizeilichen Beschränkungen zu bieten vermag. Die Wohnungen gehören übrigens zu den neuesten und besten und stehen weit über dem allgemeinen Durchschnitt des Wohnungsbestandes. Das nächste Ergebnis gegenüber den älteren Bauten ist der Wegfall eines Stockwerks — 5 Geschosse statt 6 Geschosse —, die Verbreiterung des Hofes und im Innern die Verbreiterung der Treppen. Ein Neubau, insbesondere von Kleinwohnungen,

Bebauungsplan und Bodenparzellierung. 201

macht ferner immer einen besseren Eindruck, als ein Gebäude, das einige Jahrzehnte heruntergewohnt ist. Das System ist im übrigen gänzlich unverändert das alte geblieben. Ob wir Grundriß oder Aufriß betrachten, es ist die Kasernierung in ihrer abstoßendsten Form, die jedes Gefühl der Häuslichkeit ertötet.

Wir können aus der Gegenüberstellung der Abb. 34 u. 35 ferner entnehmen, welche Fortschritte in dem Bautypus der Mietskaserne überhaupt denkbar und möglich sind. Es wäre möglich, die Höfe baupolizeilich noch mehr zu verbreitern, die Bauhöhe noch weiter herabzumindern. Die Verschwendung an Bauland, zu der der Typus der Mietskaserne zwingt, könnte noch weiter getrieben werden. Eine weitere Verteuerung der Mieten wäre die einzige sichere Folge; eine Besserung der Wohnverhältnisse ist bei dieser Bauform ausgeschlossen.

Das Haus enthält (Abb. 36) auf jedem Stockwerk 2 Wohnungen von 5 Räumen, 5 Wohnungen von 1 Stube, Kammer und Küche und 6 Wohnungen von Stube und Küche, zerfallend in drei Vorderwohnungen und 10 Hofwohnungen. Beachtenswert sind insbesondere die Eckwohnungen (*E*, *H*, *K* u.

[5] Rudolf Eberstadt, floor plan of a Berlin "Mietskaserne", 1909.

Source: Rudolf Eberstadt, *Handbuch des Wohnungswesens und der Wohnungsfrage* (Jena: Gustav Fischer, 1909), pp. 200–201.

phase was primarily devoted to involvement in matters of urban development, omitting economic considerations.[28]

The development of his *Handbuch des Wohnungswesens* cannot be understood without considering his numerous texts published before and during the period from 1909 to 1920. Various topics covered by these publications were addressed directly in the handbook, and arranged there systematically. In this sense, it forms the actual core of Eberstadt's published work; on the one hand it represented the thematic and methodical underpinning by which he gained recognition for the various editions of his handbook, and at the same time it provided material for an increasing number of new publications.

Besides his written work, Eberstadt was active in urban planning and design, although—unlike Unwin—he had not benefitted from any kind of architectural or engineering training. During the 1910s, he participated in urbanistic competitions and the design of planning layouts alongside various architects. In 1910, he won third prize for his entry in the widely discussed "Greater Berlin Competition" (*Wettbewerb Gross-Berlin*), developed with Bruno Möhring and Richard Petersen.[29] With Möhring, Eberstadt designed the master plan for Berlin Treptow (1914),[30] and with Hermann Muthesius he drew up the plan for the extension of the Freie Scholle housing estate in Berlin (1912) as well as the small housing estate in Hermsdorf ("Kleinsiedlung der Hermsdorfer Bodengesellschaft", 1918).[31]

Eberstadt's *Handbuch des Wohnungswesens* was released in four successively revised and extended editions in 1909, 1910, 1917, and 1920. Despite this remarkable number of reissues and the author's evident presence in the international discourse on housing and urban planning, no attempts were made to translate his book—a fact which clearly reflects its characteristic cultural and geographical limitations, particularly when compared to the international success of Unwin's handbook. First of all, Eberstadt's publication deals with the German context; it only occasionally refers to foreign examples to support the author's arguments. Its systematic structure fully meets the criteria of the genre of handbooks, including a table of contents, bibliographic references at the end of each chapter, an informative appendix, and a detailed subject index. A glance at the contents, divided into eight parts, reveals three main areas of emphasis: while the first part tends towards historical arguments, and the fourth part promises a practical explanation of urban development, all other parts demonstrate a clear economic focus. [5]

In contrast to Unwin's formal approach to town planning as an architect, Eberstadt didn't regard himself as an urban designer or town planner but rather as a scientist. For him, urban design was primarily a question of urban housing, not of art or even aesthetics; again, from his point of view, it was largely influenced by "land development," which involved ownership structures and the trading of land property. It was therefore important first to acquire a thorough understanding of housing, both in terms of its historical evolution as well as its current (and at that time poor) conditions. He called it the "science of housing and urban planning," which could only be achieved by interaction between the disciplines of administration, technology and economics.

Eberstadt presented his own analysis of contemporary urban development and housing, writing a socially and economically oriented structural history rather than a history of form or style. His understanding of the history of urban planning—and of cities themselves—can be perceived as resulting from a paradigm shift which he described as follows:

In studies on urban planning, so far has been asked only the question, "by whom were the cities built?" However, my point of view raises the question, "for whom are our cities built?" This essentially changes the subject matter. The second question is not intended to exclude the first one. Rather, it is always of great importance in the present as well as in the past to know the creator and the driving forces in urban planning and to determine the organizers of the city structure and the supporters of urban development. But the question of the object of urban planning is no less important than the one of the subject.[32]

Moreover, in his early-twentieth-century analysis of the city, Eberstadt identified a very large discrepancy between the existing and newly created urban structures and the needs of the time. He criticized contemporary German urban design (*NB* also in his speech at the 1910 conference in London)[33] for

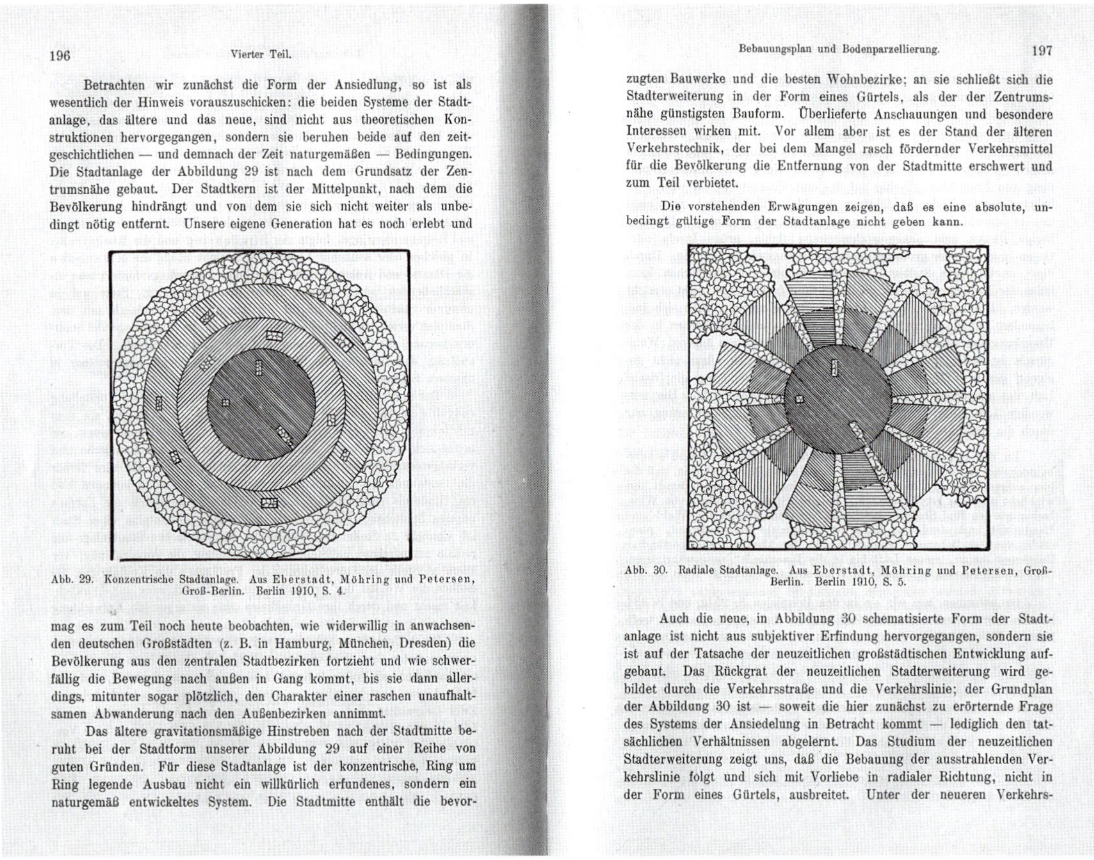

196 Vierter Teil.

Betrachten wir zunächst die Form der Ansiedlung, so ist als wesentlich der Hinweis vorauszuschicken: die beiden Systeme der Stadtanlage, das ältere und das neue, sind nicht aus theoretischen Konstruktionen hervorgegangen, sondern sie beruhen beide auf den zeitgeschichtlichen — und demnach der Zeit naturgemäßen — Bedingungen. Die Stadtanlage der Abbildung 29 ist nach dem Grundsatz der Zentrumsnähe gebaut. Der Stadtkern ist der Mittelpunkt, nach dem die Bevölkerung hindrängt und von dem sie sich nicht weiter als unbedingt nötig entfernt. Unsere eigene Generation hat es noch erlebt und

Abb. 29. Konzentrische Stadtanlage. Aus Eberstadt, Möhring und Petersen, Groß-Berlin. Berlin 1910, S. 4.

mag es zum Teil noch heute beobachten, wie widerwillig in anwachsenden deutschen Großstädten (z. B. in Hamburg, München, Dresden) die Bevölkerung aus den zentralen Stadtbezirken fortzieht und wie schwerfällig die Bewegung nach außen in Gang kommt, bis sie dann allerdings, mitunter sogar plötzlich, den Charakter einer raschen unaufhaltsamen Abwanderung nach den Außenbezirken annimmt.

Das ältere gravitationsmäßige Hinstreben nach der Stadtmitte beruht bei der Stadtform unserer Abbildung 29 auf einer Reihe von guten Gründen. Für diese Stadtanlage ist der konzentrische, Ring um Ring legende Ausbau nicht ein willkürlich erfundenes, sondern ein naturgemäß entwickeltes System. Die Stadtmitte enthält die bevor-

Bebauungsplan und Bodenparzellierung. 197

zugten Bauwerke und die besten Wohnbezirke; an sie schließt sich die Stadterweiterung in der Form eines Gürtels, als der der Zentrumsnähe günstigsten Bauform. Überlieferte Anschauungen und besondere Interessen wirken mit. Vor allem aber ist es der Stand der älteren Verkehrstechnik, der bei dem Mangel rasch fördernder Verkehrsmittel für die Bevölkerung die Entfernung von der Stadtmitte erschwert und zum Teil verbietet.

Die vorstehenden Erwägungen zeigen, daß es eine absolute, unbedingt gültige Form der Stadtanlage nicht geben kann.

Abb. 30. Radiale Stadtanlage. Aus Eberstadt, Möhring und Petersen, Groß-Berlin. Berlin 1910, S. 5.

Auch die neue, in Abbildung 30 schematisierte Form der Stadtanlage ist nicht aus subjektiver Erfindung hervorgegangen, sondern sie ist auf der Tatsache der neuzeitlichen großstädtischen Entwicklung aufgebaut. Das Rückgrat der neuzeitlichen Stadterweiterung wird gebildet durch die Verkehrsstraße und die Verkehrslinie; der Grundplan der Abbildung 30 ist — soweit die hier zunächst zu erörternde Frage des Systems der Ansiedelung in Betracht kommt — lediglich den tatsächlichen Verhältnissen abgelernt. Das Studium der neuzeitlichen Stadterweiterung zeigt uns, daß die Bebauung der ausstrahlenden Verkehrslinie folgt und sich mit Vorliebe in radialer Richtung, nicht in der Form eines Gürtels, ausbreitet. Unter der neueren Verkehrs-

[6] Rudolf Eberstadt, diagrams of a "concentric" and a "radial" city layout, 1910.

Source: Eberstadt, *Handbuch des Wohnungswesens und der Wohnungsfrage* (Jena: Gustav Fischer, 1910), pp. 196–197.

its formalism and for being too strongly oriented toward the layout and construction of streets. Eberstadt considered the German *Städtebau* ("building of cities") rather to be a *Strassenbau* ("building of streets") and, therefore, inadequate to meet the requirements of his time. He cited the "complete reversal of the position of the center and the outskirts," the separation of dwellings from workplaces, a completely altered class of urban population, and a tendency toward urban expansion across municipal boundaries as unresolved problems.[34] Eberstadt's assessments of urban planning were exceptional because he took into account all its essential factors and a large range of scales, from the basic form of the city layout, extension plans, parceling plans, street configurations, and housing floor plans to the examination of different types of streets and houses, building regulations, land values, rents, and the quality of the dwellings.[35] Concerning the urban layout, he formulated two basic principles: the radial development of a city (*radiale Stadtanlage*) and the mixed construction style (*gemischte Bauweise*), two planning ideals which he had conceived and adopted together with Möhring and Petersen at the time of the "Greater Berlin Competition." Eberstadt was convinced that a radial city layout would better meet the demands of modern traffic and open-space planning than the outdated concentric model based on the extension of the city by means of added belts. The mixed construction—dating back to an idea formulated by Theodor Goecke from the 1890s [36]—was Eberstadt's response to the "Mietskaserne," a type of oversized residential building housing cramming in too many apartments, which were additionally too small, in huge, impractical blocks. Due to land speculation, these had become particularly common in Berlin.[37] [6]

He vehemently criticized the miserable living conditions dominating these residential blocks. According to him—and similarly in Unwin's opinion, who himself derived his critique from the poor environment of industrial cities like London and Manchester—the "Mietskaserne" building type was an inevitable outcome of a system that had been set up within an inadequate legislative, administrative, and economic framework. Eberstadt identified the combination of poor planning caused by the restrictions on building lines (*Fluchtlinienplanung*) and weak building regulations, both cemented in Berlin by James Hobrecht's 1862 plan, as one of the worst and most clearly implicated causes of this. As a way out, he promoted the radical move to concrete development planning, which would also prevent excessive exploitation in private properties by means of mandatory guidelines regarding building types. In addition, the development plans should stipulate the differentiation between traffic routes and residential streets, as well as the provision of special types of houses with small apartments.[38]

The illustrations shown in Eberstadt's handbook underline the fundamental nature of his arguments. Some of the images had already become well known through the discourse on civic art. He combined them with site plans, elevations, and floor plans for dwellings according to the requirements of each part of the book. His own plans and drawings were also gradually incorporated into the various editions to serve as case studies and key examples. Furthermore, it is evident that Eberstadt regarded the tabular form of representation to be an important means of presenting an argument, especially when dealing with economic values. In terms of historical references, too, the images reflect the author's general attitude: while he idealized the Middle Ages, he maintained a rather more nuanced view of seventeenth- and eighteenth-century town planning—but criticized the contemporary situation that had arisen since the mid-nineteenth century.

With his *Handbuch des Wohnungswesens*, Eberstadt strongly influenced the debate on housing matters, the use of urban design handbooks, and the general urban planning discourse. However, its effect didn't last long: by the end of the 1920s, his economic theses had been refuted by liberal academics, and his urbanistic ideals were superseded by the emergence of modernist urban planning. His rather technical and economic approach was tailored to particular needs and conditions, and consequently his statements were less universal and transferable than the formal interpretation and theories presented by Unwin. The reasons for the brief, but nevertheless high, appreciation of Eberstadt's ideas can be found in the wide distribution of his publications and the central

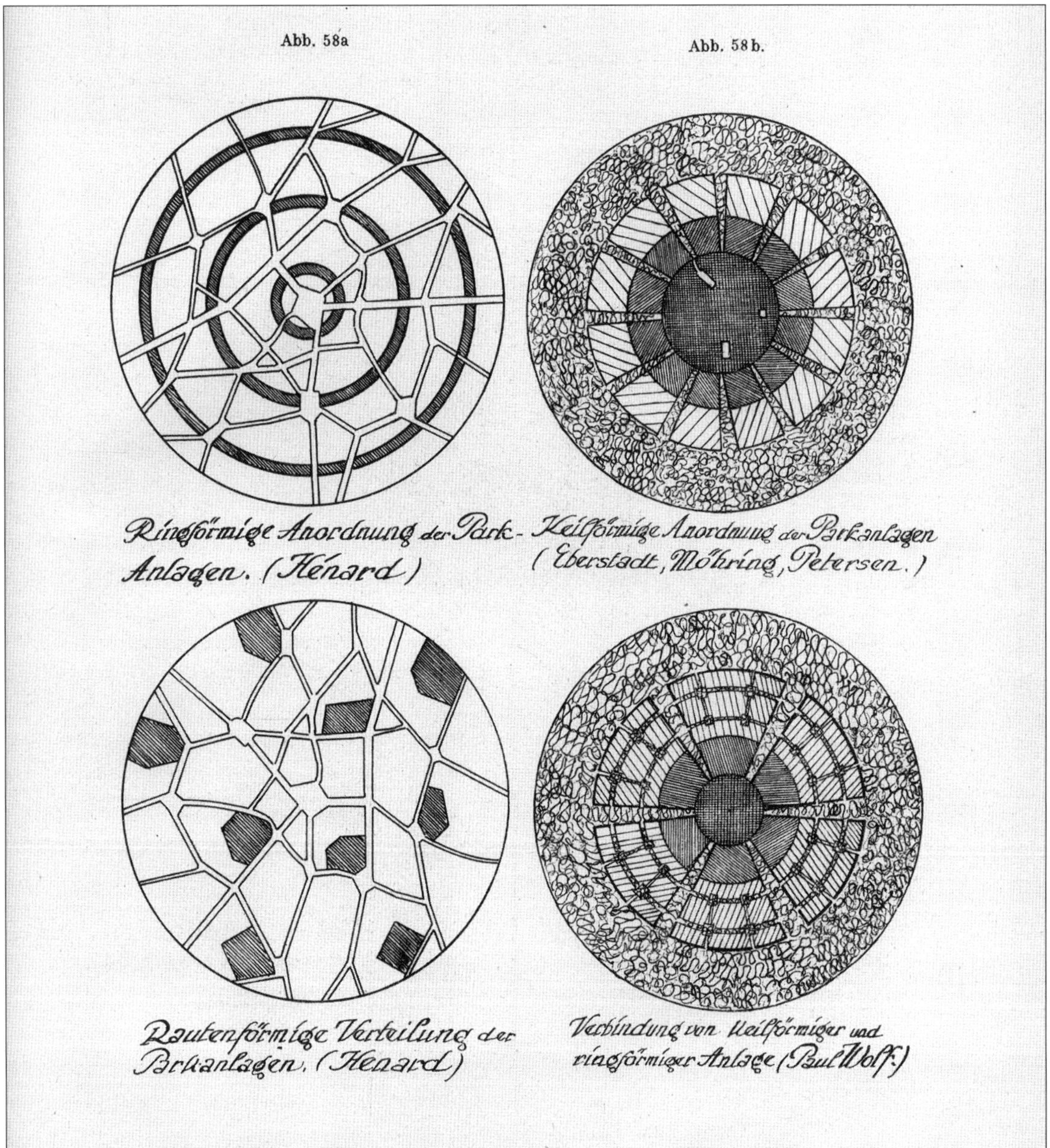

Abb. 58a und 58b. Verschiedene Verteilungsarten der Grünflächen.

role he played in the highly controversial debate on "small houses versus big blocks" (*Kleinhaus oder Mietskaserne*), as well as in the author's considerable presence at international congresses on housing and urban planning. Furthermore, Eberstadt was well-connected among experts and was an active member of the *Deutsche Gartenstadtgesellschaft* and the *Verein für Socialpolitik*.[39]

[7] Roman Heiligenthal, diagram of a "radiant city layout" by Rudolf Eberstadt, Bruno Möhring and Richard Petersen in comparison to drawings by Paul Wolf and Eugène Hénard, redrawn in *Deutscher Städtebau*, 1921.

Source: Roman Heiligenthal, *Deutscher Städtebau: Ein Handbuch für Architekten, Ingenieure, Verwaltungsbeamte und Volkswirte* (Heidelberg: Carl Winter, 1921).

With respect to the specific use of handbooks in urban planning, it is noteworthy that Eberstadt's publication had a surprisingly wide reception outside of Germany, although unlike Unwin's book it was never translated into other languages.[40] However, it was principally studied by German-speaking readers—among them other authors of handbooks such as Paul Wolf, Cornelius Gurlitt and Roman Heiligenthal, who referred to Eberstadt's work in their own writings on the subject.[41] The handbook's influence and popularity can be measured by the considerable dissemination of its two famous diagrams showing a "concentric" and a "radial" city layout. After publishing them for the first time in the context of the "Greater Berlin Competition," Eberstadt presented both diagrams at the "Town Planning Conference" in London in 1910 and integrated them into the second edition of his manual, released the same year.[42] From then on, they enjoyed a veritable cavalcade of successes within the international urban planning literature.[43] They were often used by other authors to draw direct comparisons to related images or to promote their own ideas about urban development. Among the most prominent references is the one by Ernst May, who proposed "Urban Expansion through Satellites" as an urban model for the future in his article published in *Der Städtebau* in 1922.[44] Incidentally, it was also May who instrumented in arranging a last significant discussion of Eberstadt's *Handbuch des Wohnungswesens* on the occasion of the publication on the CIAM congress "Die Wohnung für das Existenzminimum" held in Frankfurt in 1929.[45] [7]

Handbooks as Means of Reflection and Regulation

The two handbooks on urban planning and design written by Raymond Unwin and Rudolf Eberstadt respectively offer a revealing juxtaposition not only due to the temporal coincidence of their first publication in 1909. Despite their obvious formal, ideological, and methodological differences, both publications are characterized by their comprehensive and systematic approach to the compilation of the problems and tasks of town planning, which, at the time, was about to become established in architectural and engineering practice as an independent discipline.

The two authors actively participated in the international discourse on the topic and occasionally met at conferences and exhibitions. They shared the conviction that urban development was primarily a social task, equating urban planning and design with the planning and construction of society. The most important component of their social and morphological vision was comprised of the organization of residential buildings combined with the classification of streets. They were particularly concerned with the issues of social housing and the improvement of working-class living conditions. Their keen commitment was driven by their well-founded criticism of the fast-growing cities, of misdirected urban expansion, and of its harmful social consequences, which they attempted to control by means of new building legislation.

In terms of references, Unwin as well as Eberstadt showed a strong orientation toward the medieval form of towns and society. Nevertheless, fundamental

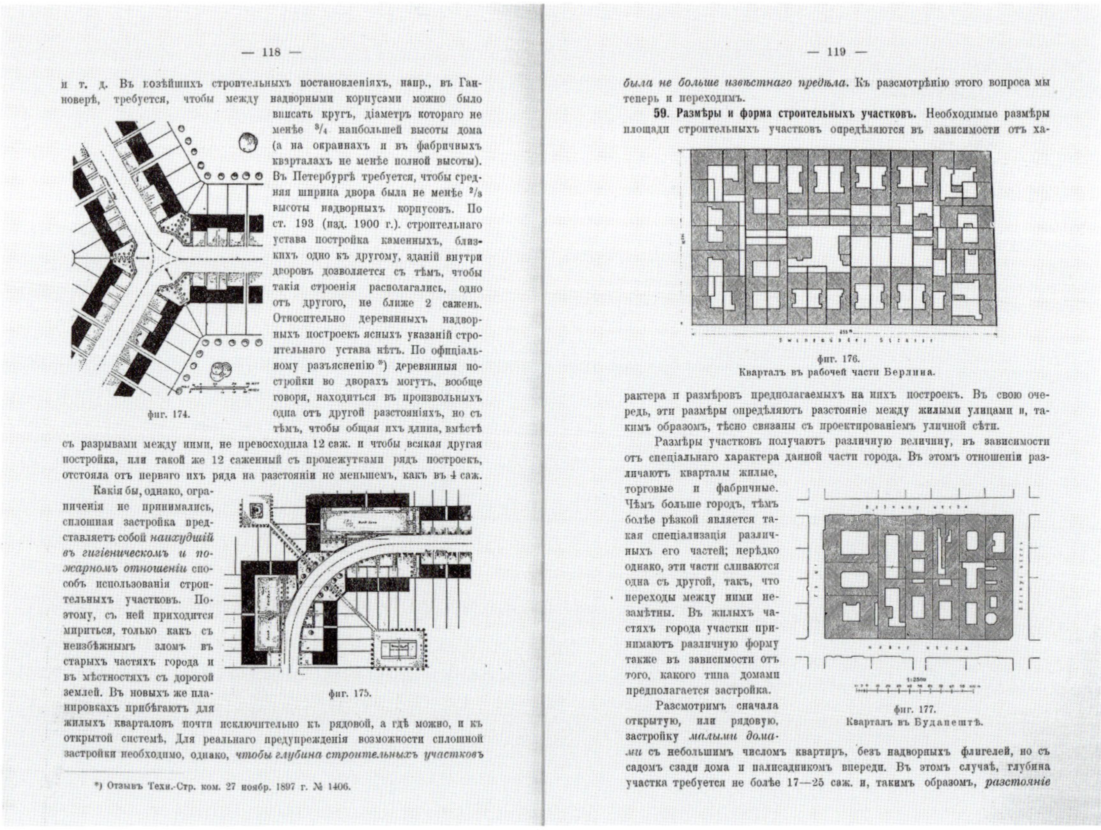

— 118 —

и т. д. Въ позднѣйшихъ строительныхъ постановленіяхъ, напр., въ Ганноверѣ, требуется, чтобы между надворными корпусами можно было вписать кругъ, діаметръ котораго не менѣе 3/4 наибольшей высоты дома (а на окраинахъ и въ фабричныхъ кварталахъ не менѣе полной высоты). Въ Петербургѣ требуется, чтобы средняя ширина двора была не менѣе 2/3 высоты надворныхъ корпусовъ. По ст. 193 (изд. 1900 г.). строительнаго устава постройка каменныхъ, близкихъ одно къ другому, зданій внутри дворовъ дозволяется съ тѣмъ, чтобы такія строенія располагались, одно отъ другого, не ближе 2 саженъ. Относительно деревянныхъ надворныхъ построекъ ясныхъ указаній строительнаго устава нѣтъ. По официальному разъясненію *) деревянныя постройки во дворахъ могутъ, вообще говоря, находиться въ произвольныхъ одна отъ другой разстояніяхъ, но съ тѣмъ, чтобы общая ихъ длина, вмѣстѣ съ разрывами между ними, не превосходила 12 саж. и чтобы всякая другая постройка, или такой же 12 саженный съ промежутками рядъ построекъ, отстояла отъ перваго ихъ ряда на разстояніи не меньшемъ, какъ въ 4 саж.

фиг. 174.

Какія бы, однако, ограниченія не принимались, сплошная застройка представляетъ собой *наихудшій въ гигіеническомъ и пожарномъ отношеніи* способъ использованія строительныхъ участковъ. Поэтому, съ ней приходится мириться, только какъ съ неизбѣжнымъ зломъ въ старыхъ частяхъ города и въ мѣстностяхъ съ дорогой землей. Въ новыхъ же планировкахъ прибѣгаютъ для жилыхъ кварталовъ почти исключительно къ рядовой, а гдѣ можно, и къ открытой системѣ, Для реальнаго предупрежденія возможности сплошной застройки необходимо, однако, *чтобы глубина строительныхъ участковъ*

фиг. 175.

*) Отзывъ Техн.-Стр. ком. 27 ноябр. 1897 г. № 1406.

— 119 —

была не больше извѣстнаго предѣла. Къ разсмотрѣнію этого вопроса мы теперь и переходимъ.

59. Размѣры и форма строительныхъ участковъ. Необходимые размѣры площади строительныхъ участковъ опредѣляются въ зависимости отъ характера и размѣровъ предполагаемыхъ на нихъ построекъ. Въ свою очередь, эти размѣры опредѣляютъ разстояніе между жилыми улицами и, такимъ образомъ, тѣсно связаны съ проектированіемъ уличной сѣти.

фиг. 176.
Кварталъ въ рабочей части Берлина.

Размѣры участковъ получаютъ различную величину, въ зависимости отъ спеціальнаго характера данной части города. Въ этомъ отношеніи различаютъ кварталы жилые, торговые и фабричные. Чѣмъ больше городъ, тѣмъ болѣе рѣзкой является такая специализація различныхъ его частей; нерѣдко однако, эти части сливаются одна съ другой, такъ, что переходы между ними незамѣтны. Въ жилыхъ частяхъ города участки принимаютъ различную форму также въ зависимости отъ того, какого типа домами предполагается застройка.

фиг. 177.
Кварталъ въ Будапештѣ.

Разсмотримъ сначала открытую, или рядовую, застройку *малыми домами* съ небольшимъ числомъ квартиръ, безъ надворныхъ флигелей, но съ садомъ сзади дома и палисадникомъ впереди. Въ этомъ случаѣ, глубина участка требуется не болѣе 17—25 саж. и, такимъ образомъ, *разстояніе*

[8] Grigorij Dmitrievič Dubelir, reprints of Raymond Unwin's and Rudolf Eberstadt's original drawings in his Russian handbook, 1912.

Source: Grigorij Dmitrievič Dubelir, *Gorodskie ulicy i mostovye (Städtische Straßen und Straßenbau)*, Kiew: tip. A. M. Ponomareva, 1912, S. 118–119.

differences can be identified: whereas the former related his reforming efforts to the way of life and the quality of craftsmanship of the Middle Ages—which gave him the rather dubious reputation of being a romantic[46]—the latter was interested more pragmatically in the medieval guild system and economics, as well as in the housing structures then predominantly represented by the "Kleinhaus". Differences can also be found in their common dedication to the Garden City movement: in contrast to Unwin, who became a central figure of the British and international discourse on Garden Cities after having won the competition for the planning of Letchworth Garden City in 1904, Eberstadt's role in the movement remained rather administrative. Although he was a member of the extended directory board of the *Deutsche Gartenstadtgesellschaft*, the ideals of the Garden City were only incidentally discussed in his handbook.

It is therefore possible to say that, apart from obvious, rather outward similarities, there are significant ideological differences between Eberstadt's *Handbuch des Wohnungswesens* und Unwin's *Town Planning in Practice*, not least due to the disciplinary and cultural background of the two authors. Eberstadt—the German economist and expert in matters of housing and land reform—based his assumptions on economic and sociopolitical matters, primarily addressing German readers who approached urban planning from a legislative and administrative point of view. By contrast, Unwin—the English architect and social reformer—developed his theories mainly against a backdrop of spatial and aesthetic demands, addressing an international audience that was interested in social, technical, and artistic tasks as well as philosophical issues.

Concerning the methodologies of urban planning, they both argued that every intervention must be preceded by a systematic and objective quasi-scientific analysis of the existing structures. While Unwin requested a detailed "survey"—a comprehensive analysis of the historical, sociological, economic, climatic, topographical, vegetative, structural, and infrastructural conditions—Eberstadt confined himself to a general, more tabular representation of economic values such as population distribution, types of housing, and the cost of land and rents. Based on these perspectives, the two authors proposed urban planning as the main instrument in building the city.

They agreed that only a concrete "development plan"—not merely the existing building regulations—could ultimately lead to an improved contemporary urban design which was able to take into account all the actual needs of society. This implied that prior to the effective configuration of new town districts, a general layout had to be defined which differentiated streets, open spaces, and built areas, as well as their types of use and densities. Unwin as much as Eberstadt considered the differentiation of traffic routes and residential streets to be one of the most urgent issues to be tackled. However, their handbooks reveal very different methodological approaches. Whereas Unwin included formal proposals for the practical implementation of specific questions of design, visualizing his ideas with atmospheric and often suggestive illustrations, Eberstadt didn't focus on the formal design. Consistent with his view as an economist, he emphasized the legislative, economic, and structural conception of urban interventions, a fact which is also reflected in the schematic, often numerical way he illustrated his arguments.

Considering the role of the two handbooks and their impact on urban planning, one can say that they considerably shaped their respective national as well as international discourse. They truly set new standard for the discipline, both in terms of form and content. The *Handbuch des Wohnungswesens* and *Town Planning in Practice* represented, each in their own way, turning points in the trend toward the use of manuals on urban planning. Both Eberstadt and Unwin referred to the previous discourse of technical and artistic urbanism introduced by Baumeister, Sitte, and Stübben. However, they qualified and extended it significantly: Unwin by incorporating the British discussion on the Garden City, and Eberstadt by bringing up land and housing issues and the economic, legal, and administrative aspects associated with them. In this sense, both manuals can be regarded as means of reflection and regulation—and not only with reference to urban structures and planning, but beyond that, to the general discourse on urban planning and the use of corresponding manuals in particular. [8]

Endnotes

1 Joseph Gantner, *Grundformen der europäischen Stadt: Versuch eines historischen Aufbaues in Genealogien* (Vienna: Schroll, 1928), p. 12. "Civic art" is used in the sense of the German *Stadtbaukunst* (comparable to the British "art of town planning" of the early twentieth century), as a more specific term than the more general *Städtebau*, defining itself primarily as an artistic, formal, as well as social task and commitment.

2 Reinhard Baumeister, *Stadt-Erweiterungen in technischer, baupolizeilicher und wirtschaftlicher Beziehung* (Berlin: Ernst & Korn, 1876).

3 Josef Stübben, "Der Städtebau," in *Handbuch der Architektur: Vierter Theil: Entwerfen, Anlage und Einrichtung der Gebäude: 9. Halb-Band*, ed. Josef Durm et al. (Darmstadt: Arnold Bergstrasser, 1890).

4 Camillo Sitte, *Der Städte-Bau nach seinen künstlerischen Grundsätzen: Ein Beitrag zur Lösung modernster Fragen der Architektur und monumentalen Plastik unter besonderer Beziehung auf Wien* (Vienna: Carl Graeser, 1889).

5 Ebenezer Howard, *To-Morrow: A Peaceful Path to Real Reform* (London: Swan Sonnenschein, 1898). The revised edition *Garden Cities of To-Morrow* was reissued in 1902 and received wide international attention. In 1899, Howard founded the British Garden City Association.

6 Raymond Unwin, *Town Planning in Practice: An Introduction to the Art of Designing Cities and Suburbs* (London/Leipzig: T. Fisher Unwin, 1909); Rudolf Eberstadt, *Handbuch des Wohnungswesens und der Wohnungsfrage* (Jena: Gustav Fischer, 1909). A more exhaustive analysis of the two manuals was published by Katrin Albrecht and Lukas Zurfluh in *Manuale zum Städtebau: Die Systematisierung des Wissens von der Stadt 1870–1950* (Berlin: Dom publishers, 2017), pp. 112–131, pp. 132–155.

7 Charles Mulford Robinson, *Modern Civic Art or The City Made Beautiful* (New York/London: G. P. Putnam's Sons, 1903); Thomas H. Mawson, *Civic Art: Studies in Town Planning Parks Boulevards and Open Spaces* (London: B. T. Batsford, 1911).

8 Paul Schultze-Naumburg, "Städtebau," in *Kulturarbeiten*, Vol. 4 (Munich: Kunstwartverlag Georg D. W. Callwey, 1906); Cornelius Gurlitt, *Handbuch des Städtebaues* (Berlin: Der Zirkel, 1920).

9 Apart from the books cited, see other publications by Baumeister and Stübben as well as Franz Adickes, Johannes Classen, Adelheid Dohna-Poninska (Arminius), Theodor Fritsch, Ewald and Felix Genzmer, Theodor Goecke, Karl Henrici, James Hobrecht, and so on. In Germany, the pioneering *Preußische Fluchtlinien-Gesetz* was enacted in 1875, urbanistic education started in 1890 at the Technische Hochschule Karlsruhe, and the first issue of *Der Städtebau* was published in 1904. A clear statement on the pioneering role of German town planning was given by John W. Simpson, "The Planning of Cities and Public Spaces," *Journal of the Royal Institute of Britisch Architects* 12 (April 8, 1905), pp. 341–342.

10 In France, the *Société française des architectes urbanistes* was founded in 1913 and the *École supérieure d'art public* in 1917, and then in 1919 the journal *La vie urbaine* was first published and the *Loi Cornudet* passed. In Italy, urbanistic education started in the 1920s, the Istituto Nazionale di Urbanistica was founded in 1930, and two years later it issued the journal *Urbanistica*; however, the *legge urbanistica* was not enacted until 1942.

11 See *The Transactions of the Royal Institute of British Architects Town Planning Conference, London, 10–15 October 1910* (London: Royal Institute of British Architects, 1911; reprinted ed. William Whyte, Abingdon/New York: Routledge, 2011), pp. 247–336.

12 Among them also Patrick Abercrombie, Thomas Adams, Stanley D. Adshead, Henry R. Aldridge, Patrick Geddes, Henry V. Lanchester, Thomas H. Mawson, John S. Nettlefold, George L. Pepler, Charles B. Purdom. See Gordon E. Cherry, *Pioneers in British Town Planning* (London: The Architectural Press, 1981).

13 On Unwin's work and biography see "The Royal Gold Medal. Presentation to Sir Raymond Unwin (F.), Past President at the Royal Institute of British Architects on Monday, 12 April 1937," *Journal of the Royal Institute of British Architects* 44 (April 24, 1937), pp. 580–590; "Memories of Raymond Unwin," *Town and Country Planning* 31 (November 1963), pp. 422–433; Walter L. Creese, ed., *The Legacy of Raymond Unwin: A Human Pattern for Planning* (Cambridge MA/London: MIT Press, 1967); Frank Jackson, *Sir Raymond Unwin: Architect, Planner and Visionary* (London: A. Zwemmer, 1985); Mervyn Miller, *Raymond Unwin: Garden Cities and Town Planning* (Leicester/London/New York: Leicester University Press, 1992).

14 Howard, *To-Morrow*; Thomas C. Horsfall, *The Improvement of the Dwellings and Surroundings of the People: The Example of Germany* (Manchester: Manchester University Press, 1904); Patrick Geddes, *City Development: A Study of Parks, Gardens and Culture-Institutes: A Report to the Carnegie Dunfermline Trust* (Edinburgh: Geddes, 1904). See also the early writings of Thomas Adams, Henry V. Lanchester, James E. Budgett Meakin, John S. Nettlefold, Benjamin S. Rowntree, Alfred R. Sennett, William Thompson, and H. Inigo Triggs.

15 Raymond Unwin, *Grundlagen des Städtebaus: Eine Anleitung zum Entwerfen städtebaulicher Anlagen*, trans. Lauchlan Mac Lean (Berlin: Otto Baumgärtel, 1910); Raymond Unwin, *L'étude pratique des plans de villes: Introduction à l'art de dessiner les plans d'aménagement et d'extension*, trans. William Mooser and Léon Jaussely (Paris: Librairie Centrale des Beaux-Arts, [1923?]). The eighth English edition was printed in 1932.

16 It was translated into Italian in 1971, Spanish 1984 and reissued in English, French and Italian. For a more complete editorial story see Katrin Albrecht, "Raymond Unwin: Town Planning in Practice, 1909," in *Manuale zum Städtebau*, pp. 137–38.

17 Unwin, *Town Planning*, pp. 13–14.

18 See Charles B. Purdom, "An introductory chapter," in *Town Theory and Practice*, ed. Charles B. Purdom (London: Benn Brothers, 1921), pp. 45–46.

19 Cf. Ernst May, "Stadterweiterung mittels Trabanten," *Der Städtebau* 19 (1922/23), pp. 51–55; Charles B. Purdom, *The Building of Satellite Towns: A Contribution to the Study of Town Development and Regional Planning* (London: Dent & Sons, 1925)

20 Unwin, *Town Planning*, p. 10.

21 The Hampstead Garden Suburb Act was enacted in 1906 to enable the implementation of the project. It provided the basis for the Housing, Town Planning etc. Act, which was reinforced by a new edict in 1919. See Edmund G. Bentley and Samuel Pointon Taylor, *A Practical Guide in the Preparation of Town Planning Schemes* (London: George Philip & Son, 1911), pp. 105–144.

22 See "Co-operation in building," in *The Art of Building a Home*, ed. Barry Parker and Raymond Unwin (London/New York/Bombay: Longmans, Green & Co., 1901), pp. 91–108; Unwin, *Town Planning* (see note 6), pp. 319–320; Raymond Unwin, *Nothing Gained by Overcrowding! How the Garden City*

Type of Development May Benefit Both Owner and Occupier (Westminster: P. S. King & Son, 1912).
23 Unwin, *Town Planning*, pp. 319–359.
24 Ibid., p. 197.
25 The images were based on photographs published in Richard Woernle's and Robert Schwerdtfeger's article "Buttstedt," *Der Städtebau* 5 (1908), no. 12, pp. 155–157, plates 89–94.
26 For example: Rudolf Eberstadt, *Magisterium und Fraternitas: Eine verwaltungsgeschichtliche Darstellung der Entstehung des Zunftwesens* (1897); Rudolf Eberstadt, *Der Ursprung des Zunftwesens und die älteren Handwerkerverbände des Mittelalters* (1900); Rudolf Eberstadt, *Der deutsche Kapitalmarkt* (1901).
27 For example: *Städtische Bodenfragen: Vier Abhandlungen (1894); Rheinische Wohnverhältnisse und ihre Bedeutung für das Wohnungswesen in Deutschland* (1903); "Das Wohnungswesen," in *Handbuch der Hygiene: Soziale Hygiene*, ed. Theodor Weyl (Jena: Gustav Fischer, 1904), pp. 307–388; *Die Spekulation im neuzeitlichen Städtebau: Eine Untersuchung der Grundlagen des städtischen Wohnungswesens: Zugleich eine Abwehr der gegen die systematische Wohnungsreform gerichteten Angriffe* (1907); *Neue Studien über Städtebau und Wohnungswesen* (1912); *Neue Studien über Städtebau und Wohnungswesen, Band II: Städtebau und Wohnungswesen in Holland* (1914); *Neue Studien über Städtebau und Wohnungswesen, Band III: Die Kleinwohnungen und das städtebauliche System in Brüssel und Antwerpen* (1919).
28 For example: "Zur Geschichte des Städtebaus," *Kunst und Künstler* 14 (1916), no. 9, pp. 419–432; "Städtebau und Siedlungswesen," in *Die Technik im zwanzigsten Jahrhundert: Fünfter (Ergänzungs-) Band: Bauingenieurwesen, Küstenbefeuerung, Luftbilderkundung*, ed. Adolf Miethe (Braunschweig: Georg Westermann, 1920), pp. 1–78.
29 Rudolf Eberstadt, Bruno Möhring and Richard Petersen, *Gross-Berlin: Ein Programm für die Planung der neuzeitlichen Grossstadt* (Berlin: Ernst Wasmuth, 1910); "III. 'Et in terra pax' – Rud. Eberstadt, Bruno Möhring und Richard Petersen: Erläuterungsbericht mit 16 Abbildungen im Text und 5 Extratafeln," in *Wettbewerb Gross-Berlin 1910: die preisgekrönten Entwürfe mit Erläuterungsberichten* (Berlin: Wasmuth, 1911).
30 *Bebauungsplan für den mittleren Ortsteil Treptow nebst Erläuterungsberichten von Rudolf Eberstadt/Bruno Möhring und Hermann Jansen*, ed. Magistrat Berlin (Berlin: Ernst Wasmuth, 1914).
31 On the Freie Scholle plan see Eberstadt, *Handbuch des Wohnungswesens*, p. 347 (Edn. 1917); Harald Bodenschatz, "Städtebau von den Neunziger Jahren des 19. Jahrhunderts bis zum Ersten Weltkrieg," in *Berlin und seine Bauten: Teil I – Städtebau* (Berlin: DOM Publishers, 2009), pp. 13–109, here p. 93. On Hermsdorf see Rudolf Eberstadt and Hermann Muthesius, "Kleinsiedlung der Hermsdorfer Bodengesellschaft in Hermsdorf bei Berlin," *Der Städtebau* 16 (1919), n. 1/2, pp. 6–9, plates 1–4; Hermann Muthesius, *Kleinhaus und Kleinsiedlung* (München: F. Bruckmann, 1920), p. 205; Bodenschatz, *Städtebau*, p. 77.
32 "Bisher wurde in städtebaulichen Untersuchungen nur die Frage gestellt: durch wen wurden die Städte gebaut? Die von mir vertretene Auffassung wirft dagegen die Frage auf: für wen werden unsere Städte gebaut? Hiermit wird der Gegenstand der Betrachtung wesentlich verändert. Durch die zweite Frage soll nicht etwa die erste ausgeschaltet werden. Vielmehr ist es in der Gegenwart wie in der Vergangenheit stets von großer Bedeutung, den Urheber und die bewegenden Kräfte im Städtebau zu kennen und festzustellen, wie die Veranstalter der Stadtanlage und die Träger der städtebaulichen Entwicklung sind. Aber nicht minder bedeutsam als die Frage nach dem Subjekt ist die nach dem Objekt des Städtebaues." Eberstadt, *Geschichte des Städtebaus*, p. 420.
33 Rudolf Eberstadt, "Town Planning in Germany: The Greater Berlin Competition," in *The Transactions of the Royal Institute of British Architects Town Planning Conference, London, 10–15 October 1910* (London: Royal Institute of British Architects, 1911; reprinted ed. William Whyte, Abingdon/New York: Routledge, 2011), pp. 313–333.
34 Eberstadt, *Handbuch des Wohnungswesens*, pp. 167–169 (Edn. 1909).
35 For further specifications see Lukas Zurfluh, "Rudolf Eberstadt: Handbuch des Wohnungswesens, 1909," in *Manuale zum Städtebau*, pp. 116–130.
36 Cf. Theodor Goecke, "Verkehrstraße und Wohnstraße," in *Preußische Jahrbücher* 73 (1893): pp. 85–104.
37 Eberstadt, Möhring, Petersen, *Gross-Berlin*, pp. 3–7; Eberstadt, *Handbuch des Wohnungswesens*, pp. 194–98 (Ed. 1910); Eberstadt, "Town Planning," pp. 326, 328.
38 Eberstadt, *Handbuch des Wohnungswesens*, pp. 207–217 (Edn. 1909), pp. 243–256 (Edn. 1910).
39 For further specifics see Zurfluh, "Eberstadt", pp. 127–129.
40 Unwin referred to Eberstadt's writings as well as those of the Dutch author Joachimus Pieter Fockema Andreae (1912) and the Russians Grigorij Dmitrievič Dubelir (1912) and Moisej Grigorievič Dikanskij (1915).
41 Paul Wolf, *Städtebau: Das Formproblem der Stadt in Vergangenheit und Zukunft* (Leipzig: Klinkhardt & Biermann, [1919]); Gurlitt, *Handbuch des Städtebaues*; Roman Heiligenthal, *Deutscher Städtebau: Ein Handbuch für Architekten, Ingenieure, Verwaltungsbeamte und Volkswirte* (Heidelberg: Carl Winter, 1921).
42 Eberstadt, Möhring, Petersen, *Gross-Berlin*, pp. 4–5; Eberstadt, *Handbuch des Wohnungswesens*, pp. 196–197 (Edn. 1910); *Wettbewerb Gross-Berlin 1910: Die preisgekrönten Entwürfe mit Erläuterungsberichten* (Berlin: Ernst Wasmuth, 1911), p. 4; Eberstadt, *Town Planning*, p. 328.
43 The diagrams can be found in the manuals and theoretical writings of Thomas H. Mawson (1911), Vladimir Nikolaevič Semenov (1912), Gustav Langen (1912), Martin Wagner (1915), Paul Wolf (1919) or Roman Heiligenthal (1921), and they were discussed in lectures on urban planning such as those by Hans Bernoulli held at the ETH in 1917/18, cf. sketchbook of Hans Schmidt, gta Archiv, ETH Zürich, 61-3-4.
44 Ernst May, "Stadterweiterungen mittels Trabanten," *Städtebau* 19 (1922/23), pp. 51–55.
45 Ernst May, "Die Wohnung für das Existenzminimum," in *Die Wohnung für das Existenzminimum*, ed. Internationale Kongresse für Neues Bauen (Frankfurt a. M.: Englert & Schlosser, 1930), pp. 10–16.
46 Unwin, however, was well aware that the wheel of time couldn't be turned back. For him, the Middle Ages were rather synonymous with the pre-industrial society and its form of towns.

PUBLIC SPACES AND SOCIAL CONCEPTS IN TOWN PLANNING SCHEMES

Recoding Urban Formations in Transatlantic Transfer Processes

Anna Minta

In the history of urban planning we can observe constant attempts to code and recode cityscapes. In many cases, these attempts at, and processes of, ascribing symbolic qualities to certain urbanistic forms not only follow aesthetic endeavors and changes in widespread public taste, but often comprise efforts to inscribe normative meaning into urban layouts and architectural forms which are expected to be understood by the majority of the public. This applies particularly to public spaces in large towns, where designed environments exert influence on the social practices of a wider public.[1] Despite this often-hegemonic intention to shape social behavior through the layout of cities and public spaces, I will demonstrate in this paper that, at least in the times of modernity, there exists no normative system that assigns fixed symbolic interpretations to specific urban formations. On the contrary: I argue that, instead of a strict system of images of the city that convey a consensus on collective political values and social order, there is a certain flexibility that allows the recoding of political iconography. The relationship of urban form to social meaning often depends on specific, rather individual circumstances. The political system, social conditions, economic situation, and historical and cultural traditions, as much as the urban and natural environment, all have an impact on the construction of meaning in cityscapes. As a provocative thesis I argue that urban patterns and spatial formations are often flexible "containers" which may accommodate a broad and heterogeneous spectrum of interpretations, and whose readability is dependent on the accompanying rhetoric and mediation strategies. As I will demonstrate, intentional practices of coding urban formations and cityscapes in their entirety are often rather successful. In some cases, rhetoric and symbolic acts manage to counteract earlier common conventions in interpreting specific urbanistic features and their symbolic qualities. I will use the US capital Washington, D.C. is used as a case study for flexible

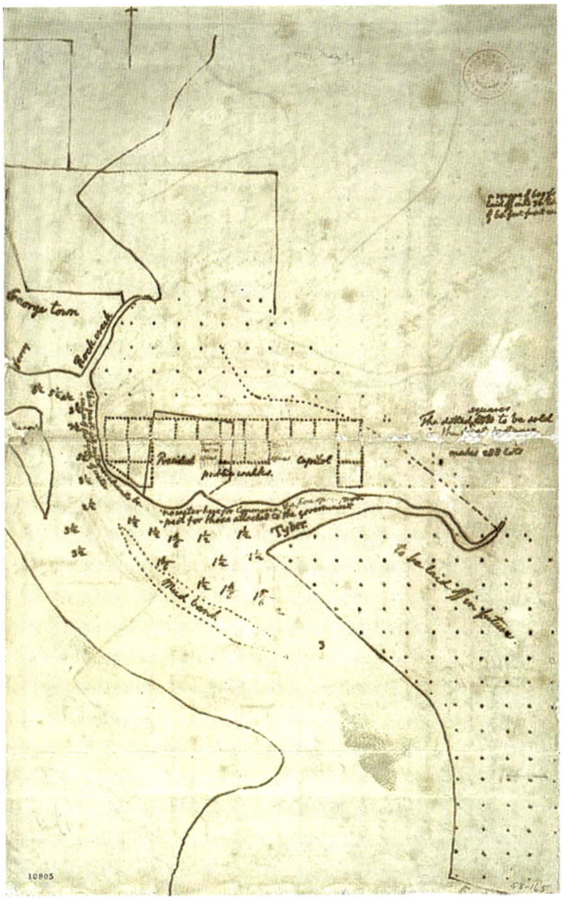

[1] Thomas Jefferson, *Master Plan for the Federal City*, Sketch, circa March 1791.

Source: Library of Congress, Washington, D.C., Manuscript Division, Thomas Jefferson Papers, Series 1. General Correspondence. 1651–1827, George Washington, March 31, 1791, Proclamation of Federal District with Map; Digital ID# us0074.

appropriations and coding processes of urban town planning formations.

After the capital's foundation in 1790, the city was continuously developed as a patriotic space symbolizing national history and identity. In its first master plan, the city was already laid out as a social space for learning and practicing civic virtues. With the United States having declared political independence from Europe in 1776, a liberation from the normative aesthetic doctrines of European art academies followed. Consequently, a new artistic liberty allowed for flexibility in adopting urban formations, removing them from their original context and layers of meaning, and incorporating new symbolic qualities. These appropriations, I argue, are not a consequence of ignorant backwardness but the sovereign result of adopting and reinterpreting urban and architectural forms with the explicit intention of superseding European traditions and establishing new urbanistic and symbolic schemes for the new American republic. The process of recoding the city resulted from America's increasing national self-conceptualization as an empire.

Furthermore, after exploring the ideological appropriation of town planning schemes and the manifold attempts to inscribe patriotic meaning into Washington's cityscape, I will compare this master plan and its inherent urban iconography to other contemporary town planning schemes, particularly in colonial contexts, which show similar planning patterns. By demonstrating that, despite formal similarities, they have in mind different urban images and sociopolitical concepts, I will support my argument that the symbolism of urban formations is not self-evident: official narratives and normative interpretations have always seemed to be necessary to establish and consolidate symbolic qualities in urban structures.

Washington, D.C.: Baroque Models for a Republican City

Long before current sociological and architectural discussions on the symbiotic relationship between the built environment and social behavior patterns (the socio-spatial dialectic[2]), the importance of town planning and its influence on structuring society and forming social practices had already been acknowledged by both planners and politicians. With the awareness of the prominent position of a capital city with respect to national and international representation, as well as its influence on shaping national consciousness, the founding of the city

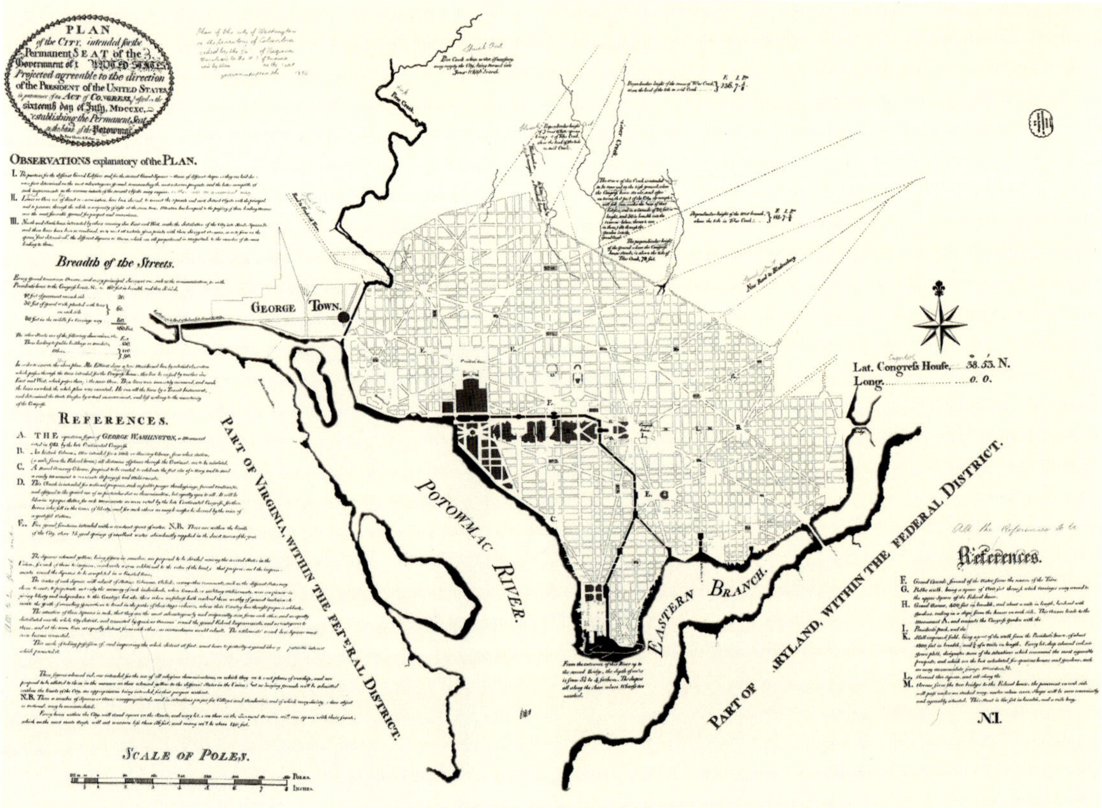

[2] Pierre Charles L'Enfant, *Plan of the city intended for the permanent seat of the government of t[he] United States […]*, ([n.p.], 1791, repr. [n.p.]: U.S. Geological Survey, 1991).

Source: Library of Congress, Washington, D.C., Geography and Map Division, G3850 1791. L41 1991.

of Washington as the capital of the United States was a highly symbolic act.[3] On June 16, 1790, Congress voted for the "Residence Act"— instead of naming an established city like Philadelphia or New York as the capital of the United States, a new city was to be founded.[4] Already, its geographic position—in the middle of the thirteen colonies that existed at the time—was meant to be a mediator between the southern and northern states.

From its very beginning, the capital was a contested space. Discussions regarding the design of the master plan were closely linked to the self-conception and political understanding of the newly founded republic. In this way, the perception of the United States as a confederate union with rather autonomous individual states was challenged by the image of a strong centralist state with ambitions of empire.[5] This conception of itself as a prospering empire was translated into a founding master plan—freely adopting urban formations of Baroque origin hereby translating the political absolutist hierarchy in spatial conceptions into a multi-focused conception of a republic.

US Secretary of State Thomas Jefferson opposed a grand imperial master plan. He was a supporter of a strong federal structure and therefore granted only limited representational power to a capital. He sketched a rough master plan in

March 1791 and repeatedly described his concept to President George Washington. [1] He explicitly traced his layout of a rigid checkerboard structure back to Babylonian urban settlements, explaining that the US could only benefit from this more than 3,000-year-old tradition of a highly civilized culture.[6] The regular grid of streets, claimed Jefferson, provided for an egalitarian division of building plots, symbolizing social equality. For the President's House and the Congress Building he reserved bigger plots, separated from each other. With two equal but independent solitary buildings, Jefferson attempted to illustrate the constitutional principle of the separation of powers. In the center of the future capital he outlined a large park area ("public walk"), envisioning it as a space for social gatherings. In summary, Jefferson envisioned a modest capital, placing public activities at the center of his sketch.

President Washington, by contrast, being convinced of the representational and therefore powerful function of the capital, decided on a monumental scheme laid out for massive future expansion presented in 1791 by the French-born engineer Charles Pierre L'Enfant, who had worked closely with George Washington before. [2] Aware of the importance and representational function of the capital, L'Enfant explained in a letter to Washington that his plans were "laid out on a dimension proportional to the greatness which ... the Capital of a powerful Empire ought to manifest."[7] Having grown up in Paris, he used Versailles and other European cities of grand scale as models for the axial layout of streets, as well as in locating important buildings as focal points-de-vue within a complex spatial design of streets, public spaces, and parks.[8] Similarly to Jefferson's sketch, the general layout and the placement of the democratic institutions in L'Enfant's design were meant to represent the constitutional principles of the American republic. The balance of legislative and executive power is represented by locating Congress and the White House on two distinctive hills within the rigid grid of city streets, with major diagonal roads radiating from them. At that time, the Supreme Court—as the third representational power in the republic—was not given a prominent location, but was housed in the Capitol building until 1935, as it had not yet developed its eventual functions and power.[9]

L'Enfant concentrated on establishing the center as a symbolic space celebrating the nation's history. He developed a scheme with which to visualize patriotic history and identity by providing numerous public sites and monuments. An equestrian statue of George Washington (today's Washington Monument) was supposed to mark the meeting-point of the two major axes that shape the Mall, with the White House and Capitol as reference points. Additionally, L'Enfant developed a series of squares in his master plan that were "most advantageously and reciprocally seen from each other and ... equally distributed over the whole City district, and connected by spacious avenues."[10] By spreading these spaces for national monuments ("Statues, Columns, and Obelisks, or any other ornament such as the different States may choose to erect") and monumental institutional buildings throughout the city, L'Enfant intended to architecturally manifest patriotic history; to "perpetuate memory" and to

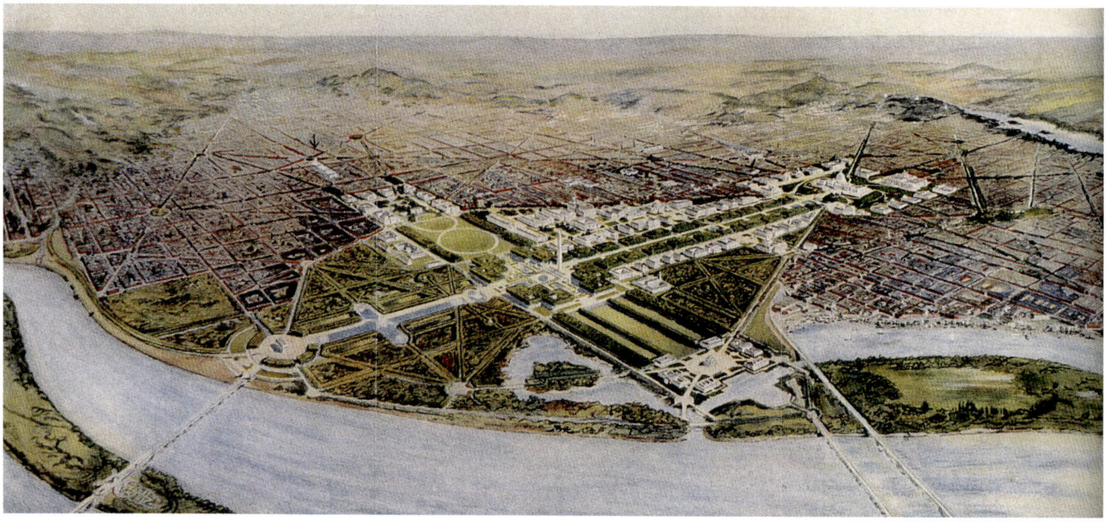

[3] F.L.V. Hoppin, *Senate Park Plan for Washington, D.C.*, 1901.

Source: Courtesy of the U.S. Commission of Fine Arts.

"invite the youth of succeeding generations to tread in the paths of those sages, or heroes whom their country has thought proper to celebrate".[11] This presence of the past in the form of normative national narratives in the urban environment was expected to support the collective reaffirmation of state and nation for present and future generations. Furthermore, L'Enfant projected a major ceremonial space in the city center in the form of a "national church" to ritually celebrate America's history and its protagonists: "This Church is intended for national purposes, such as public prayer, thanksgiving, funeral orations etc.... It will be likewise a proper shelter for such monuments as were voted by the late Continental Congress for those heroes who fell in the cause of liberty, and for such others as may hereafter be decreed by the voice of a grateful Nation."[12] L'Enfant's national church was never built, but over the years, numerous national monuments were located in the city center, thus establishing the Mall as a symbolic space for commemorating American history.[13]

Articles in newspapers and magazines in the eighteenth and nineteenth centuries reiterated the symbolic interpretation of Washington as a public, patriotic, and somehow sacred space. Early descriptions, like the anonymous "Essay on the City of Washington"[14] from 1795, already understood in their interpretations of the capital's urban structures the cultural concept of "civil religion"—the institutionalized collection of sacred beliefs about the American nation that is fundamental to hegemonic claims of America's superiority. The essay projects a visual translation of American history and values onto the capital's building politics.

It is remarkable that neither L'Enfant, the government, nor the people felt uncomfortable appropriating a formal city layout with hierarchical structured axes and public squares that had its origin in Baroque absolutist city and garden planning. L'Enfant must have observed similar planning principles in his native town of Versailles, where Louis XIV of France developed his palace and garden

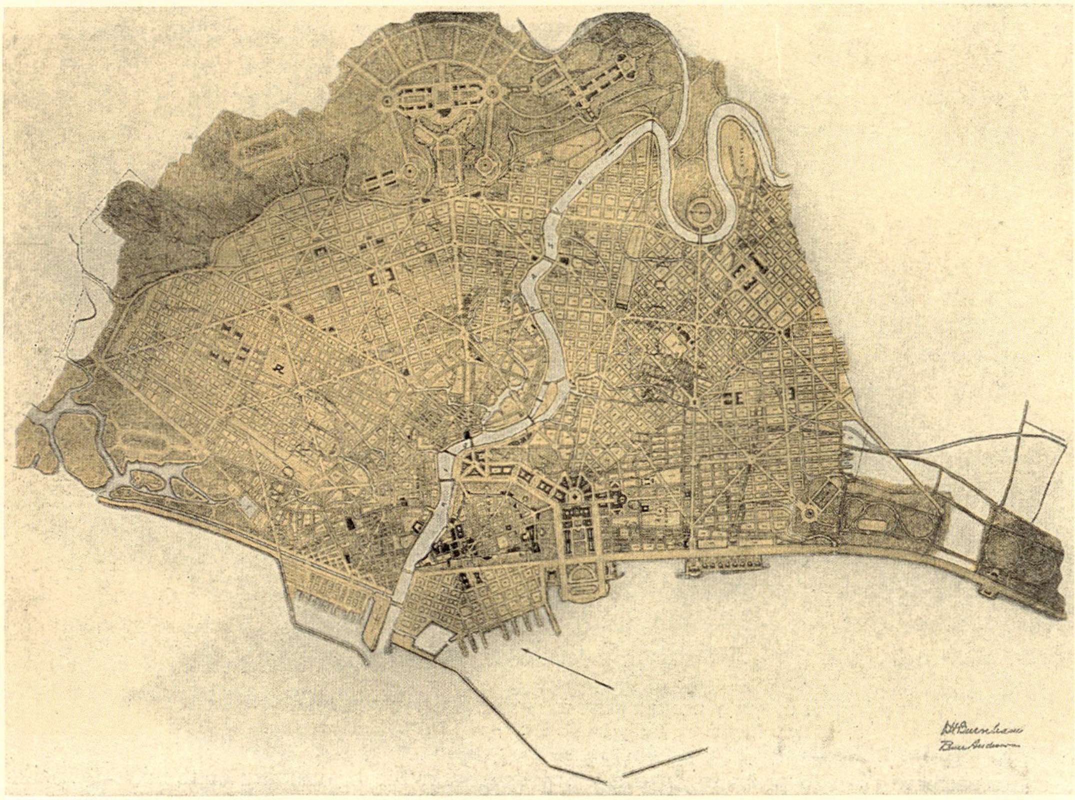

XXXI. PLANS FOR THE DEVELOPMENT OF MANILA, SUBMITTED TO THE PHILIPPINE COMMISSION BY D. H. BURNHAM, 1905.
The essential elements of this plan are the government center and system of proposed arteries radiating from it, the railway station, and the shore road.

[4] Daniel Burnham, *Manila, Philippines, Master plan* (1905).

Source: Daniel H. Burnham and Edward H. Bennett, Plan of Chicago (Chicago: The Commercial Club, 1909). Courtesy of Wikimedia.

in similar hierarchical patterns from 1661 onward. The Versailles Palace and gardens became the most prominent and most frequently copied model for the residence of an absolute monarch, translating the political system of a strictly centralized power into an overall master plan which manifests the absolutist power in the monarch's centrally located palace. L'Enfant instrumentalized urban formations which were traditionally and ideologically strongly related to absolutist planning patterns that celebrated the supremacy and exclusive power of an absolute monarch in their hierarchical spatial structure. L'Enfant integrated these formal principles into his master plan for the confederate capital of the United States. He recoded planning principles for republican purposes—most prominently establishing, besides the seat of the President, a second major *point-de-vue* for the Capitol in order to demonstrate the separation of powers in a democratic state. Additionally, he provided monuments and squares commemorating national history and its multiplicity of political, military, and civilian protagonists—thereby expanding the mono-focus of the absolutist Baroque plan into the multi-focus cityscape of a republican capital.

The process of the democratic-republican recoding of urban formations was well accepted by the American public. In 1898 the Board of Commissioners of the District called for intensified design efforts in developing and beautifying the capital, thereby further disconnecting the urban formations from their absolutist planning background. In 1901–02 the Senate Park Commission, chaired by the Chicago architect Daniel H. Burnham, increased the number of monumental structures to "inspire patriotism and a broader love of country."[15] Embedded in the urbanist reform theories of the City Beautiful movement, and referring to L'Enfant's ideas of "a grand city", "grand buildings", majestic aspect" and "grandest prospect,"[16] town planners promoted grandeur and beauty in public spaces in order to create social harmony and to spread civic and moral virtue among the urban population. [3]

Although the name of the City Beautiful movement hints primarily at aesthetic concerns, there are immanent sociopolitical concerns in its town planning ambitions too.[17] Overlaying the physical city structure with a symbolic scheme of political, social, and cultural values was clearly aimed at representing national self-understanding and international supremacy. Town planning discussions around 1900 frequently combined aesthetic concepts with moral values—beauty became a synonym for better citizenship. Town planning was understood as an instrument with which to educate the public. The American Journalist Charles Mulford Robinson, who became the first Professor for Civic Design at the University of Illinois in 1913 (along with Harvard one of the only two US universities offering Urban Planning courses), published his very successful book *Modern Civic Art or, The City Made Beautiful* in 1903, which in 1917 had already run to a fourth edition. In it, he describes "Civic Art" as something that "stands for more than beauty in the city. It represents a moral, intellectual, and administrative progress."[18] By defining civic qualities within City Beautiful theories he places moral values first. Municipal beauty, Robinson continues, is the result of an art in urban planning and architecture that serves social benefits and is aimed at improving urban living. He ignores the pressing social welfare concerns in urban planning of his time, such as that of affordable housing, and focuses exclusively on harmonious social order in aesthetic town planning concepts. Like the US concept of "civil religion," civic art is expected to combine moral, social, and political values in being thoroughly democratic and Christian. Robinson compares Washington, in its interrelation of urban layout and civic vision, with the biblical vision of a "new Jerusalem," providing in its urban structure and its grouping of public buildings an excellent example of a patriotic, democratic, and "beautiful" urban landscape. To emphasize the importance of public buildings and their function in communicating patriotic beliefs and civic consciousness, Robinson recommends elevating monumental buildings above adjacent buildings and separating them, preferably using parks, from everyday infrastructure. Broad avenues are to ensure the eminent presence of public buildings, thereby turning architecture and space into unavoidable educators of the public. Robinson, like other supporters of the City Beautiful, promoted urban reform and aimed

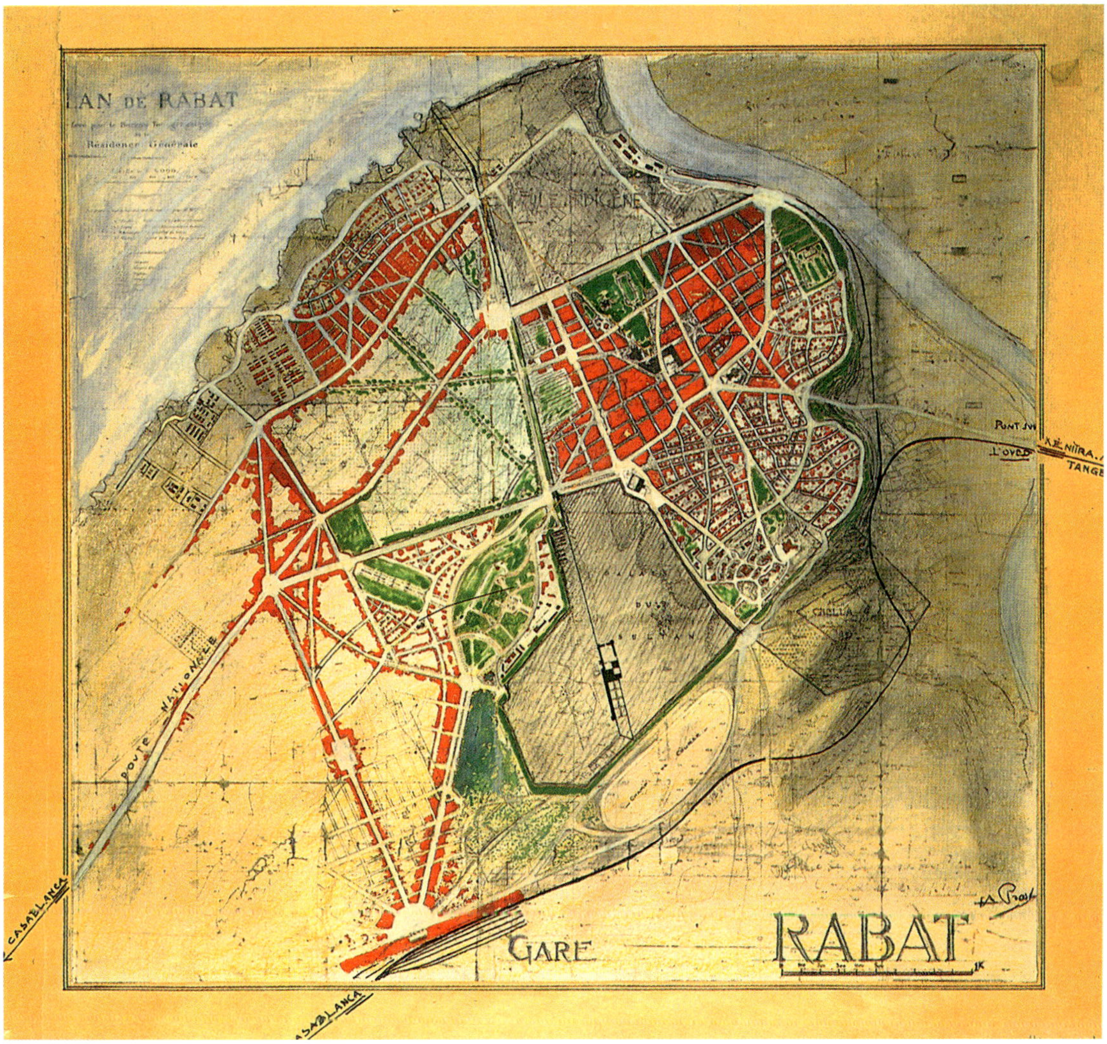

[5] Henri Prost, *Rabat, Morocco, Master plan*, ca. 1920.

Source: *L'Oeuvre de Henri Prost* (Paris: 1930), in *At the End of the Century. Hundert Jahre Gebaute Vision*. Exhibition catalog. (Cologne: Museum Ludwig Köln, 1998), p. 196.

for social reform and civic education at the same time. Urbanistic features, no matter their historic and ideological background, were instrumentalized through complex practices of recoding in order to communicate social meaning. Publications such as Werner Hegemann and Elbert Peets's *The American Vitruvius: An Architect's Handbook of Civic Art*, published in 1922, functioned as manuals for architects and town planners which offered a "thesaurus" of urban formations as civic art which could be integrated into various cityscapes but required symbolic interpretation to be coded with specific meaning.[19] In Washington, following City Beautiful concepts, this thesaurus of forms was instrumentalized to communicate civil virtues, sociopolitical values, and patriotic narratives—urban forms being successively depleted of their original absolutist planning background.

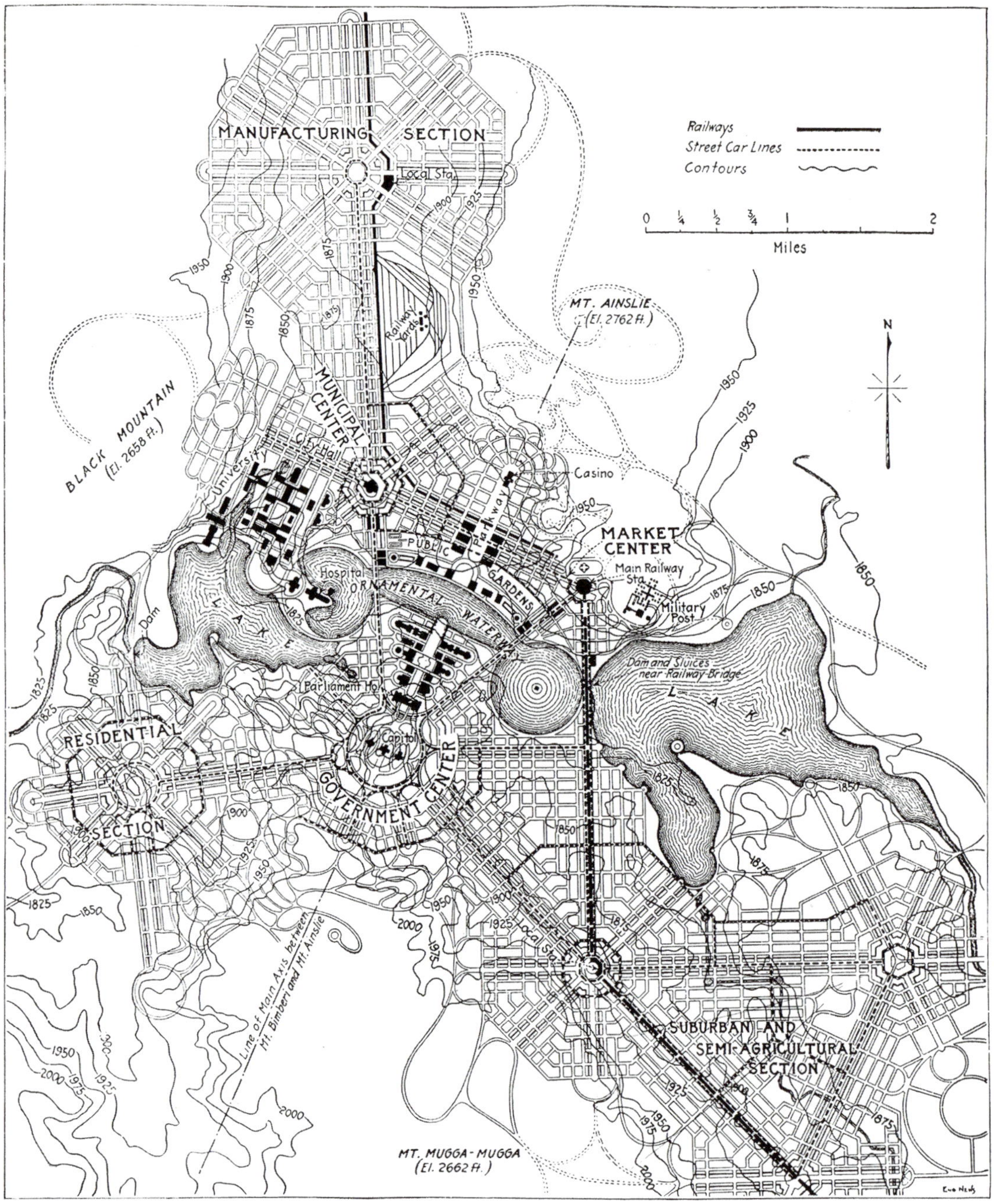

[6] Walter Burley Griffin and Marion Mahony Griffin, *Canberra, Australia, Master plan, 1911–1913.*

Reprinted from: Werner Hegemann and Elbert Peets, *The American Vitruvius: An Architect's Handbook of Civic Art* (New York: Architectural Book Publishing, 1922), p. 250.

The City Beautiful in the Colonial Context

The conception of the city as a work of art and the idea of a close interrelation between spatial order and social cohesion were fairly widespread from the late nineteenth century until the late 1920s. Key concepts in urban planning in the context of the City Beautiful movement were the beautification and introduction of monumental grandeur into urban environments in order to enhance moral and civic virtue among the urban population. Widespread urbanistic features for grand gestures were sets of ceremonial axes, hierarchical avenues, and public places framed by monumental Neo-Classical buildings, decorated with nationalistic artwork—all arranged in a harmonious balance of formality, symmetry and staged informality. Comparable to the British Garden City movement that exerted international influence on town planning debates, the American City Beautiful movement found its worldwide dissemination through competitions, consultancy, and colonial expansionism in the twentieth century.[20] Translated into different cultural and political environments, City Beautiful concepts were adapted to democratically inspired town planning processes as much as to authoritarian top-down plans—communicating ideas of loyalty, hegemony, control, and social order. Breaking with historical continuity in urban developments, imposed City Beautiful formations, grand spaces, and monumental structures were often used to showcase political power and prestige.

US planners and politicians, too, changed the intended sociopolitical meanings within their proposed urbanistic formations. In 1902, after the end of the Spanish-American and Philippine-American Wars, the United States was aiming for colonial expansion and became, for the first time, the imperial ruler of a distant territory. Since the Americans considered the Philippines to be in great need of civilizing improvements, the idea of bringing about social reform by imposing new city plans was propagated. The architect Daniel H. Burnham, who had previously worked on the Senate Park Commission expansion plan for Washington in 1901–02, and later on the *Plan for Chicago* in 1908, now drew redevelopment plans for the Philippine cities of Manila (as the winter capital) [4] and Baguio in the North (as the summer capital) in 1905.[21] On a formal level they show formations similar to those which were previously—in the US context—explicated as expressions of civic progress and its republican character. Burnham himself might have considered them to represent a translation of civic beauty ideals into a context outside the US. However, in the colonial context they suggest the imperialistic consciousness of the US, convinced of its own political hegemony and cultural superiority, by creating exclusive city structures, and thereby imposing rigid grid structures and ignoring local terrain. The grouping of public buildings and the layout of street patterns were intended to manifest Western values and to imprint American rule (and trade protectionism) upon the Philippines. A new monumental government district consisting of symmetrically grouped monumental buildings was proposed as a new central core for governmental activities. It was located next to the old town, which itself was preserved both for its picturesqueness and to demonstrate urban progress by juxtaposing the old and new town. Streets radiate from the central plaza to provide far-reaching visibility; as Burnham described it, "every part of the Capital City should look with deference toward the symbol of the Nation's power."[22]

Other colonial master plans, like Henri Prost's for Rabat (circa 1910–20) [5] in French Morocco and Ernest Hébrard's for Hanoi (1924) in French Indochina, likewise implemented urbanistic City Beautiful ideas: geometric structures and monumental buildings as urban figurations of an imperial policy aimed at perpetuating colonial power in the authoritarian cityscape. Better known are the master plans for the Australian capital Canberra [6], by Walter Burley Griffin and his wife Marion Mahony in 1911, and Edwin Lutyens and Herbert Baker's plans for imperial New Delhi in India (1912–30).[23]

These examples demonstrate that City Beautiful influences can be found in a wide range of master plans—spanning political backgrounds from democratic federalism to authoritarian imperialism. In most cases, the newly implemented city structures break with historical continuity in urban growth to showcase civic progress, cultural superiority, and political power with new monumental settings. Thus, urban forms are, to a certain extent, susceptible to symbolic coding activities. The appropriation of town planning schemes, manifold attempts to inscribe political, social, and moral meaning into aesthetic urban structures, and the implementation of similar planning patterns in heterogeneous contexts—all of these underline the importance of purposeful and selective strategies for coding and recoding urban and architectural forms and traditions in order to manifest performative social qualities.

Endnotes

1 As introduction to the wide field of sociology of space, see among others: Martina Löw, *Raumsoziologie* (Frankfurt am Main: Suhrkamp, 2001); Jörg Dünne and Stephan Günzel, eds., *Raumtheorie. Grundlagentexte aus Philosophie und Kulturwissenschaften* (Frankfurt am Main: Suhrkamp, 2006).

2 Edward W. Soja, "The Socio-Spatial Dialectic," *Annals of the Association of American Geographers* 70, no. 2 (1980): pp. 207–225; Edward W. Soja, *Postmodern Geographies. The Reassertion of Space in Critical Social Theory* (London and New York: Verso, 1989).

3 For a complex study of Washington's planning history and architectural debates, see Anna Minta, *Staatsbauten und Sakralarchitektur in Washington/DC. Stilkonzepte patriotischer Baukunst* (Berlin: Dietrich Reimer, 2015).

4 *An Act for Establishing the Temporary and Permanent Seat of the Government of the United States*, 1st Cong., 2nd Sess., CPAP XXVIII (July 16, 1790), p. 130. Secretary of State Thomas Jefferson compiled a list of possible cities appropriate to become the capital; see Thomas Jefferson, *Notes on the Permanent Seat of Congress, March 13, 1784," in Thomas Jefferson and the National Capital. 1783–1818*, ed. Saul K. Padover (Washington D.C.: U.S. Govt. Printing Office, 1946), pp. 6–9.

5 Lucie-Patrizia Arndt, *"Imperial city" versus "federal town": Die Vision einer Hauptstadt für die USA* (Berlin: LIT, 2008).

6 Letter from Thomas Jefferson to George Washington, April 10, 1791, in Padover, ed. *Thomas Jefferson*, pp. 60–61; see also John W. Reps, "Thomas Jefferson's Checkerboard Towns," in *Journal of the Society of Architectural Historians* 20, no. 3 (1961): pp. 108–114.

7 Pierre Charles L'Enfant to George Washington, n. d. (circa 1791), in *L'Enfant and Washington. 1791–1792. Published and Unpublished Documents Now Brought Together for the First Time*, ed. Elizabeth S. Kite (Baltimore, MD: Johns Hopkins University Press, 1929), p. 47.

8 Thomas Jefferson, who kept a large library, sent L'Enfant plans from Amsterdam, Bordeaux, Frankfurt, Karlsruhe, Lyon, Marseilles, Milan, Montpellier, Orleans, Paris, Strasbourg, and Turin; see John W. Reps, *Monumental Washington. The Planning and Development of the Capital Center* (Princeton, NJ: Princeton University Press, 1967), p. 15.

9 For a building history of the United States Supreme Court, see Minta, *Staatsbauten*, pp. 202–234.

10 Quote from L'Enfant's captions provided for the 1791 master plan; see Kite, *L'Enfant and Washington*, pp. 65–66.

11 Ibid.

12 Ibid. See also Anna Minta, "Planning a National Pantheon: Monuments in Washington/DC and the Creation of Symbolic Space," in *Public Space and the Ideology of Place in American Culture*, ed. M. Orvell and J. L. Meikle (Amsterdam and New York: Rodopi 2009), pp. 21–50.

13 For the development of the Mall, see Richard Longstreth, ed. *The Mall in Washington, 1791–1991* (Hanover and London: University Press of New England, 1991).

14 Anonymous, "Essay on the City of Washington," in *Gazette of the United States and Daily Evening Advertiser*, 11–13 February, 1795; reprint in Vittorio M. Lampugnani et al. eds., *Anthologie zum Städtebau Vol. 1* (Berlin: Gebr. Mann, 2008), pp. 107–115.

15 Petition by the Board of Commissioners of the District (Doc. No. 552, House of Representatives, 56th Congress, 2nd Session) reprinted in William V. Cox, *Celebration of the One Hundredth Anniversary of the Establishment of the Seat of Government in the District of Columbia* (Washington D.C.: U.S. Govt. Printing Office, 1901), p. 21. For the Senate Park Plan see Sue A. Kohler and Pamela Scott, eds., *Designing the Nation's Capital. The 1901 Plan for Washington, D.C.* (Washington D.C.:

U.S. Commission of Fine Arts, 2006).

16 Pierre Charles L'Enfant, "Note relative to the ground … for the seat of the Federal City," n.d. (circa end of March 1791), in Kite, *L'Enfant and Washington*, pp. 43–48.

17 William H. Wilson, *The City Beautiful Movement* (Baltimore, MD: Johns Hopkins University Press, 1989); Gilbert A. Stelter, "Rethinking the significance of the city beautiful idea," in *Urban Planning in a Changing World*, ed. Robert Freestone (London and New York: E & FN Spon, 2000), pp. 98–117. The City Beautiful has one of its origins in the Garden City movement. The British town planner Raymond Unwin published *Town Planning in Practice* in 1909, which was influential in Europe and the US: a compendium of images and theories on Garden City design influenced by the work of Camillo Sitte in Austria and Germany, William Morris and the British Arts and Crafts Movement, socialist ideas like those of Ebenezer Howard, and the biologist and town planner Patrick Geddes.

18 Charles Mulford Robinson, *Modern Civic Art or, The City Made Beautiful*, 2nd edn. (New York and London: G.B. Putnam's & Sons, 1904), p. 17.

19 Werner Hegemann and Elbert Peets, *The American Vitruvius: An Architects' Handbook of Civic Art* (New York: Architectural Book Publishing, 1922) illustrated and with comments on about 1200 examples of urban features.

20 Robert Freestone, "The Internationalization of the City Beautiful," *International Planning Studies* 23, no. 1 (2007): pp. 21–34. See also Jean Royer, *L'Urbanisme Aux Colonies et Dans Le Pays Tropicaux* (La Charité-sur-Loire: Delayance, 1932–35).

21 Thomas S. Hines, *Burnham of Chicago: Architect and Planner*, 2nd ed. (Chicago: University of Chicago Press, 1979); Ian Morley, "City Designing and Nationhood During the Early 1900s: Civic Design in the Philippines" (paper, International Planning History Society Conference, 2012). http://www.fau.usp.br/15-iphs-conference-sao-paulo-2012/abstractsAndPapersFiles/Sessions/33/Morley.pdf

22 Daniel H. Burnham et al., *Manila, P.I.: Plan of Proposed Improvements* (Washington D.C.: US Government Printing Office, 1906), cited after Hines, *Burnham of Chicago*, p. 203; reprint in Charles Moore, *Daniel H. Burnham: Architect, Planner of Cities* (Boston: Houghton Mifflin, Vol. 2, 1921).

23 Wolfgang Sonne, *Representing the State: Capital City Planning in the Early Twentieth Century* (Munich: Prestel, 2003).

CONSTRUCTING THE EVERYDAY
Housing Dr. Lassar's Urban Shower in Nineteenth-Century Berlin

Laila Seewang

In the summer of 1883, the German Hygiene Exhibition opened in Moabit a few hundred meters west of today's central train station in Berlin. There, located on a leftover triangle of land at the fringe of the city between a prison, two train stations, two hospitals, a military exercise ground, a new high school, and the Borsig factory, hygiene officially, if at first only temporarily, took its place among the other institutions ushering in modern life. Unfortunately, four days before the originally planned opening in 1882, the temporary wooden pavilions had proven themselves an architectural hazard to life and burned to the ground. This delayed the opening until the following year and provided the opportunity to erect a new steel and glass structure which could fully embody the sentiment of the exhibition's title: "The General German Exhibition in the Area of Hygiene and Safety" (Allgemeine Deutsche Ausstellung auf dem Gebiete der Hygiene und des Rettungswesens). Modern engineering would now take responsibility for the life and safety of both the visiting public and the exhibited artifacts. A grand forty-five-meter-high glass dome shone out over the city, bounded by four finial-topped towers, one of which showcased a novel elevator. The exhibition and its architecture, like all exhibitions, clearly had a representative function to fulfill, creating a temporary identity around which various narratives of public health coalesced.[1] It was thus both a catalyst and a reflection of the larger urban reality of hygiene changes already underway in Berlin. [1]

In 1883, Berlin was emerging from a notorious past; a time when pollution ran amok in the streets and cholera epidemics struck with regular ferocity, and when Berlin was known in the international press as a muddy, inefficient, infested, and overall smelly city—and this in an era not known for its cleanliness.[2] According to August Bebel, founding member of the Social Democrats in Germany, it was only in the 1870s that Berlin would transition from barbarism

Hauptansicht der Hygiene-Ausstellung.

Bilder aus der Hygiene-Ausstellung in Berlin. Originalzeichnungen von A. Plinke.

[1] Engraving of the Berlin Hygiene Exhibition of 1882–1883.

Source: "Die Hygiene-Austellung in Berlin," Über Land und Meer ([n.p.], 1883), p. 740.

to civilization through "a scientific-technological transformation of the urban environment."[3] This transformation would be to a large degree infrastructural, and restructure the lives of the entire population. This sets it apart from earlier recoding efforts, such as that by Schinkel, whose concert halls and palaces for the aristocratic elite in the earlier part of the century drew a cultural city out of its military shadows. If the exhibition represented the broader efforts of the municipality, that was attempting to bring order to the unruly urban environment, it was by no means the most visible aspect of this project. Many parts of Berlin were a huge construction site as the city laid, amongst other infrastructural works, its first municipal water supply and sewer system: the primary weapon in a war waged against dirt as the harbinger of physical and moral disease. Although the fresh water network (which brought in water to drink and to clean the streets), and the subaltern sewers (which removed wastewater in the blink of an eye) were largely invisible, their construction was altering the image of the city at multiple scales.

Within the city, this hygiene project produced a recognizable network of public works that began to aesthetically recode municipal architecture in red brick. Throughout the long construction period by various architects, the majority of the buildings for the water projects were built in the Neo-Gothic style: pump houses, water towers, reservoirs, machine rooms, housing for workers, and twelve pumping stations. This architectural identity wove together four distinct, heavily loaded historical narratives to form a complex set of meanings in a period of nation-building. If Goethe had popularized the Gothic as a German architectural style in his 1773 essay "Von deutscher Baukunst," by the nineteenth century Prussian restoration of, and conservation efforts on, medieval architecture and Teutonic fortresses had renewed the image of the Holy Roman Empire as a model upon which to build the new nation, and the Prussian Ministry of Public Works promulgated this style through funded research projects.[4] But most importantly, the municipality had appropriated this style and utilized it for most of the civic buildings in Berlin, of which the Red Town Hall (Rotes Rathaus) is the most notable. This architecture—of town halls, city gates, and other civic institutions—was identified most strongly with the municipal strength of the Hanseatic cities in the Middle Ages. In fact, the confusion over which of the overlapping narratives was being claimed by the buildings possibly led to a stronger architectural identification; that they could be interpreted as simultaneously Berlin-ish, Brandenburg-ish, Prussian, or German cemented the symbolic role they performed in the city. While the details of their architecture may not have been readable by the public the way in which, according to Victor Hugo, the average twelfth-century Parisian could still understand the messages contained within the façade of Notre Dame, there was at least a sense that this municipal network of buildings was historically and culturally appropriate.

The water projects also forged a dramatically new relationship with the environment at large. Although the symbolic meaning of the land itself had been changing rapidly since the Prussian Reform Edict was imposed by Napoleon in 1807—allowing, amongst other things, for the marketization of land and the abolition of serfdom—idealized landscapes were still integral to pre- and post-unification narratives of Germanness, not least that of the German forest. The introduction of major water infrastructure in Berlin resulted in concrete changes that shifted the understanding of the city's relationship to its countryside. Most noticeably, the pine forests around the Tegeler See and Müggelsee lakes were replaced by waterworks, a cultural loss that was lamented by poets and inhabitants alike.[5] With an impact that was less tangible to city dwellers but certainly more sizeable, increased land speculation and expropriation rights enabled Berlin to purchase estates outside of its boundaries upon which to build extensive sewage farms (*Rieselfelder)* to recycle the city's sewage, almost tripling the area of the municipality.[6] By 1890, when the first *Rieselfelder* were in operation, land in Brandenburg no longer brought with it images of aristocratic estates and small-scale farms, but rather of industrial-scale agriculture; this landscape was a service arena that processed the capital city's waste and produced its vegetables. With the customs wall torn down in 1860, and a water infrastructure that extended far beyond the city limits, Berlin was no longer seen to be in binary opposition to its hinterland, but had merged with it, and was managing its commodities.

The exhibition therefore represented the broader efforts of the municipality, which was attempting to bring order to the unruly urban environment. But it also played a role in distributing objects that would simultaneously help construct new identities and practices forecast by the technologies on display. Critical to this process was the intended audience, which in this case was largely German. Though the Hygiene Exhibition was aimed at the educated Berlin public in general, it was, according to reviews, mainly of interest only to "scientific and technical experts" leading Berlin's transformation into a modern and hygienic capital.[7] In their hands, the exhibited medical and technical products would radiate out from the pavilion into the city to effect this revolution from the ground up. Unlike previous exhibitions that had promoted First-Industrial-Revolution inventions that would define large industry at the outskirts of cities, these *applied* technological objects of the Second Industrial Revolution—in the hands of this scientific elite—would reach a mass population and recode not only the city but the everyday lives of most of its inhabitants.[8] These small items nested within a temporary exhibition were thus invested with large-scale expectations, which explains why the Prussian Crown Prince inaugurated the event as a "truly philanthropic endeavor" that would, thanks to the cooperation of state and industry, "elevate the wellbeing of the people." It heralded a future of modern enlightenment led by a bourgeois elite, "alleviating adversity and establishing welfare."[9]

By 1872, obligatory household connection to the new sewer system was accelerating attendant changes to the Berlin bathroom. It was here that the new apparatuses emerging from the Hygiene Exhibition began to connect citizens to their new aqueous environment—and thereby generated a wave of social ramifications. One hygiene installation in particular caught the attention of the media and viewing public in 1883, amidst a host of other apparatuses—such as sterilization equipment, embryoscopes, groundwater sensors, school desks, and orthopedic shoes—that mediated between society and its environment. Co-designed by public health advocate and founding member of the German Association for Public Baths Dr. Oskar Lassar and military engineer David Grove, a public shower was exhibited: a novel, upright bathing structure with individual cubicles, which entered the exhibition as a medical technology in the "Apparel and Skin Care" category. It was a wooden pavilion with entrances for women and men on either side of a cashier's booth. While doctors, engineers, scientists, and educated visitors were the audience for this new technology, the attendant documentation made it clear that it was intended for use on the bodies of the working classes: "the proletariat to whom such a moldy smell adhered," and for whom the more expensive, spatially demanding, and time-consuming practice of washing in a bathtub was still a luxury or a prescribed medical activity, rather than a daily necessity.[10] The shower would regulate the operative qualities of the

Dr. Lassar's Volksbad. Ansicht.

[2] Oskar Lassar and David Grove's model showers at the German Hygiene Exhibition, 1883.

Source: *Bericht über die Allgemeine deutsche Ausstellung auf dem Gebiete der Hygiene und des Rettungswesens* (Breslau: S. Schottlaender, 1885), p. 339.

skin—the opening and closing of pores—which was recast as the most important bio-technical organ at "the border between the self and the external world"; the external world consisting primarily of dirty and contagious air stagnating in dense living quarters.[11] [2]

It was at this scale that the battle for cleanliness would be fought, an effort by no means underestimated by Lassar. The shower—or more specifically the space under the running water from the showerhead and above the drain in the floor—became an interface where the body inserted itself into the infrastructure of the city at large. At the time of the Hygiene Exhibition in 1883, access to private forms of bathing was not within the reach of most Berliners, with cleanliness itself a concept more associated with white linen and moral living than water. In aristocratic households, the practice of maids bringing bathtubs and hot water into the bedroom persisted, while working-class houses generally had no access to private facilities at all. It was within the bourgeois world that private bathing practices as we know them today would germinate: urban households not luxurious enough to have a full staff of attendants to assist in bathing practices, but wealthy enough to embrace new technological fixtures and a private water supply. Lassar's shower was a novelty aimed at bringing bathing out of the private realm and into the public, transferring practices from one social group to a practice designed for public, universal use. Like other aspects of cultural modernity—associated with media, technology, banking, and political and educational institutions—the public realm was being constructed by bourgeois practice.[12] The shower was born of this world: a domesticated technology directed at the biological surface of the body.

Transferring this practice to the entire population would build upon two strands of resurgence in public bathing that had already begun to overcome the Victorian resistance to water at the beginning of the nineteenth century, with their respective architectures reflecting their differences. River baths (*Flussbäder*) had originated within the military both as a means of cleaning and of learning to swim, but soon spread to public use within the city—an example being the *Pfuelsche Flussbad*, founded in 1817. The first municipal public bath in Berlin was approved in 1850 and located on the banks of the Spree, with free bathing areas and changing rooms for men, and later for women, regulated by the police department who oversaw all commercial river use.[13] Simultaneous to the river baths, a growing interest existed in bathing as a restorative practice. Focused less on external cleaning and more on what Sigfried Giedion might later call "rejuvenation," these baths were modeled on ancient Roman or Greek baths or Turkish hammams, extensive histories of which were published both in architectural journals, as well as scientific ones such as the *Deutsche Vierteljahresschrift für öffentliche Gesundheitspflege* (German Quarterly for Public Hygiene).[14] The earliest baths built in Berlin followed on the heels of the better-known Mariannenbad in Vienna of 1818, and from 1873 included the luxurious Admiralsgartenbad.[15] Despite these two strands of bathing culture, it was clear that neither option was going to solve the problem of dirt at the right scale. The river baths were only available seven months of the year, the water itself was becoming increasingly polluted by private and commercial waste, and the luxury baths treated only a small fraction of the population. Lassar's urban shower was a radical departure from these models in that it attempted a universal application—cleaning all people, all year round—and could only have been imagined in conjunction with the new municipal water supply and removal networks. Bringing cleanliness to the working classes, however, demanded an efficiency that could not be met by existing means. He recognized that providing baths for the entire population would be neither economically nor spatially feasible.

In developing his shower prototype, Lassar looked to the Prussian military, where Grove had already constructed an early shower-bath in 1878.[16] The Prussian military were pioneers in cleaning efficiency and had been the first to test the shower as a method for mass cleaning. The speed of cleaning an entire regiment had been timed to the second. Grove had led experiments with a "primitive" installation that positioned and poured water over the heads of passing soldiers so that the entire Kaiserfranzgrenadier Regiment could be "cleaned and refreshed" every one to two weeks.[17] Lassar also documented and catalogued factories that provided bathing facilities for their workers. Before the municipal works, water was costly, piped to commercial and some residential customers either through a combination of small, private, discontiguous networks, or by the private Berlin Water Company (an English firm operating in Berlin). Only because of the clear threat of disease that accompanied large masses of bodies was it offered to (and enforced for) workers at all. Mining works and other types of visibly dirty work—those involving dye and lead, for

| 3

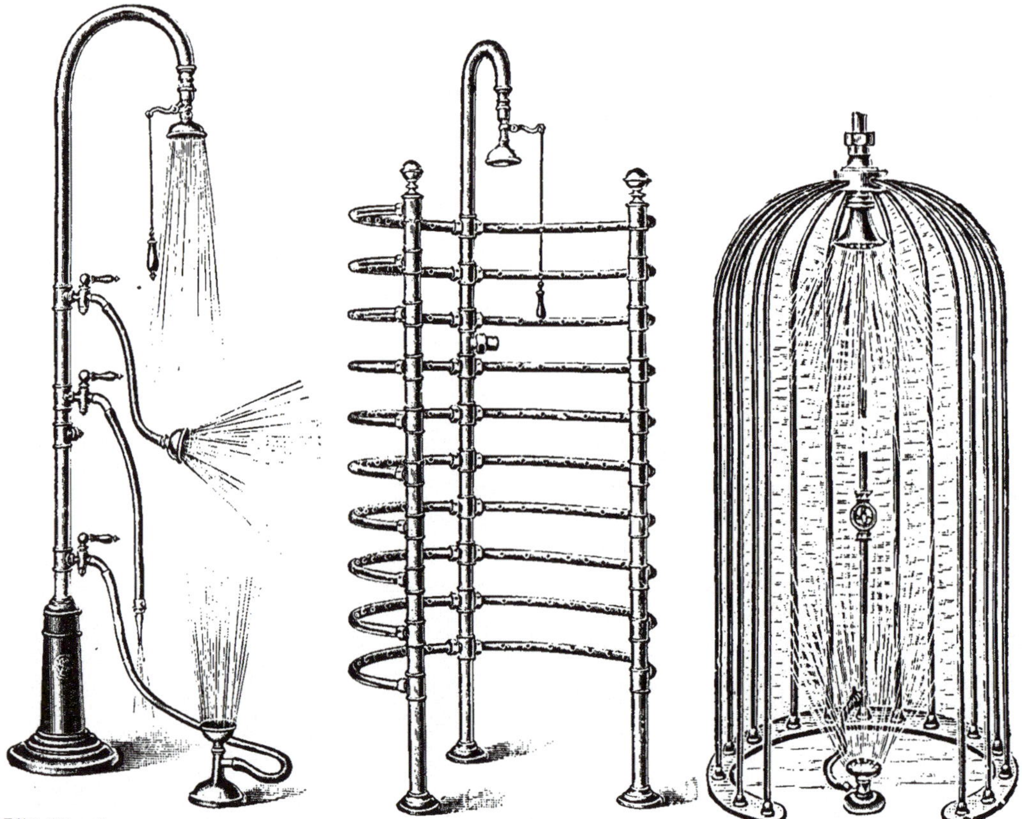

Bild 261. Brauseapparat mit Kopfbrause, Seiten- und Unterdusche nebst Strahl.

Bild 262. Manteldusche.

Bild 263. Kapellendusche.

[3] Experiments with shower formats.

Source: W. Schleyer, *Bäder und Badeanstalten* (Leipzig: Carl Scholtze Verlag für Architektur, Technik und Gewerbe, 1909), p. 346.

Example of a single shower unit for municipal use. Illustration by author: plan redrawn from Schleyer, *Bäder und Badeanstalten* (1909), p. 357.

example—were the first factories to shower their workers, often throwing in a clean uniform and a piece of soap. While Lassar considered some facilities, such as the Leipziger Wollkämmerei—with its separate male and female facilities, a bathing supervisor (*Bademeister)*, soap, and hand towels—to be excellent models, others were noted with some disapproval; for example the Krupp steelworks, which, though maintaining a workforce of over 10,000, had only seven cubicles for washing.[18]

Ultimately, as the drawings at the Hygiene Exhibition showed, Lassar envisaged his structure as part of the public street. Like the municipality's public urinal from 1879, it would service a newly mobile commuting population, and its architecture would combine sufficient light and airflow with a carefully calibrated privacy, regulating the oft-conflicting demands of visibility and propriety. Lassar concluded that, if located as visibly as possible on public squares, at busy traffic intersections, and at train stations, the structures would become both a functional part of the daily experience for the working population and a symbol of urban cleanliness, reminding them to wash themselves.[19] Although the model showers were ultimately built in the shape of a rectangle at the exhibition, the exhibited plan and axonometric drawing showed an octagonal structure, similar to both the urinals and an earlier shower design in Hamburg, which allowed for a core of centralized plumbing with an array of shower stalls around it. This minimized the floor area and made a freestanding facility in a public location feasible. Architectural considerations aside, the key difference between Lassar's pavilion-style urban showers and their factory and military precedents lay in the free use of the city's new fresh water supply, drawn in a constant flow from the hyporheic zones near the outlying lakes Tegeler See and Müggelsee. Pumped under pressure to the showerheads in the center of the pavilion, water would drench the bathers' bodies. The same water would be flushed through the streets and bathrooms of the city in volumes inconceivable before 1874, and it is this supply that made it possible to remove dirt from both bodies and streets, washing it away to the periphery of the city in seconds via the new underground sewers. [3]

The architectural problem of matching the right technology to the right structure and location had been solved, but Lassar realised that finding an appropriate form of bathing was only half the battle. His struggle to provide public baths to the whole population did not meet an existing demand, as the population was as yet unconvinced that visiting a bath was either necessary or safe. Instead, in order to fight the ever-present danger of epidemics, he had to instil the practice of bathing in the face of this social and moral resistance. Firstly, fears surrounding the sensitivity of the pores to air-borne miasma had to be replaced with a fear of dirt, the elimination of which required water-based cleansing and a piece of soap. More importantly, Lassar believed that the only way to ensure that the entire population bathed was to create a culture of cleanliness. In using the term "culture," Lassar appealed to popular discourses of nationality to consider cleanliness integral to German identity, just as ideas of "Germanness" infiltrated practically every other cultural discourse after the creation of the German nation in 1871. This culture would have to transcend the social differences that had hitherto defined a variety of heterogeneous bathing cultures: all classes, genders, ages, and religions would have to be considered equal in the face of hygiene re-education. With a universal application, the shower was a medical technology that would be applied to bodies (classless and genderless), rather than to persons (which came with social connotations). His battle cries, "Every German, one bath per week!" and "The Germans are a clean nation!" highlight that public water supply and waste water removal could be pitched as a national project, even though similar sanitation projects might have been undertaken in other European cities at the time.[20] This sentiment was echoed by architects, even going so far as to characterize nations by their bathing habits: "The cleanliness of a people is an exact measure of their level of culture, which we can see by an example: Japan has very developed bathing methods, while bathing in China is as good as unknown."[21]

Although one version of Lassar's design for a freestanding facility was built in Frankfurt, on the whole the shower-bath found little success on the streets—perhaps because the streets were too far removed from the pedagogy necessary to promote cleaning. Instead, the institutionalization of bathing and its municipal sponsorship and endorsement encouraged this cultural transition, which occurred most notably through the construction of affordable public baths in the inner city. In 1873, the Berlin Association for Public Baths (*Berliner Verein für Volksbäder*) opened its first bathing institution (*Volksbad*) and by 1886 was collaborating with the municipality on a public bath program, building large bathhouses that could serve everyone. As in his original proposal, Lassar pushed for a decentralized network of facilities to be located in the densest parts of the city, if possible next to the new municipal parks, in order to easily reach the largest number, and poorest, of bodies.[22] Competitions were held and published by the association, with designs being judged on symmetry, function, and materials, especially as certain material choices were easier to keep clean. Lighting and the ability to see dirt were critical parts of the designs, as were shiny tiles with rounded corners which allowed them to be more effectively cleaned: the bright, white bathroom proliferated. Most of the association's baths included shower facilities, private baths, and a large swimming pool. Lessons, hot water, soap, and a towel were provided, and surveys were taken. Everything—attendance, the age and gender of bathers, times of use, and amount of time spent cleaning—was documented and supervised under the strict eye of the superintendent (*Bademeister*) who was often housed in a small apartment at the top of the new institution.[23] The collection of data in turn led to the development of a more nuanced architectural program: for example, women were seen to favor bathing over showering, which led to more bath-rooms on the women's side of the facility, and certain groups were found to use the large swimming hall at different times, leading to different hours for women, men, and children. Attendance was highest on the days before public holidays—in 1899 this was the day before Pentecost—highlighting the association of bodily cleansing with religious and cultural rituals.[24]

The baths also acted as a space for material experimentation: one facility constructed at the beginning of the 1890s included two zinc bathtubs for cold-water showers, and another from a few years earlier included two copper bath tubs, which were at the time considered to be the most favorable for bathers.[25] While hot water was carefully limited, cold water arrived free and in seemingly limitless quantities, and a cold rinse soon became the universal standard after a modestly warm bath or short shower. The moral and cultural effects of this linger to this day, someone who "bathes in warm water" still being given a derogatory label in Germany.[26] With the adaptation of the shower to institutional buildings such as bathhouses, the semi-private shower unit now won out. Lassar proposed a compromise whereby three men could use one cubicle for the combination of the fastest cleaning with the most privacy, balancing technical efficiency with cultural norms: one man dries off and dresses behind a screen while another one showers and the third is waiting. This solution was deemed to be the most "German" way of cleaning, in contrast to "American" public bathing facilities with mass-changing areas or "English" bathtubs. In justifying the small-group changing rooms, which were clearly less spatially efficient than group changing areas, the debate also had recourse to cultural influences, claiming that Germans were less comfortable than their American counterparts with nudity, particularly when it came to the mixing of different age groups.[27] The program, as much as it supported and encouraged year-round cleaning for all classes, didn't reach as much of the population as desired. It was not always possible to place bath houses in the areas of the city where they were most needed, and integrating bathing into working schedules was not always feasible. The city thus redirected its efforts from providing baths to instilling bathing discipline, consciously focusing on urban schools. Here, the shower adopted explicitly pedagogic responsibilities: school children learned that cleaning the body was no longer a luxury but a medical necessity. The first school showers were installed in Göttingen in 1884, and it was within these types of facilities that the collected data from earlier *Volksbäder* would be standardized, habits would become internalized, and new practices would be introduced to the population at large. A Ministerial Decree in 1910 set institutionalized standards regulating such details as water temperature and length of showers, changing room layouts, and materials.[28] The school showers, directed at a socially homogeneous group of young boys, employed a more open architectural layout: one communal washing room with a grid of overhead showers and one changing room with individual cubicles and lockers became the norm. Discipline was achieved within these rooms, with showering, the temperature of the water (30°C), the use of soap, and the cleaning of feet regulated not only architecturally but also by the attendant superintendent or teacher. The development of a rigorous technique in practical cleanliness was seen as critical to both physical and moral pedagogy. Even today, young children in Germany are subjected to didactic hygiene narratives that draw upon nineteenth-century children's fables such as *Struwwelpeter* to instill the morality of cleanliness.[29] Although it was well into the twentieth century before showers and bathtubs in domestic bathrooms became standard—in many parts of Berlin not until after World War II had destroyed much of the rental housing built between the 1860s and 1880s—the practice began to permeate public expectations. A clean appearance in public reflected good morals and upbringing, and by the turn of the century advertisements for soap relied on a normalized image of cleanliness and domestic hygiene.[30] [4] The shower at the German Hygiene Exhibition was wildly successful, drawing over 10,000 paying customers. In some ways, the small installation could be seen as the silent recipient of the Crown Prince's praise for heralding the sanitary future in its entire moral and physical splendor. It is clear that infrastructure can be representative of political and cultural narratives—such as, for example, when Roosevelt turned a golden key to start the turbines of the Hoover Dam in 1936, dedicating it "in the name of the people of the United States, to whom you, Boulder Dam, are a symbol of greater things in the future," or when Hitler posed for photos shoveling gravel to build "his" Autobahn. Garibaldi's plans for diverting the Tiber River were the symbol around which he hoped to create a new Rome, and Tulla's straightening of the Rhine saved

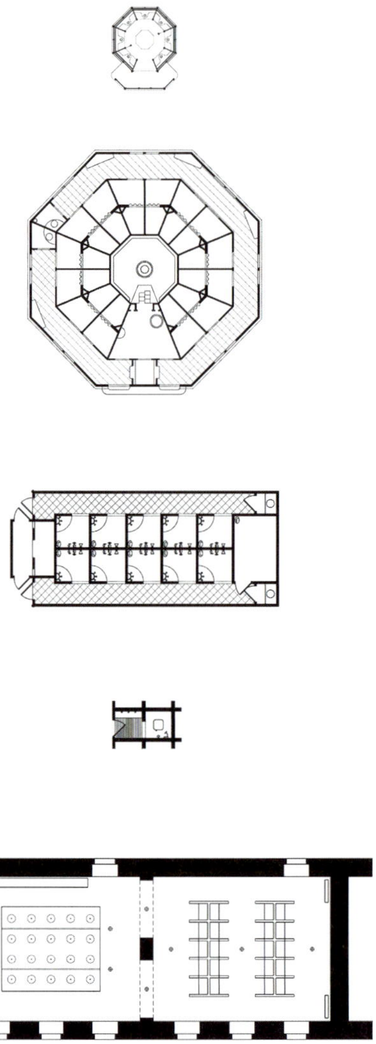

[4] The development of shower models. Illustrations by the author, from top:
"Achteck" municipal urinal, 1879; Lassar's urban shower, Meriansplatz, Frankfurt, 1888, plan redrawn from Schultze, Bau und Betrieb von Volksbadeanstalten (1893), p. 10;
Lassar and Grove's model showers as built at the Hygiene Exhibition of 1879, plan redrawn from Lassar, Über Volksbäder (1888), p. 19;
Example of a single shower unit for municipal use ca. 1909, plan redrawn from Schleyer, Bäder und Badeanstalten (1909), p. 357;
Berlin municipal school shower room, plan redrawn from Matzdorff, "Die Entwicklung des städtischen Volksbadewesens in Berlin," (1899), p. 20.

farms and created a new regional focus, simultaneously mobilizing the whole apparatus of state.[31] But infrastructure as small as the showerhead that emerged as a way of interacting with these large-scale systems can also be responsible for tangible cultural change. In the period, ideas of "Germanness" infiltrated practically every cultural discourse, which means that it is difficult to separate what was merely discussed as a national characteristic at the time and what aesthetic messages and habitual practices were truly at play in constructing identities and affinities within the population. Although Lassar's octagonal structure never graced the streets of Berlin, it generated an after-effect that was to contribute to the identity of the city and the public for a century to come.[32] It implemented a pedagogy of hygiene that ultimately became daily practice within the domestic realm, and co-constructed a public body that was diligently regulated by the networks of water infrastructure at both the scale of the skin and that of the municipal city at large. By the turn of the century the morning toilette of the whole city would generate the daily peak demands on its water infrastructure and the shower joined the myriad of technological interfaces that made up Berlin's physical and cultural every-day.

Endnotes

1 Alexander Geppert, *Fleeting Cities. Imperial Expositions in Fin-de-Siècle Europe* (London: Palgrave Macmillan, 2010), pp. 16–61. Geppert discusses the limitation of the German Industrial Exhibition of 1896 to a national, and largely Berlin-based audience, and in doing so expands on Georg Simmel's review of the exhibition "Die Berliner Gewerbe-Ausstellung" (*Die Zeit*, 1896)—in particular his claim that exhibitions create momentary centers of world civilization—to explore the representative and economic aspects of the exhibition.

2 Jules Huret, *Berlin um Neunzehnhundert* (Munich: Nicolai, 1909). In this collection of essays, Huret provides particularly detailed scathing reviews of the physical state of the city in the late-nineteenth century.

3 Martina Hessler, "Damned always to alter, but never to be: Berlin's Culture of Change around 1900," in Levin et al., eds., *Urban Modernity: Cultural Innovation in the Second Industrial Revolution* (Cambridge, MA and London: MIT Press, 2010), p. 170.

4 The notion that Gothic architecture, and by association the northern German brick Gothic architecture, is German dates back to early treatises on art from the sixteenth and seventeenth centuries, including those by Alberti, Scribanius and Sandrart. These references to the architecture of the Goths during the Renaissance were uncomplimentary at best, while most bordered on opprobrious. It was considered a vulgar, Christian style that was used to rebuild the cities of southern Europe in the wake of the devastation wrought on Rome after it fell to barbarian hordes. It was Goethe's "Von deutscher Baukunst" from 1773 that most loudly claimed the Gothic style as German within Germany, despite the fact that Viollet-le-Duc would soon prove that the style developed in France. The movement centered on Prussia was concerned with identifying the state with a Teutonic history, for which medieval fortresses were in the nineteenth century (as well as today) the most visible sign of the period of eastward colonization in the twelfth and thirteenth centuries; relics of the high point of the German-dominated Holy Roman Empire. The efforts of this movement are captured most notably in the monumental work by Friedrich Adler, *Mittelalterliche Backstein-Bauwerke des Preussischen Staates*, published serially between 1859 and 1898 (collected as a volume in 1862) in the *Zeitschrift für Bauwesen* and commissioned by the Prussian Ministry for Public Works. It is the first comprehensive documentation of medieval architecture in Prussia. The publication, eventually compiled as two volumes with two atlases of topographical studies and measured drawings and details, declares in its introduction that the homeland and source of this architecture was in northern Germany—specifically in the vicinity of the town Brandenburg. Also in its foreword, the author clearly states that the purpose of this survey and collection is to furnish contemporary Neo-Gothic building efforts with scientific, accurate, and detailed knowledge regarding medieval construction. Many historical narratives, most popularly that of Theodor Fontane in his *Wanderungen durch die Mark Brandenburg (1862–1889)*, recount the narrative of the founding of the Mark of Brandenburg as the start of the "Germanisation" and *"Christianisation" of the region, a process accompanied by rampant church*, cloister, and fortress building.

5 Willy Brandt—a poet living near the site of the second municipal waterworks—and his circle were particularly vocal regarding the cultural loss of the pine forests to make way for the new waterworks buildings.

6 For the size of the *Rieselfelder*, see: *Umweltatlas Berlin: Rieselfelder*, Senatsverwaltung für Stadtentwicklung und Umwelt, accessed 3/11/2016, http://www.stadtentwicklung.berlin.de/umwelt/umweltatlas/d110_02.htm

7 "Die Hygiene-Austellung in Berlin," *Über Land und Meer*, Vol. 37 ([n.p.], 1883), p. 739.

8 Thomas Hughes, "The City as Creator and Creation," in Christina Rathgeber and Josef Kleihues, eds., *Berlin New York: Like and Unlike* (New York City: Rizzoli Press, 1993), pp. 13–14. The characteristic differences in urban impact between the First and Second Industrial Revolutions are summarized as: "Smoke, fire, and masses of workers comprise our image of the First Industrial Revolution; humming dynamos, city streets illuminated by electric arcs and incandescents, intraurban electric transit, city planning and urban housing developments of an international style, engineers bent over drawing boards, Edisonian inventiveness, scientific managers, and white-coated scientists working in industrial laboratories and research institutes characterize the Second. Berlin and New York, not smoky Pennsylvania or Ruhr Valley towns, were the sites of the managerial, institutional, technical, and scientific developments of the second industrial revolution."

9 "Die Hygiene-Ausstellung in Berlin," *Über Land und Meer*, Vol. 37 ([n.p.], 1883), p. 739. The author writes: "Betont muß werden, daß diese Hygiene-Ausstellung für den Fachmann—und dieß sind in diesem Falle die Aerzte, Apotheker, Lazarethvorstände, Verwaltungsbeamte, Baumeister und Ingenieure—durchweg interessant sein mag, daß dieselbe jedoch dem großen Publikum nur wenig bietet." And later: "Das große, gebildete Publikum möchten wir aber bitten, nicht mit allzu großen Erwartungen zur 'Hygiene-Ausstellung' zu kommen." The Crown Prince's opening remarks as quoted by the article's author in full are: "Der großen Aufgabe, an welcher zu arbeiten Staat und Gesellschaft des wieder aufgerichteten Deutschen Reichs immer mehr als eine hohe Pflicht erkennen—der Hebung des Volkswohls—soll auch diese Hygiene-Ausstellung dienen und ein Zeugniß ablegen von dem, was Kunst und Wissenschaft, was Industrie und Gewerbe im Dienste dieser echt menschenfreundlichen Idee bisher zu leisten vermocht haben. Und so wird die Ausstellung auch für die Zukunft durch Aufklärung und Anregung segensreich wirken; wird ihren idealen, ihren edlen Zweck, Noth zu lindern und Wohlfahrt zu begründen, voll und ganz erfüllen."

10 Oskar Lassar, "Bade- und Waschanstalten," in *Bericht über die Allgemeine deutsche Ausstellung auf dem Gebiete der Hygiene und*

des Rettungswesens (Berlin: S. Schottlaender, 1885), p. 331. Lassar places the environmental blame on "der schimmelartige Geruch, der so vielen Angehörigen des Proletariats anhaftet, der mephitische Dunst in schlecht gelüfteten Schulstuben, die Dumpfheit in Gefängnissen und die kaum durch die kräftigste Ventilation zu reinigende Kasernenluft." Dillon elaborates on the exhibition, highlighting the split between the bourgeois generation of hygienic practices and their application to working class bodies: "The bath functioned at the boundary of the body, the skin, and was introduced as a medical technology." Jennifer Dillon, "Modernity, Sanitation and the Public Bath: Berlin, 1896-1930, as Archetype" (doctoral dissertation submitted to Duke University, 2007), pp. 48–60.

11 Oskar Lassar, "Bade- und Waschanstalten," in *Bericht über die Allgemeine deutsche Ausstellung auf dem Gebiete der Hygiene und des Rettungswesens* (Berlin: S. Schottlaender, 1885), p. 330; E. Bäumer, "Über Volksbäder," *Veröffentlichungen der Deutschen Gesellschaft für Volksbäder Band 1* (Berlin: August Hirschwald, 1902), p. 34: "Die Haut bildet die Grenze zwischen unserem Ich und der Aussenwelt, sie ist daher eher als alle andere Organe den schädlichen Einwirkungen der uns umgebenden Welt ausgesetzt."

12 For the bourgeois construction of public life in the nineteenth century, with particular relevance to the German context, see Jürgen Habermas, *The Structural Transformation of the Public Sphere: An Inquiry into a Category of Bourgeois Society*, trans. Thomas Burger with Frederick Lawrence (Cambridge, MA: MIT Press, 1991). For specific analysis of its cultural development through bourgeois male associations and clubs in Germany, see Geoff Eley, "Nations, Publics, and Political Cultures: Placing Habermas in the Nineteenth Century," in *Habermas and the Public Sphere*, ed. Craig Calhoun (Cambridge, MA: MIT Press, 2011).

13 Georg Matzdorff, "Die Entwicklung des städtischen Volksbadewesens in Berlin," *Veröffentlichungen der Deutschen Gesellschaft für Volksbäder Band 1 Heft 5* (1902), p. 11.

14 Sigfried Giedion, *Mechanization takes command: A contribution to anonymous history* (Minneapolis: University of Minnesota Press, 2013), p. 629.

15 Jennifer Dillon, "Modernity, Sanitation and the Public Bath: Berlin, 1896–1930" (doctoral dissertation submitted to Duke University, 2007), p. 148.

16 Rudolf Schultze, *Bau und Betrieb von Volksbadeanstalten* (Bonn: Emil Strauss Verlag, 1893), p. 8.

17 Oskar Lassar, "Das Volksbad," in *Thätigkeit des Berliner Vereins für Volksbäder* (Berlin: Julius Springer, 1896), p. 15.

18 Oskar Lassar, *Über Volksbäder* (Braunschweig: Friedrich Vieweg und Sohn, 1888), p. 12.

19 Oskar Lassar, "Bade- und Waschanstalten," in *Bericht über die Allgemeine deutsche Ausstellung auf dem Gebiete der Hygiene und des Rettungswesens* (Berlin: S. Schottlaender, 1885), p. 340.

20 Lassar, *Über Volksbäder*, p.13; Georg Matzdorff, "Die Entwicklung des städtischen Volksbadewesens in Berlin," *Veröffentlichungen der Deutschen Gesellschaft für Volksbäder Band 1* (Berlin: August Hirschwald, 1902), pp. 11–22; E. Bäumer discusses the cultural value of a nation's cleanliness in "Über Volksbäder" in the same volume, pp. 33–48.

21 E. Bäumer, "Über Volksbäder," *Veröffentlichungen der Deutschen Gesellschaft für Volksbäder Band 1* (1902), p. 41. In the original: "Die Reinlichkeit eines Volkes ist geradezu ein Maßstab für seine Kulturhöhe, daß sehen Sie an einem gerade jetzt sehr naheliegenden Beispiele: Japan besitzt ein sehr entwickeltes Badewesen, während das Baden in China so gut wie unbekannt ist."

22 Ende and Böckmann, "Die neuen Volks-Badeanstalten in Berlin," *Deutsche Bauzeitung* No. 32 (21. April 1888), p. 194.

23 Ibid. Ende and Bockmann here discuss the two Volks-Badeanstalten in Gartenstrasse 5 and Wallstrasse 50 built by the Gesellschaft für Volksbäder in 1888.

24 Georg Matzdorff, "Die Entwicklung des städtischen Volksbadewesens in Berlin," *Veröffentlichungen der Deutschen Gesellschaft für Volksbäder, Band 1* (1902), p. 14.

25 Ibid., pp. 11–22; Ende and Böckmann, "Die neuen Volks-Badeanstalten in Berlin," in *Deutsche Bauzeitung* No. 32 (21. April 1888), pp. 193–195.

26 For the cold-water apparatuses that were installed above bath tubs, see Ende and Böckmann, "Die neuen Volks-Badeanstalten in Berlin," in *Deutsche Bauzeitung* No. 32 (21. April 1888), p. 194. The term "Warmduscher" is a derogatory slang term used to describe a soft or wimpy character.

27 W. Schleyer, *Bäder und Badeanstalten* (Leipzig: Carl Scholtze Verlag für Architektur, Technik und Gewerbe, 1909), p. 23.

28 See Bäumer, "Die Entwicklung des städtischen Volksbadewesens in Berlin," in *Veröffentlichungen der Deutschen Gesellschaft für Volksbäder, Band 1* (1899), p. 37 and Deutsche Gesellschaft für Volksbäder, *Das Volksbad. Seine Errichtung und sein Betrieb* (Berlin: Julius Springer, 1919), pp. 41–46.

29 eDidact, *Gesund durch Körperpflege und Sauberkeit (1.–2. Klasse)* (Landsberg: Olzog Verlag, 2012).

30 Ute Daniel, "Der unaufhaltsame Aufstieg des sauberen Individuums. Seifen- und Waschmittelwerbung im historischen Kontext," in Imbke Behnken, ed. *Stadtgesellschaft und Kindheit im Prozess der Zivilisation. Konfigurationen städtischer Lebensweise zu Beginn des 20. Jahrhunderts* (Opalden: Leske + Budrich, 1990), p. 48.

31 *The New York Times*, September 12, 1936. Blackbourn, in discussing the straightening of the Rhine in the eighteenth and nineteenth centuries, writes: "Tulla's project meant, in effect, that the whole apparatus of state was mobilized." David Blackbourn, *The Conquest of Nature: Water, Landscape, and the Making of Modern Germany* (New York: W. W. Norton, 2006), p. 94.

32 Paul Gerhard, *Modern Baths and Bath Houses* (New York: John Wiley and Sons, 1908), pp. 30–36.

ABOVE AND BELOW THE STREET LEVEL

Recoding the Street Façade and the Urban Soil

Harald R. Stühlinger

Over the course of the nineteenth century, the face of street surfaces began to change in every city, both large and small, following the introduction of constantly growing infrastructural equipment into the urban below-ground. This new coding—but also recoding—of the neglected fifth façade of urban space was ignited by a change in production methods and design, and the proliferation of man- and handhole covers. What started almost two centuries ago is—in different ways—still going on today.

In antiquity, canalization infrastructure already existed in various regions of the world. By this term we understand an underground system of pipes to dispose waste water—pluvial or waste—away from the city. An outstanding and prominent ancient example of the disposal of water was the Cloaca Maxima in Rome, which at the same time drained the lower part of the then-important Forum Romanum. It gives its name to one of the two systems used in different European cities in the beginning of modernity. Simultaneously, other infrastructural networks such as those for gas, the telegraph, telephones, electricity, and others were being laid into the urban soil. When creating an underground network for these different systems, maintenance openings had to be introduced in order to allow access to the pipes, tubes, and conduits. These openings—manhole and handhole covers and so forth—were first executed in wood and stone, but these materials were replaced with longer-lasting iron over the course of the Industrial Revolution.

In the first half of the nineteenth century, and much more so in the second half, European cities and metropolises exerted a tremendous pull on the rural population. This fostered not only an accumulation of manpower and a rise in population density, but also led to hygiene issues which resulted in epidemics of tuberculosis and cholera. In order to resolve this problem, which was intrinsically linked to the urbanization phenomenon of the nineteenth century,

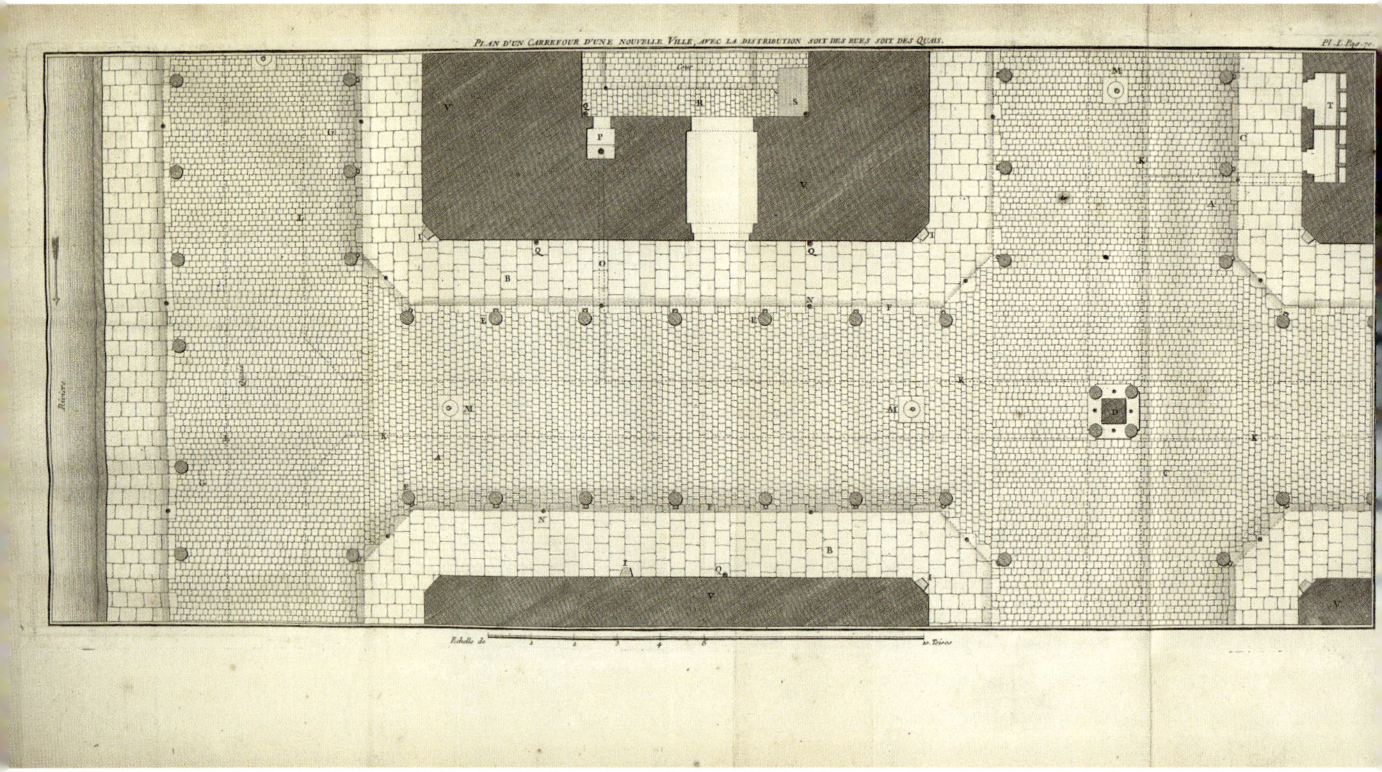

[1] Pierre Patte, section and a plan of a street in an ideal city, 1769 ("Plate I").

Source: Pierre Patte, *Mémoires sur les objets les plus importans de l'architecture* (Paris: Rozet, 1769).

hygiene systems were first tested in and introduced to larger metropolises, and then to smaller cities, towns, and villages. Engineers, doctors, and politicians discussed two systems which were already in use: cesspits and sewers (in the German speaking world these were also called "Cloaken"). Cities like Paris believed that their system of cesspits was the best way to avoid the epidemics, while other cities, like Vienna, saw in their sewer system—although still quite primitive and dating back to the eighteenth century—the future of canalization.

Drawings of ideal street sections are known from as early as 1693, when the French planner Henri Gautier systematized streets hierarchically.[1] He only depicted the elements above ground, but by the middle of the eighteenth century already street sections could also be found for the area underground. Subsequently, with the potential of the urban soil as a means of housing infrastructural networks, the street section began to fill up with more and more infrastructures, and holistic urban planning processes became necessary.

Early Depictions of Canalization and Covers

From the seventeenth to the nineteenth century, planners, philosophers, artists, and church officials alike questioned the condition of the city of Paris as an aesthetic object and called for its beautification. For most of those years, Paris served as a role model in urban planning, as can be seen in embellishment plans for many European cities.

The eighteenth-century French architect Pierre Patte published two plates in his *Mémoires sur les objets les plus importans de l'architecture*[2] showing a section and a plan of a street in an ideal city [1]. There, he shows the course of pluvial water from the roofs of the houses and streets as well as the wastewater from kitchens and toilets to a canal centrally located in the middle of the street. In the ground plan, he indicates not only the gutters on either side of the paved streets but also manhole covers located above the canals. In his drawing, the manhole covers are round objects perhaps considered to be obviously executed in stone. In a contemporary drawing by Eugénio dos Santos, the lead planner for the reconstruction of Lisbon after the earthquake, tsunami, and fire of 1755, he shows standardized houses which line a uniformed street with sidewalks separated from the road.[3] In the middle of the road, one can discern a square manhole cover. Unlike Patte's monolithic round stone covers, it seems to be an iron grille with several openings for water to enter the canal underneath. None of these eighteenth-century examples—even if they were executed in exactly the proposed way—can be found in situ today. The only remnants of these ideal and avant-garde plans are the drawings.

The Conquest of the Urban Ground

Over the course of the nineteenth century, the introduction of gas lighting and the supply of water through an ingenious network of water reservoirs, as well as the disposal of wastewater, fostered a reorganization of the urban ground. What subsequently occurred was the proliferation and sprawl of infrastructure into the soils of European cities. Much like the technical equipment building the infrastructure, several popular magazines and illustrated newspapers delivered surgically precise views into the dissected urban underground. During Paris's enormous second wave of embellishment under Napoleon III and Georges-Eugène Haussmann, the new underground infrastructure was of great interest. As early as the beginning of the Second Empire in 1852, the magazine *Tableau de Paris* published a fictional perspective of a street section [2]. The reader could not only make out the pipes for the water and gas supply, but also the workers manipulating devices, doing maintenance work, and removing manhole covers from a shaft with a pole. A few years later, in 1866, an even more elaborate section was shown in the popular magazine *Daheim*.[4] The keen interest of the bourgeoisie in their modern urban surroundings was satisfied through images and explanations of the systems under their feet, as well as through tourist-like visits to the canals—the first ones in Paris, with tours later being offered in other metropolises. The new medium of photography played—at least in Paris—an important role. As early as the late 1850s, one of the proponents of photography in the French capital was Nadar (Gaspar-Félix Tournachon), who with his camera and an early example of flash equipment strode through the uncanny world of the Parisian canals to create some of the most illuminating views of nineteenth-century urban photography.

Une rue souterraine à Paris.

[2] *Une rue souterraine à Paris.*
Source: Edmond Texier, Tableau de Paris (1852), p. 75.

The best-known planning figure in Berlin in the late 1850s and early 1860s was the hydrotechnical engineer James Hobrecht, who created an extension plan for the city of Berlin. Being an expert in canalization, he conceived of a structural network of wastewater canals and adapted the newly developed neighborhoods to follow the main arteries of his canal system. Later in his career, he published the results of his work in Berlin, which consisted of a textbook and an atlas in which he presented interventions from the largest to the smallest scale.[5] In one plate, he explains—exactly like Pierre Patte—how wastewater from the toilet and kitchen found its way to the sewer. While the fountain in the French planner's image was a public fountain in the center of a crossroads, Hobrecht's was a private one located in the garden behind the house. In another plate, he shows the different dimensions of the canals—but, more importantly, provides detailed drawings of manhole covers and gullies [3]. These are among the first accurate depictions of manhole covers in technical publications, while the catalogues of foundries at the same time showed them as commercial objects. [4]
The planners who first dealt with the organization of the urban underground found no limitations in this new "terrain," as the ground under the streets

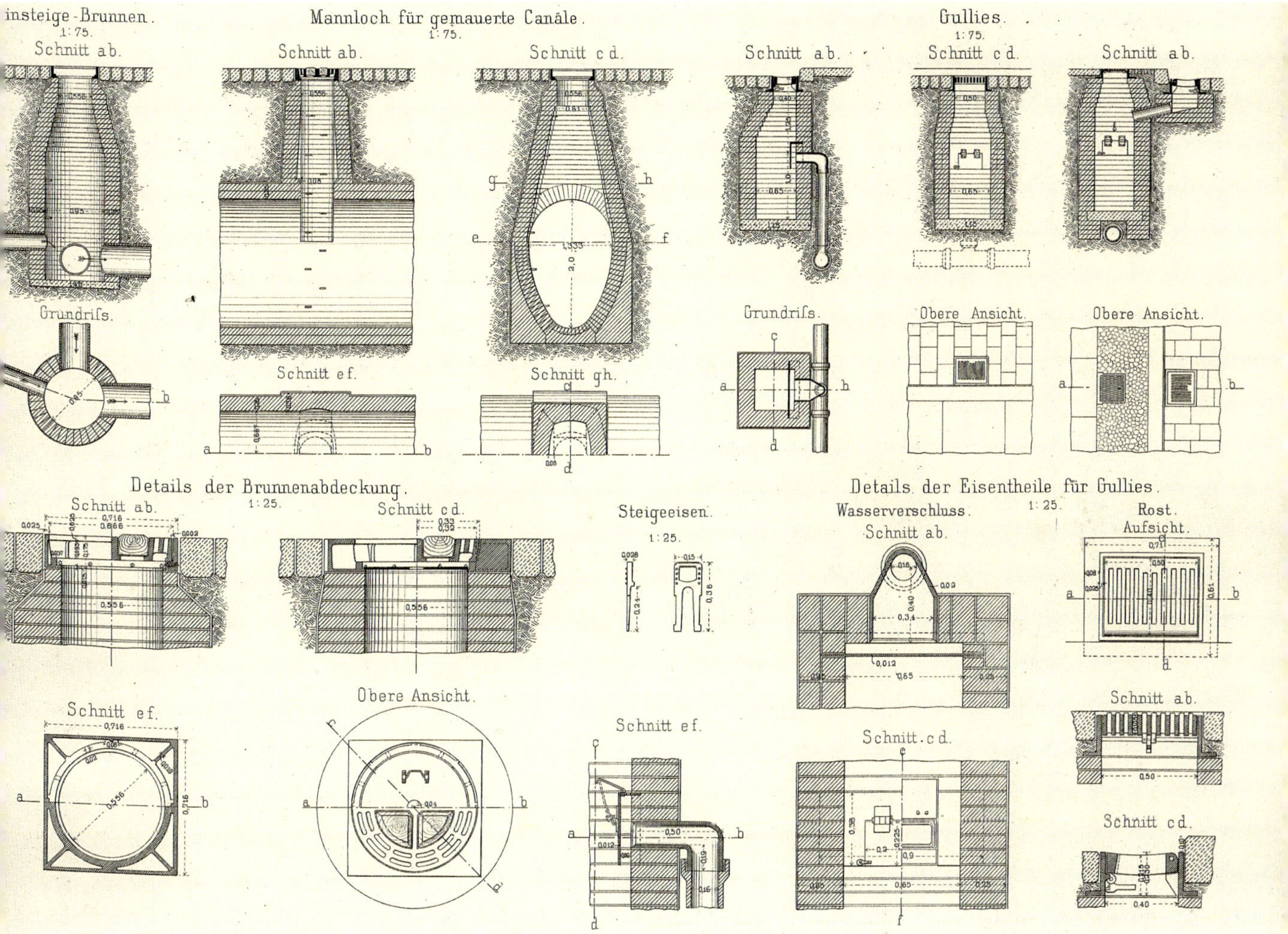

[3] James Hobrecht, drawings of manhole covers and gullies ("Plate 9"), 1884.

Source: James Hobrecht, *Die Canalisation von Berlin: im Auftrage des Magistrats der königl. Haupt- und Residenzstadt Berlin* (Berlin: Ernst & Korn, 1884).

was practically devoid of any technical devices. In the first half of the nineteenth century, gas and water pipes and sewers slowly conquered the soil under the streets—but by the end of the nineteenth century, the lack of available space had become an issue and a meticulous organization of the ground was arranged, in which each infrastructural line had its own assigned location. Joseph Brix demonstrated how to organize the manifold infrastructural pipes (telegraph and telephone lines, electricity cables, and communication cables for fire fighters or the police, and so on) under a medium-sized four-meter-wide sidewalk.[6] It is obvious why these pipes were put under the sidewalk; the obstruction in case of maintenance, repair, or replacement would affect only the easily diverted pedestrian traffic, instead of the still-chaotic and only barely organized vehicular traffic.

At the turn of the twentieth century, the infrastructural systems were depicted in technical publications. Books and brochures were dedicated to representations

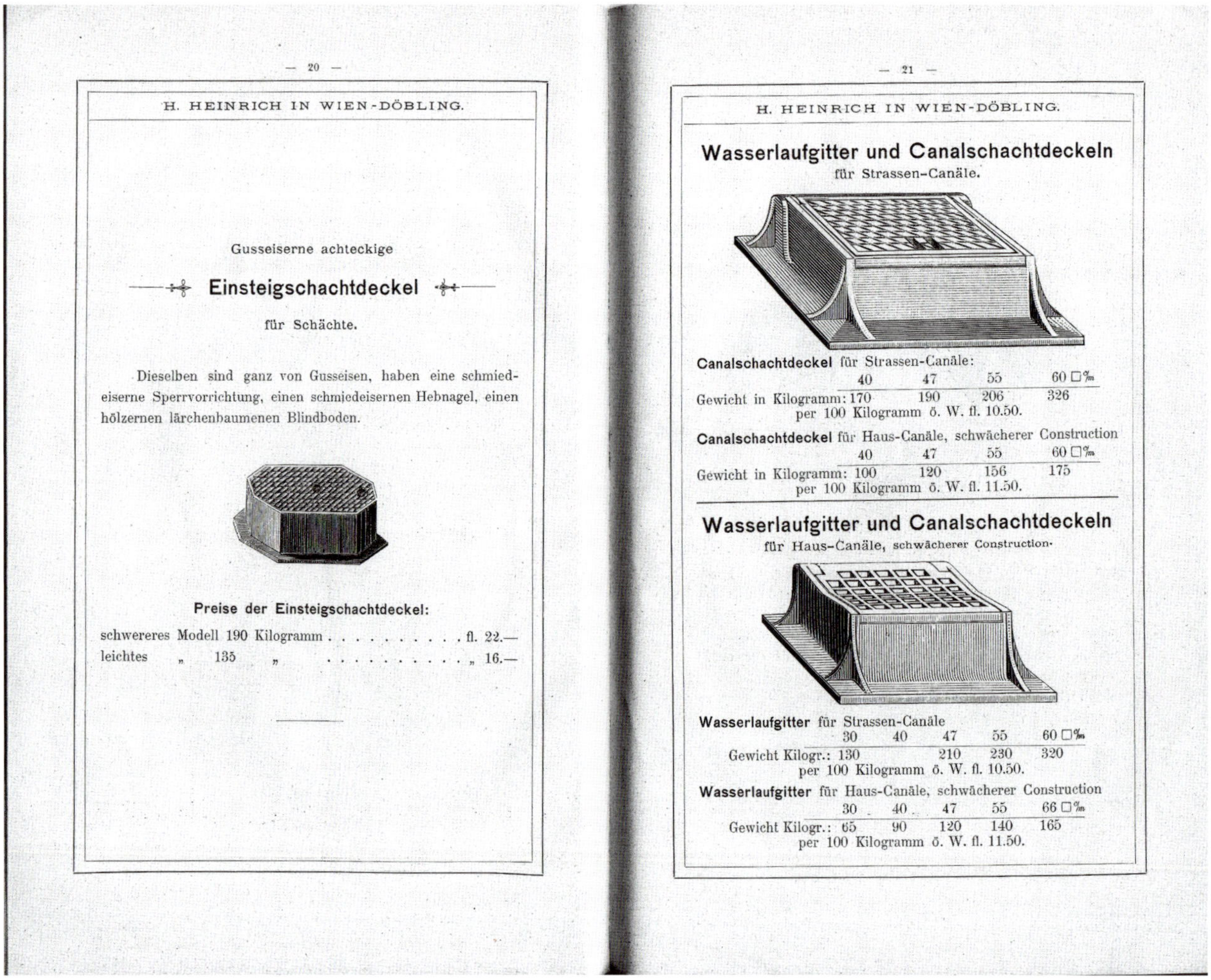

— 20 —

H. HEINRICH IN WIEN-DÖBLING.

Gusseiserne achteckige

Einsteigschachtdeckel

für Schächte.

Dieselben sind ganz von Gusseisen, haben eine schmiedeiserne Sperrvorrichtung, einen schmiedeisernen Hebnagel, einen hölzernen lärchenbaumenen Blindboden.

Preise der Einsteigschachtdeckel:

schwereres Modell 190 Kilogramm . . . . fl. 22.—
leichtes „ 135 „ . . . . „ 16.—

— 21 —

H. HEINRICH IN WIEN-DÖBLING.

Wasserlaufgitter und Canalschachtdeckeln

für Strassen-Canäle.

Canalschachtdeckel für Strassen-Canäle:

	40	47	55	60 □%
Gewicht in Kilogramm:	170	190	206	326

per 100 Kilogramm ö. W. fl. 10.50.

Canalschachtdeckel für Haus-Canäle, schwächerer Construction

	40	47	55	60 □%
Gewicht in Kilogramm:	100	120	156	175

per 100 Kilogramm ö. W. fl. 11.50.

Wasserlaufgitter und Canalschachtdeckeln

für Haus-Canäle, schwächerer Construction.

Wasserlaufgitter für Strassen-Canäle

	30	40	47	55	60 □%
Gewicht Kilogr.:	130		210	230	320

per 100 Kilogramm ö. W. fl. 10.50.

Wasserlaufgitter für Haus-Canäle, schwächerer Construction

	30	40	47	55	66 □%
Gewicht Kilogr.:	65	90	120	140	165

per 100 Kilogramm ö. W. fl. 11.50.

[4] Catalogue of the company H. Heinrich, [no date], p. 20–21.

of the use of these hygiene systems. This coincided with the first urban design exhibitions held in Germany [5].[7] The exhibition in Dresden in 1903 made visible the different systems and networks of pipes in the urban underground and explained them visually in street sections at 1:1 scale, as well as in model streets with pavements, manhole covers, street lights, benches, and trees. Visitors could acquaint themselves with the technical infrastructure and fully comprehend what was going on underneath their feet.

Manhole Covers as Documents and Storytellers: Semantics and Symbols

When metal manhole covers were widely introduced in the second quarter of the nineteenth century, they indicated the presence of a system of pipes in the urban ground, making it visually evident that an underground infrastructure made life in urban centers easier. Above ground, at the threshold between the

[5] Illustrations for cleaning canals ("Plate 79", 1904.

Source: Robert Wuttke, *Die deutschen Städte geschildert nach den Ergebnissen der ersten deutschen Städteausstellung zu Dresden 1903, vol. 2* (Leipzig: F. Brandstetter, 1904).

public space and the eerie underworld, the manhole cover had to be a safe surface upon which the passersby would not slip or stumble. Therefore, the surface was designed with raised elements in order to prevent such accidents from the outset. While the earliest examples showed only different graphic patterns, at later stages they included the name of the foundry and date of production. As these metal covers were produced locally in the beginning, a variety of covers were made and no normative designs appeared.

A decade after the demolition of the Viennese city fortifications, an area that had been used as a military exercise field was turned into an urban development zone. The first building to be erected was the new city hall. Before the foundations of the Neo-Gothic monument were dug, canals were laid in the large

[6] Manhole cover, with inscription "Stadt Trier 1901", Trier, Germany.

Photograph by the author.

field. The city hall was set back from the Ringstraße, leaving space for an extensive urban park. Walking through the park, one can still find in situ manhole covers dated 1872 which were cast in Pest (today Budapest). Manhole covers with the name of the same producer and the same date can be found in the inner courtyards of the building, all indicating the approximate date of the start of the construction work. This peculiar and quite informative arrangement can also be found in other, even larger urban situations, such as streets.

If manhole covers are dated, other historical urban processes can be studied. The Swiss Telephone Administration (*Schweizerische Telephonverwaltung*, or STV) installed its telephone network in several districts of Zurich from the 1890s onward. All over the city, dated manhole covers can be found indicating that the extensive network dates back to the nineteenth century but is still in existence and operating. In addition to documents and administrative papers, these metal plates prove the resilience and sustainability of the urban infrastructure already laid out in the nineteenth century.

In the last decade of the twentieth century, there was a new fashion in manhole covers. Proud mayors and directors of public works in cities started to display their municipal pride on the covers, depicting the monuments of their city or the city's coat of arms. The city of Trier was an early trendsetter, having already presented its coat of arms on manhole covers at the start of the last century [6].

Globalization Takes Control: Knowledge Transfer and Standardization of Design

There was as yet little expertise available regarding the implementation of a functional sewerage system, and the various methods used were contested until the middle of the nineteenth century. Debate among scientists, architects, engineers, and doctors was unable to settle on a single optimal solution for the disposal of human waste. Finally, the development and successful implementation of a sewer system was accomplished by the engineer Joseph Bazalgette in London. Knowledge of this beacon of hygienic urban management spread all over Europe through reports, drawings, and of course visits. The urban renewal of Paris in the reign of Napoleon III and his administrator Georges-Eugène Haussmann achieved a new dimension as the new technical infrastructure was systematically integrated into the urban realm. The urban landscape planner Jean-Charles Adolphe Alphand published his *magnum opus, Les Promenades de Paris*, showing not only the design of parks, streets with avenues of trees, and urban gardens, but also street sections with canals and means by which pluvial water was discharged into the urban underground. With this visual information, the concept of the combination of an embellished and equally hygienic city was promulgated throughout Europe and even onto other continents. But Paris was not only a reference in terms of theoretical and practical planning. Mysteriously, and to the present day, a Parisian manhole cover dated 1871 lies in the streets of Athens, proving that a material and physical transfer was also taking place [7].

As previously mentioned, manhole covers were produced at a local or at least regional level over the course of the nineteenth and into the twentieth century. With the centralization and growth of the steel industry, fewer and fewer local foundries continued operating and many subsequently closed their doors. The big industrial producers now offer a limited number of designs to customers worldwide. Even prior to this development, some kinds of standardization or proto-globalization processes were already underway in the last quarter of the nineteenth century. One early example can be found throughout the territory of the German Empire. Square-shaped manhole covers have survived in Weimar, and the same design was used in other German foundries hundreds of kilometers away [8]. In Strasbourg, the capital of the newly annexed state of Alsace, manhole covers which were produced in Frankfurt am Main can still be found *in situ* with the same design as the ones from Weimar.

Deciphering the City

The evolution of the production mechanisms of manhole covers, as well as the distribution of the products, shows that the development which started in the second half of the nineteenth became even more dramatic in the course of the twentieth century, culminating in an advanced standardization process and an early form of globalization. If we look back on the diversity of manhole covers and other plaques in the urban environments of the last fifteen decades, we see urban idiosyncrasies and local peculiarities which add to the richness of the

[7] Manhole cover, Parisian foundry, produced in 1871, found in Athens.

Photograph by the author.

[8] Manhole cover, with the inscription “Canalbau Weimar 1889”, Weimar.

Photograph by the author

design of urban space, and which tell us on the one hand about local foundries, and on the other about local characteristics.

Using the dates given on covers, we can identify developments in, and the proliferation of, urban infrastructure, leaving us with a variety of different kinds of information about historical stratas in our urban surroundings. With the representation of cities' coats of arms, the companies' names, and with other representational paraphernalia, a recoding process was started in the public realm. Traces were left, and the attentive user of streets and squares in the nineteenth century would read and decipher these signs and codes. The strategy of adding names to advertise a foundry, or to name the infrastructural company or city administration, started long ago. This is not much different today, although fewer and fewer dates of production can be found, making the reading of the manhole covers more difficult than it used to be.

The location, the site, the *genius loci* is also created through the endless minor and often-overlooked details which make up the atmosphere of the public realm. It would be an enriching experience for architects, urban planners, and city administrators alike to rekindle an interest in the design of manhole covers.

Endnotes

1 Henri Gautier, *Traité de la construction des chemins. Où il est parlé de ceux des Romains, & de ceux des Modernes, de leur figure, de leur matière, & de leur disposition dans toute sorte de lieux* (Toulouse: Dominique Camusat, 1693).

2 Pierre Patte, *Mémoires sur les objets les plus importans de l'architecture* (Paris: Rozet, 1769).

3 Eugénio dos Santos, *Ideal facade and ideal plan of a street of Lisbon*, drawing, 1756, Arquivo Histórico, Lisbon.

4 Illustration in *Daheim: ein deutsches Familienblatt mit Illustrationen*, Jahrgang 1, 1866, p. 88

5 James Hobrecht, *Die Canalisation von Berlin: im Auftrage des Magistrats der königl. Haupt- und Residenzstadt Berlin* (Berlin: Ernst & Korn, 1884).

6 Joseph Brix, *Berliner Normalquerschnitte für die Unterbringung der Versorgungsleitungen in Straßen mit 4m breiten Bürgersteigen* (Berlin: [n.p.], 1909).

7 For example, the "Deutsche Städtebauaustellung Dresden" in 1903, "Städtebauaustellung Berlin" in 1910, and "Städtebauausstellung Düsseldorf" in 1912.

AUTHORS

Dragan Damjanović is a researcher at the Art History Department of the Faculty of Humanities and Social Sciences, University of Zagreb and works on 19th and early 20th century architecture in Croatia and Central Europe.

Sarah M. Whiting is Dean and William Ward Watkin Professor of Architecture at Rice University, and is also a principal of WW Architecture, based in Houston.

Florian Hutterer is a researcher at the Institute for Urban and Regional Planning of TU Berlin. He works on history of urban development and planning, public space and urban mobility.

Britta Hentschel is a university lecturer and researcher in the history and theory of art, architecture, and urbanism. She currently works on her habilitation thesis at ETH Zürich and in the preservation of historical monuments in Switzerland.

Richard Kurdiovsky is a researcher at the Institute for History of Art and Musicology of the Austrian Academy of Sciences and works on architecture and urban culture of the long 19th century in Central Europe.

Irina Davidovici is a researcher at ETH Zurich and works on the history of social housing in Europe.

Ágnes Anna Sebestyén is an art historian at the Hungarian Museum of Architecture and Monument Protection Documentation Center and has research expertise in the history of modern architecture and architectural photography in Hungary.

Bradley Fratello is a Professor of Art History at St. Louis Community College, Meramec completing a book titled Manet & Globalization: Policing the Boundaries of French Identity in Second Empire Paris.

Katrin Albrecht is a researcher at ETH Zurich and lecturer at the FHS St. Gallen working on Italian and Swiss architecture of the 19th an 20th century.

Lukas Zurfluh is a researcher and lecturer at the FHS St. Gallen working on Swiss and international Architecture of the 19th and 20th century.

Anna Minta is Professor for the History and Theory of Architecture at the Catholic Private University Linz and analyzes architecture as social environments that contribute to the formation of identity and social order in transcultural perspectives.

Laila Seewang is an architect and PhD candidate at the Institute for History and Theory of Architecture at the ETH, Zürich. Her research centers on the role played by large-scale infrastructural projects in reflecting the political, social and economic forces that drive urban change.

Harald R. Stühlinger is Professor for the History of Architecture and Urban Design at FHNW in Muttenz and publishes in the history of architecture, urban design and photography.

IMPRINT

© 2019 by jovis Verlag GmbH
Texts by kind permission of the authors.
Pictures by kind permission of the photographers/holders of the picture rights.

All rights reserved.

Cover: Adolphe Alphand, Les Promenades de Paris, Paris: J. Rothschild 1867–1873 (detail)

Copy-editing: Jessica Glanz
Design and setting: jovis, Susanne Rösler
Lithography: Bild1Druck GmbH
Printed in the European Union

Bibliographic information published by the Deutsche Nationalbibliothek
The Deutsche Nationalbibliothek lists this publication in the Deutsche Nationalbibliografie; detailed bibliographic data are available on the Internet at http://dnb.d-nb.de

jovis Verlag GmbH
Kurfürstenstraße 15/16
10785 Berlin

www.jovis.de

jovis books are available worldwide in select bookstores. Please contact your nearest bookseller or visit www.jovis.de for information concerning your local distribution.

ISBN 978-3-86859-459-1